Romans in Britain

Also by Rodney Legg

Purbeck Island
Ghosts of Dorset, Devon and Somerset
Steep Holm
Exploring Ancient Wiltshire with George Osborn
Monumenta Britannica with John Fowles
Purbeck Walks
Old Swanage

Romans in Britain

RODNEY LEGG

Heinemann : London

William Heinemann Ltd
10 Upper Grosvenor Street,
London W1X 9PA

LONDON MELBOURNE TORONTO
JOHANNESBURG AUCKLAND

First published in Great Britain 1983
Copyright ©Rodney Legg 1983

434 41330 5

Printed and bound in Great Britain by
Billing and Sons Ltd, Worcester

Contents

For John Pitfield

Preface

THE TITLE OF this book is the same as one of the opening chapters in William Camden's *Britannia*. It is also that of a play by Howard Brenton, presented by the National Theatre in 1981, which transposed British adventurism in Ireland to the context of the Romans in Britain. Both give cause for reflection.

Camden's monolithic treatment was the result of ten years' travel and study into antiquarianism, which he completed on the 2nd May 1586 at the age of thirty-five. It frequently tells us what we have lost. William of Malmesbury, writing before 1125, noted there was a Roman vaulted building in Carlisle with an inscription on the façade to "Mars the Victor". By Camden's time all traces of this shrine and its inscription had been swept away. Most of our Roman vestiges are now confined to the crags on the moors, or retrieved from an archaeological underworld of trenches and trowels. It would somehow have been living proof of the existence of the Province of Britannia if just one Roman building had survived long enough to be incorporated into a mediaeval street – though, on reflection, if this had really happened, some council would doubtless have bulldozed the thing in the 1960s.

Brenton's play is a reminder that history is about people. The machinations of a political state – and there is no other kind – invariably turn against its own peoples. The thought still lingers that the Roman invasion of Britain was never truly completed for, despite its ebb and flow through Scotland, it did not come within a hundred miles of Cape Wrath, and had to fall back on a circumnavigation. It was entirely an egotistical creation for making Roman reputations, but it had to rely on military occupation and a constant investment of manpower and capital. Perhaps it should be a matter for national pride that these islands offered a resistance that was sustained over thirteen generations – four hundred years – and attempted reasserting their independence through a succession of usurpers and separatists. This nationalist spirit has still not been lost from the British Isles, and the fact that it has been wilfully ignored for so long has now brought it to a bursting point where continued dissatisfaction can only be at our peril. On the Roman side this troublesome colony was an uncomfortable land which required constant maintenance. It is a tribute to the firm structure of Roman bureaucracy, as well as to the strength of individual emperors, that this drain on resources was successfully in-stitutionalised for so long.

But there was a value to owning Britain, both for its mineral wealth and its grain exports. It is worth remembering that an imperial state can function in chronic deficit. Britain at the time of Queen Victoria's Golden Jubilee was overspending enor-mously in its balance of payments (with cost of imports running at twice the income from exports), but the difference was met by invisible earnings from colossal interests overseas.

There is a place for twentieth century antiquarianism if it can tell us something about ourselves. Art treasures and surviving archaeological sites are the three-dimensional jigsaw of the subject, but the collective weight of the literary fragments is more than a mere surface gloss. There is a tendency for the ever-growing mass of information to provide little more than ammunition for one group of archaeologists to fire at another; this may be avoided when everything is set firmly within the literary record, though perhaps now and then the opportunity will be irresistible.

Footnotes have been avoided as an irrelevant distraction; where authors have been consulted their names are given and the titles of their books are quoted. Books disappear rapidly from print these days and whether or not they are obtainable depends upon the bookseller's microfiche or the library. Major future developments will be recorded as monographs in the growing list of British Archaeological Reports.

Other academics have been quoted from what is becoming the most important collected source of knowledge concerning Roman Britain: this is *Britannia*, the journal of this country's Roman studies, which is published by the Society for the Promotion of Roman Studies at 31 Gordon Square, London WC1. It is a breakaway from the *Journal of Roman Studies*, which covers the empire in general, and was founded in 1970 under the editorship of Sheppard Frere, in "an act of faith" that has been amply justified.

Dorset 1983   R. L.

Acknowledgements

GRATITUDE SHOULD BE expressed to Penguin Classics for making available to us most of the principal surviving works of Roman literature. One of them decided me to start this book: *The Twelve Caesars* by Suetonius, in the translation by Robert Graves, would be my choice for a desert island. This edition offers the fortunate coincidence of one of the world's greatest writers translated by another. For me it is this superb period material that brings life to analytical archaeology, which would otherwise give us only detritus, destruction and death.

Collaboration on the car-guide *Exploring Ancient Wiltshire* introduced me to the unique reconstruction of the Orphic mosaic at Littlecote Park and led me into a search for further information that proved that not only can a year be a long time in archaeology but the information always seems to start by being a decade out of date. Discussion with Richard Hattatt showed that there were still occasional niches for a new book, in his case *Ancient and Romano-British Brooches* (Dorset Publishing Co, Sherborne, 1982) where no full study on identification and dating had previously existed. Mine does not have the benefit of an unoccupied slot so I shall try to find a new approach, and look at Roman history as an adventure story. I have pinned some words from Tom Lethbridge's *The Painted Men* on to the wall as a reminder: "I cannot see why it should be necessary to make any historical study boring to the degree of tears for the sake of the imagined accuracy, which no history can ever possess."

Modern archaeological books have been obtained for me by Fox and Co of Princes Street, Yeovil, and the antiquarian titles by William Hoade at the Wimborne Bookshop in Dorset. For advice on the presentation of my text, which extended to retyping the manuscript, I am grateful to Colin Graham. Bernard C Pickard pointed out some areas that benefited from further attention. With his aid and the interest of Patrick Dunion I was able to find some particularly unusual antiquities to illustrate. My publisher, Roland Gant, had the enthusiasm necessary for the photography of Hadrian's Wall through the Northumberland mists. The main picture coverage was provided by John Pitfield and Colin Graham. For the inevitable gaps I turned to the institutions but avoided the over-used where possible. I was greatly helped by Iris Philips in the Department of Prehistoric and Romano-British Antiquities at the British Museum, and by Mr Smit at the National Monuments Record.

That it has reached this stage has been due to the phone bill of William Heinemann Limited and the calm efficiency of Claire Drew-Edwards who had become Claire Bushnell in the time it took for me to respond to one of her calls. Anita Turpin produced the dust jacket without much help from the author. My thanks have to go to Priscilla da Cunha for the layouts and to Harry, Tom and John at Hewer Text Composition Services of Edinburgh for providing typesetting that was infinitely cleaner than my manuscript. Reg Piggott gave us a highly accomplished piece of cartography from the author's apology for a map, which was in the style of John Aubrey with contradictory notes and deletions and could have passed for something out of the seventeenth century except for its extensive use of sellotape. All this searching after antiquities is a wearisome task, as my parents realised twenty-five years ago when all journeys had to follow the Ordnance Survey's *Map of Roman Britain*. It is still Britain's only decent road map.

DUMNA INSULAE

SCITIS

CALEDONIA

MALAIUS

AGRICOLA'S INCURSIONS

GASK RIDGE FORTS

ANTONINE WALL
Warwick Vase
Carriden
Bothwellhaugh
Inveresk
·Castledykes

Bodotria Aestuarium

OCEANUS

·Newstead

Crawford

High Rochester

GERMANICUS

NOVANTAE

Birrens
Glenlochar
·Risingham
Netherby HADRIAN'S WALL
Carlisle Chesterholm Corbridge
Maryport
Burrow Walls Papcastle Chester-le-Street
Moresby Penrith ·Kirkby Thore
·Ambleside
Ravenglass
Overborough· ·Catterick
Brough by Bainbridge
·Aldborough
·Lancaster
Ribchester ·Ilkley ·York
Kirkham ·Tadcaster
Wigan Slack· ·Brough
Castleford Doncaster Abus Flumen
·Manchester
·Buxton
Northwich Littleborough· Caistor ·Mablethorpe
Chesterfield Lincoln·
Burgh le Marsh
Littlechester Metaris Aestuarium
Water Eaton PROVINCIA Ancaster Brancaster
Wroxeter· ·Wall
·Leicester
Forden Gaer Mancetter Water Caistor
Leintwardine ·High Cross Newton Caistor Burgh
Droitwich BRITANNIAE Mildenhall Castle
Alcester· Treasure
·Chesterton Godmanchester
Towcester· POTTERIES ·Cambridge
Kenchester
IRON ORE
·Gloucester ·Alchester Dunstable Colchester
Usk Cirencester St Albans
Caerleon· ·Dorchester
Cardiff Caerwent Chelmsford
·Sea Mills Wanborough
Sabrina Flumen Bath Mildenhall London SALTPANS
(Cunetio)
MENDIP STONE WANSDYKE ·Speen ·Staines Tamesis
LEAD QUARRIES FRONTIER ·Silchester Flumen
MINES Old Sarum ·Ewell Rochester
Ilchester· POTTERIES IRON ORE WORKINGS Canterbury Richborough
·Winchester ·Alfoldean Dover
North Tawton Hod Hill· Porchester
·Exeter Badbury· POTTERIES Fishbourne Lympne
TIN MINES Dorchester· ·Chichester Hastings
·Nanstallon Lake Farm Pevensey Boulogne
VECTIS

OCEANUS BRITANNICUS

HIBERNIA

MANAVIA

OCEANUS HIBERNICUS

MONA
Caer Gybi ·Prestatyn
Caernarfon· COPPER AND LEAD MILES
Chester
Whitchurch·

·Pennal Caer Sws
CaeGaer·
·Llanio
WELSH
Dolaucothi GOLD MINES
Castell
Fleming· Carmarthen
IRON ORE
·Neath

BOKERLEY DYKE
STONE SHALE

N

Non-Roman Britain is stippled

English miles
0 50 100

Roman miles
0 50 100

kilometres
0 50 100

SIGNAL STATIONS

SIGNAL STATIONS

xii

The first two landings

Julius Caesar conquered Gaul, but he bungled the invasion of Britain. His campaigns of 58–57 BC had resulted in the occupation of most of modern France.

It was history being reversed. In 386 BC the attacking Gauls had entered Rome, after having held back for the summer solstice, and stayed there for seven months. Only the Capitol withstood the siege. Charcoal from that sacking is found in each excavation around the area of the forum. The basic Celtic problem was recorded by Diodorus Siculus, the Greek historian of the late first century who should be more accurately known as "Sicilus", for he was Diodorus the Sicilian. He wrote: "With their excessive love of wine, they drink so greedily of it that when drunk they fall into a deep sleep or into fits of temper."

Professor Jean Markale, writing in *Celtic Civilisation*, adds: "Livy gives this love of drink as the reason for the ease with which the exiled dictator Camillus, who had led a small army from Ardea, cut the throats of the sodden Gauls as if they were sheep." The remaining Gauls accepted a ransom, a fee, and left. It took the Romans a full fifty years to recover.

Caesar was a great continental general but he recognised that the Veneti, the seafaring tribe of the Channel coast, could only be beaten by a fleet. He established shipyards on the river Loire, and took note of the fact that "sailing in a wide ocean was

1

clearly a very different matter from sailing in a landlocked sea like the Mediterranean".

Gaul's governor, Decimus Junius Brutus – *not* the Brutus of Caesar's assassins – was in command of the fleet, "including the Gallic ships that Caesar had ordered the Pictones, Santoni, and other tribes in the conquered areas to provide". Caesar says that the new fleet won its decisive victory thanks to its boat-hooks, the poles used to maintain a hold on the seabed and steady the stern of a vessel during a difficult landing. These were used to tear down the enemy rigging.

But whatever damage had been inflicted upon the native fleet, it was to make no material difference, for by the time the Veneti realised their ships were being crippled the wind had dropped and the native fleet was then becalmed and at the mercy of the oar-powered Roman ships.

"They had already put their ships before the wind when suddenly such a dead calm fell that they could not stir. Nothing could have been more fortunate for us. It enabled us to complete the victory by pursuing and capturing the vessels one after another, and only a very few managed to make land when night came on after a battle that lasted from about ten o'clock in the morning until sunset."

In 55 BC Caesar undertook the first crossing of the Rhine, in a punitive raid to deter further German expansion into Gaul, "but a crossing by means of boats seemed to him both too risky, and beneath his dignity as a Roman commander". Through the pile-driving skills of his engineers he was able to march across a great bridge, the structure of which had been strengthened by diagonal ties held in place by the force of the current. One assumes that they broke step and shuffled across, to avoid vibrating it to destruction. Caesar may wisely have avoided an amphibious crossing of the Rhine but he had to come to terms with the Channel.

In the autumn of 55 "Caesar made active preparations for an

expedition to Britain, because he knew that in almost all the Gallic campaigns the Gauls had received reinforcements from the Britons. Even if there was not time for a campaign that season, he thought it would be of great advantage for him merely to visit the island, to see what its inhabitants were like, and to make himself acquainted with the lie of the land, the harbours, and the landing places."

These quotations, though written in the third person, are by Caesar himself from *The Conquest of Gaul*, available to us in S A Handford's edition for Penguin Classics. Caesar goes on to state that the Gauls knew next to nothing about the British coast. Only the traders went across the Channel, Caesar says, and although he interviewed traders from everywhere, he could find nothing worth knowing. It does not sound convincing. The likely explanation is that Caesar failed to realise that there would be serious tidal differences, and therefore did not inter-rogate the Gauls about them. Any merchant would have ex-perienced and respected the pattern of the tides along the coast he visited. If he had made Caesar's mistake, he would have lost his boat and ceased to be a trader.

Caesar destroys his own argument when he states the obvious, that "traders are the only people who visit Britain, and even they know only that part of the coast which faces Gaul". This was precisely the piece of coast chosen by Caesar for his landings.

The aberration here is a reminder that Caesar's military memoirs were also propaganda, for consumption in Roman circles far removed from any knowledge of the practicalities of the British coast. The importance of intelligence gathering had been neglected. The price was to be nearly total failure risking the elimination of the finest units of the Roman army. It had been a near thing, and Caesar felt compelled to introduce excuses to pre-empt criticism that might seep back to Rome.

The truth is that Caesar's first landing in Britain aborted.

From the start it was presumptive and careless. Before the crossing – from the Pas de Calais area across the Dover Straits – Gaius Volusenus Quadratus carried out a reconnaissance of the Kent coast to find a suitable beach-head. What followed was to lead to the loss of much of the Roman fleet, which had been built up only the previous summer for the war against the Veneti. The whole logistical support for the British landings was washed away when the rising tide inundated the beached transports. A cynic might point out that they may not have tides in the Mediterranean, but Bologna certainly experiences them. They do tend to build up by a third in the course of a week at the autumn equinox. Caesar describes the arrival of the eighteen transport vessels, carrying the cavalry and supplies, on the fourth day after his landing in Britain.

Caesar says: "It happened to be full moon that night, at which time the Atlantic tides are particularly high – a fact unknown to the Romans. The result was that the warships used in the crossing, which had been beached, were waterlogged, and the transports – which were riding at anchor – were knocked about by the storm, without the soldiers having any chance of interfering to save them. A number of ships were shattered, and the rest, having lost their cables, anchors, and the remainder of their tackle, were unusable, which naturally threw the whole army into great consternation. For they had no other vessels in which they could return, nor any materials for repairing the fleet. Since it had been generally understood that they were to return to Gaul for the winter, they had not provided themselves with a stock of grain for wintering in Britain."

Insufficient supplies had been landed. The Seventh Legion set out into the countryside to steal British corn. Others worked all day cannibalising the more severely damaged ships to repair those that were salvageable. In the end, the net loss was twelve ships. Meanwhile, men from the Seventh Legion were ambushed as they started to take the last available grain. Caesar then decided to return to Gaul, but two of the transports failed to find their safe harbours and were carried to the south. They found themselves surrounded by the local Gallic tribe, the Morini, in the middle of an uprising, and were saved only by the arrival of Caesar's cavalry. The whole expedition, in the water, on the beaches, and on land, had been on the point of disaster. Caesar had barely returned with his army and his life.

The legions wintered in Belgic territory. Two of the British tribes sent hostages, as they had promised, but the remainder decided this was unnecessary. Caesar's dispatches impressed and excited Rome, where the Senate decreed twenty days of public thanksgiving. Caesar left for Italy, after setting in motion a ship construction programme.

Caesar writes about himself using the third person: "He specified the dimensions and shape of the new ships. To enable them to be loaded quickly and beached easily he had them made slightly lower than those which we generally use in the Mediterranean – especially as he found that owing to the frequent ebb and flow of the tides the waves in the Channel were comparatively small. To enable them, however, to carry a heavy cargo, including a large number of animals, they were made somewhat wider than the ships we use in other waters. They were all to be of a type suitable for both sailing and rowing, an arrangement which was greatly facilitated by their low freeboard. The materials required for fitting them out were to be imported from Spain."

They built six hundred such vessels, and twenty eight warships, which were assembled at Portus Itius – Boulogne, or Wissant, eleven miles to the north. The fleet was kept in harbour for a month by continuous north-easterly winds.

The armada of 54 BC was to number more than eight hundred vessels, carrying five legions and two thousand cavalry – a total of thirty thousand men.

"The soldiers worked splendidly, and by continuous rowing enabled the heavily laden transports to keep up with the warships. When the whole fleet reached Britain about midday, no enemy was to be seen. Caesar discovered afterwards from prisoners that, although large numbers had assembled at the spot, they were frightened by the sight of so many ships and had quitted the shore to conceal themselves on higher ground."

One lesson was learned – this time the fleet stood off at sea – but the perils took a new form. A night storm dashed forty ships to pieces and the rest were immobilised or cast on to the shore, as "the anchors and cables had not held, and the sailors and their captains could not cope with such a violent gale, so that many vessels were disabled by collision".

Otherwise the rest of the expedition went well. A proper beachhead was constructed, taking ten days and nights to complete. The Roman army marched across the Thames and took St Albans, from the Catuvellauni. Several tribes, including the powerful Trinovantes of Essex, accepted peace terms from the Romans and supplied grain and hostages. British chariot skirmishes were mainly reserved for picking off the stragglers who had strayed too far from their unit.

One attack was daring and unnerving: "Throughout this unusual combat, which was fought in front of the camp in full view of everyone, it was seen that our troops were too heavily weighted by their armour to deal with such an enemy – they could not pursue them when they retreated, and dared not get separated from their standards. The cavalry also found it very dangerous work fighting the charioteers. For the Britons would often give ground on purpose, and after drawing some distance from the legions would jump down from their chariots and fight on foot, with the odds in their favour."

Caesar also made a potted travelogue describing the country. He gave the shape of Britain more or less accurately, as a triangle. The estimate was that the island was five hundred miles in length along the Channel coast, then eight hundred miles from Kent to the Orkneys, and seven hundred miles from the north down to Land's End. It is not far wrong when you allow for the confusing and indented coastline. The measurements had been converted from sailing times into Roman miles. Put into English miles, the precise figures are 475, by 760, by 665 miles. He pointed out that the western seaboard faced Ireland and Spain, though the latter association was taken too literally and classical geographers never resolved the confusion.

He discovered "by accurate measurements with a water-clock that the nights are shorter than on the continent". Caesar heard that in the smaller northern isles there was a month of perpetual darkness in mid-winter. He records that the interior of Britain was occupied by descendants of the indigenous population. In the southern regions they were displaced by Belgic immigrants "who came to plunder and make war, nearly all of them retaining the names of the tribes from which they originated, and later settled down to till the soil".

Tin was found inland, and iron near the coast, and for money the Britons used bronze or gold coins and iron currency bars. Timber of all kinds was found, as in Gaul, except for sweet chestnut and fir trees. It needs to be stressed here that translations of *The Conquest of Gaul* persist in mistaking the sweet chestnut reference for beech ('fagus' could mean either). It is ludicrous to assume that Caesar did not notice the largest trees in the country, particularly as he took his army through the great beech woods of Kent, Surrey, and the Chilterns. That beech was then present and prolific has been proved by analysis of numerous pollen samples and pieces of preserved timber.

Taboo species of game included hares, fowls, and geese – which were not eaten – though they were reared for pleasure and amusement. Rabbits, or conies, were not introduced to Britain until after 1066. The climate, Caesar found, "is more temperate than in Gaul, the cold being less severe".

He thought the people of Kent, the Cantii, the most civilised Britons, with a way of life much the same as in Gaul. Further north the tribes did not grow corn but lived on milk and meat. Caesar says the Britons wore skins, but the description as a whole is probably a deliberate exaggeration comparable to the noble savage descriptions which became so common in nineteenth century literature.

"All the Britons dye their bodies with woad, which produces a blue colour, and this gives them a more terrifying appearance in battle. They wear their hair long, and shave the whole of their bodies except the head and the upper lip. Wives are shared between groups of ten or twelve men, especially between brothers and between fathers and sons; but the offspring of these unions are counted as the children of the man with whom a particular woman cohabited first."

His point about the density of population has been borne out this century by aerial photography: "The population is exceedingly large, the ground being thickly studded with homesteads, closely resembling those of the Gauls." It was left to Ammianus Marcellinus, writing in the fourth century AD, to leave us a deeper appreciation of the Celtic mind, saying they took pleasure "in commenting on the sublime secrets of nature, their minds ever straining towards the most abstract and difficult of questions".

Caesar returned to Gaul at the end of August 54, making the return in two voyages to overcome the shortage of ships. The size of his expedition had shown Rome that there was not going to be any prospect of a quick and simple annexation of Britain. The strongest advances had been diplomatic rather than military, achieved by exploiting tribal rivalries and differences. The Romans were accomplished practitioners of that art. For Caesar himself there would have been some additions to his art collection, Gaius Suetonius Tranquillus recording: "Pearls seem to have been the lure that prompted his invasion of Britain; he

The Warwick Vase was reconstructed around fragments brought to Britain by William Hamilton after he had drained a lake near Hadrian's Villa, 15 miles from Rome, in 1770. It stands nine feet eight inches high and that excludes the plinth. The Warwick Vase was the first item on Napoleon's list of treasures that he would take back to France after the conquest of Britain.

Courtesy: Glasgow Museums

would sometimes weigh them in the palm of his hand to judge their value, and was also a keen collector of gems, carvings, statues, and Old Masters." Appreciation of art would appear to be a compelling stimulant to the conquest of continents, as with Hermann Goering in recent times. Napoleon wanted to take home the ten feet tall Roman marble Warwick vase as his personal trophy from an invasion of England. It has been standing beside the entrance to Glasgow's bus depot, but has now joined the city's Burrell Collection.

Claudius Aelianus, who taught rhetoric at the time of Hadrian, mentions those British pearls. He writes about them in his standard zoological work *On the Peculiarities of Animals*: "The best sort of pearl is the Indian and that of the Red Sea. It is produced also in the Western Ocean where the island of Britain is. This sort seems to be of a yellowish colour, like gold, while its lustre is dull and dusky. Juba tells us that the pearl is produced in the straits of the Bosporus and is inferior to the British, and not for a moment to be compared with the Indian and Red Sea kind."

Caesar had established a Roman claim to Britain, though its inhabitants withheld further tributes. Augustus, Caesar's successor, issued an edict against the further expansion of the Roman empire. There matters were to rest for three generations.

The British claim was revived by Caligula in AD 40, as a result of his one military expedition, to Germany, when he received the surrender of some exiled Britons. They were led by Adminius, the son of the British chieftain, Cunobelin. Adminius had been placed on the throne of eastern Kent but was then banished by his father. The actions of the exiles in Germany were of no practical significance but Caligula, who was insane, relished it as the high point of his reign.

Gaius Suetonius Tranquillus, writing seventy years later, though from highly detailed archives, records that Caligula "nevertheless wrote an extravagant dispatch to Rome, as if the whole island had surrendered to him, and ordered the couriers not to dismount from their post-chaise on reaching the outskirts of the city, but make straight for the Forum and the Senate House, and take his letter to the Temple of Mars the Avenger for personal delivery to the consuls, in the presence of the entire senate." Suetonius is quoted from the Penguin Classics edition of *The Twelve Caesars*, translated by Robert Graves.

Caligula proceeded to the Channel shore and assembled his bolt-firing artillery machines on the beaches: "No one had the least notion what was in his mind when, suddenly, he gave the order – 'Gather seashells!' "

Province of Britannia

CLAUDIUS TOOK THE decision to absorb Britain into the Roman empire. He had shown an immediate interest in the country on becoming emperor at the death of Caligula in AD 41. His son, born on the twenty-second day of his reign, was named Britannicus. Claudius would often hold him up to show to the troops and spectators at the games.

Already the pronouncement of Augustus against the expansion of the empire was being ignored, in the Atlas Mountains where the Roman legions were creating the new province of Mauretania. The annexation of Britain, on the other hand, would have required months of preparation and planning, particularly as the accounts of Caesar's northern wars made it clear that a successful conquest required a considerable army.

The venture would have been suicidal with anything less than Caesar's forces, and risky unless double that strength could be committed. It must have been clear from the start that 50,000 men would be needed.

The reasons for incorporating Britain into the empire had to be reasonably compelling. These, at least, would have been apparent:

1. Britain, since Caesar, had continued to absorb Gallic Druids, Celtic dissidents, refugees, and general continental overspill.

2. Peoples of Gallic extraction comprised the powerful tribes on Britain's southern seaboard, and in AD 41 they harried the French coast after the Romans had refused to return some defectors.

3. The defectors, from the Atrebates, were led by Verica, the son of Commios. Like his brother, Tincommios, who fled to the court of Augustus before AD 14, he was forced into exile. As king, Verica had adopted the Latin title 'Rex' and replaced the barley-ear emblem on his coins with a vine-leaf, which can be seen as a statement of policy that looked towards the Mediterranean. He went to Rome after fleeing from Britain, and his appeals for intervention provided Claudius with diplomatic justification for a British invasion.

4. Awareness of the growing strength of Cunobelin – latinised as Cunobelinus – who avoided antagonising the Romans, though tribal tensions would have been regarded as having a destabilising effect on the northern empire. The death of Cunobelin, in about AD 43 after a long reign, came too late to influence the invasion decision, though it may have affected its course. His capital, Camulodunum (Colchester) was given its name from the Celtic war-god Camulos.

5. Britain must have seemed economically appealing, as a quarter of the overall land area in the chalk downland districts of the south was already producing grain, and the surplus was traded.

6. The country had other known wealth, including an export business in gold, tin, iron, and lead. Strabo mentions British exports of cattle, hides, slaves, and hunting dogs – as well as corn – and the scale of this trade had increased greatly since Caesar's time.

7. Cartographical neatness – first century ideas of geo-graphy placed Britain and Ireland facing directly towards Spain, and colonising Britain was seen as completing the third side of a triangle with Gaul. The same misconception led later to Agricola considering, according to his son-in-law, Tacitus, a conquest of Ireland, "for Ireland, lying as it does midway between Britain and Spain and easily accessible from the Gaulish Sea, would have linked the strong parts of the empire together, with mutual advantages for all". Thus the Irish troubles might have started a thousand years earlier.

8. Britain was known to be an island of only medium size, of 100,000 square miles on the Roman calculations, which would not have appeared an insurmountable obstacle to an army which operated on a continental scale.

9. Its prosperous lowlands conveniently faced the main European shore and must have seemed an easy target to invade and occupy. Though the Romans knew that there were mountains behind, these were of inconsequential proportions when compared with the Alps and peaks in Italy.

10. The principle of not expanding the empire had been broken by the annexation of the North African state of Mauretania – present-day Morocco – in AD 41–42.

11. Extensive war-stores of equipment and materials had been held in reserve since the retreat of Augustus from Germany after the defeat of AD 9.

12. Prestige for Claudius, by consolidating the footsteps of Caesar, particularly as his predecessor, Caligula, had laid an empty claim to Britain. For Claudius it was to be his *iustus triumphus*, his proper triumph.

The invasion plans were set in motion. Aulus Plautius was given command of five legions, each of about 5,600 men, plus 15,000 native auxiliaries from other parts of the empire. His fleet and administrative support teams must have totalled at least a further ten thousand. This gives an overall invasion force upwards of fifty thousand.

The legions were the Second Augusta, the Ninth Hispana,

During its war against the Britons the Twentieth Legion adopted the boar, the principal sacred beast of the Celts, for its crest. This pottery antefix is one of several that would have been set at intervals along the eaves of a military building at Holt, Denbigh.

Courtesy: British Museum

the Fourteenth Gemina, the Twentieth Valeria, and all or part of the Eighth Augusta. Of these names, Augusta signifies that a legion was raised or reconstituted by Augustus. The Hispana won its honours in Spain, and Gemina was formed by amalgamating two legions. Valeria was named by Claudius after his wife, Valeria Messalina, and adopted its emblem of the boar – it is reasonable to assume this represents the Celts as it was their principal sacred beast – during the British campaign.

The invasion fleet embarked from Boulogne in the summer of 43 and landed at Richborough, Kent, where the major supply base was established. It is probable that other units landed in the harbours of Dover and Lympne. Denarius diplomacy had probably preceded the army, with agreements for money and position being made with leaders of the south-eastern tribes. Taking tributes from kings was the Roman way of neutralising as many potentially hostile peoples for an interim period, a method later to be practised themselves by the British. In both the Roman and British empires the process was that settlers created a colony, and submissions a protectorate. Pitt-Rivers,

Richborough, on the Kent coast, was the main base for the supply of Roman Britain and its principal Channel port. The first century fort was later extensively redeveloped, the outline of second century shops showing in the foreground and a late third century wall behind. By this time it had become a command point for the defence of the Saxon shore.

Courtesy: National Monuments Record

writing almost a century ago in his *Excavations in Cranborne Chase*, emphasised that for the Romans such stratagems were only intended to last a generation, as "vassal status was by nature transitional, and, as a rule, it was destined to lead ultimately to absorption".

Cogidubnus certainly came to terms, and was established as client-king of the Regni in Sussex and eastern Hampshire. The Second Legion, from Strasbourg on the Rhine, had the task of entering resisting territory. Both the Belgae and the Durotriges, the fortress peoples of the great hill-forts of Wiltshire and Dorset, had decided to fight the Romans. They were to meet their match in a future emperor, Vespasian, who had been given command of the Second Legion in Germany by Narcissus on Claudius's accession.

Celtic warfare had developed along the lines of team combat,

15

Celtic geometric patterning on another superb British shield, with a prominent central boss to protect the user's hand.

Photograph: Colin Graham

with chivalry and rules – each side represented by its warriors – rather than full-scale conflict. They were dressed for the ceremonial of war, like knights of the Middle Ages, with shields and armour of richly-coloured enamelled bronze. These reds and blues were also carried on their bodies – Caesar's painted men – with woad and other dyes. They were magnificent horsemen, and their mounts were decked with armour and finery. Their battle wagons were the chariots, light and high-speed vehicles, with wicker screens to protect the driver and steel rims to lessen the strains on the wheels.

The battle call was sounded with a long trumpet, a carnyx, its mouthpiece in the form of an animal head. The British Celts, as with the Gauls described by Polybius, "had innumerable

16

Battle for the Celts was a loud affair, this being one of their simpler horns.

Photograph: Colin Graham

horns and trumpets; and at the same time the whole army set up such a shouting that not only the instruments and the warriors but the hills around seemed to be raising their voices in echo".

This style of battle was no match for the orderly, drilled, and superior armed ranks of the grimly efficient Roman fighting

Roman charioteer: a vivid scene cast in lead on a canister found at Warwick Square, London.

Courtesy: British Museum

Vespasian, apparently, sculpted in Roman marble, from Colchester, Essex. He commanded the onslaught of the Second Legion into central southern England and was later to become emperor.

Courtesy: British Museum

machine. The great hill-fort refuges, the ultimate monuments of European prehistoric engineering, could not be sustained against an onslaught from such a force. In Britain, Vespasian was to march through determined but ineffectual opposition.

Gaius Suetonius Tranquillus records, in his usual condensed summary of events for *The Twelve Caesars*, that he "fought thirty battles, subjugated two warlike tribes, and captured more than twenty strongholds, besides the entire Isle of Vectis (Wight)".

Before Vespasian moved west the hold on south-eastern England was already secure, with treaty terms also accepted by the Iceni of Norfolk, and Claudius came for sixteen days to wallow in the triumph. The Iceni had been pressured by the expansion of the Catuvellauni, the Iron Age tribe of the east Midlands, who had spread westwards to subjugate the Dobunni of the Cotswolds and eastwards to absorb the Trinovantes' territory in Essex and Suffolk. The Roman invasion might not have been welcomed by the Iceni, but it offered relief from

18

Vespasian's portrait as emperor, three decades after the conquest of southern Britain. *Photograph: Colin Graham*

tribal tensions. Friction with the Romans, however, would lead to uprisings in 47–48 and 60.

In August 43 Vespasian was preparing his initial base for the western conquest. It appears to have been near Chichester, in the Regni territory of west Sussex, probably on nearby Selsey Bill, though nothing survives there that can be visited today. The shore has since receded by more than a mile. Three hundred Celtic gold coins were found in the nineteenth century along this coast from Selsey to Wittering, suggesting the site of an eroding tribal capital.

Offshore, where the Mixon reef marks the ancient coastline, divers from the Kingston-on-Thames branch of the British Sub-Aqua Club discovered the remains of a Roman fort in 1967. A subsequent investigation, carried out by Major Hume Wallace and a group of skin-divers in 1974, located several large pointed stones on the seabed. These are believed to be

Roman mooring bollards and the search is continuing for more conclusive evidence of Roman jetties.

The *Channel Pilot* records "a deep hole, with depths of over six fathoms off the eastern end of the Mixon", which may have been the approach channel to the fort.

The massive dyke system which cuts off the Selsey peninsula and Chichester Harbour – its defences engineered in Colchester fashion – was built to protect a settlement in the area of Selsey Bill towards the close of the Iron Age. It was only after this was threatened by coastal erosion that the tribal capital of the Regni was moved – just within the defensive cordon – to Chichester. Its very name gives this away, being known to the Romans as Noviomagus Regnensium, Newmarket of the Regini (the tribal name is generally latinised to Regni, and was formerly known to archaeologists as Regnenses).

Chichester may have started as an hibernia, or winter-quarters, for the Second Legion, but their fleet would have, at least initially, taken advantage of the existing wharves and moorings on Selsey Bill.

The account by Suetonius is sparse, but definite. It implies that Vespasian left the Isle of Wight till last. Vespasian would have passed it immediately he left Selsey, but it is logical that he would have delayed its seizure until after the collapse of the Dorset hill-forts. Vespasian's first priority was a sudden attack on central Dorset uplands and, in this, the Isle of Wight was inconsequential. Being an offshore island it could play no decisive role in the events that were taking place. It was bypassed, in the same way that the Anglo-American landings in Normandy in 1944 were able to ignore the heavily defended Channel Islands, which were left until the end of the campaign.

Vespasian's plans even appear to have taken his own men by surprise: one Roman officer buried his savings at Bredgar, near Sittingbourne, but never returned. Four of the 34 gold coins were minted in 41–42, and the hoard can therefore be dated to

20

the invasion year. Such finds are exceptional, because money was generally banked with the legion's pay corps, to ensure that there would be something for the dependents.

Vespasian landed in the heart of the Durotrigic lands on the heathy shores of Poole Harbour – landlocked and calm, with the advantage of four tides a day instead of the usual two – taking possession of the sparsely inhabited Hamworthy peninsula. He may have cut a canal from the west end of Lytchett Bay.

Hamworthy was a fort, port, and supply depot. The Second Legion cut a road straight inland, over a heathland ridge, to the River Stour six miles to the north. Here, on the meadows a mile to the west of the modern town of Wimborne Minster, they created a huge fortress. It was not rediscovered until the mid-1960s, the banks and ditches having disappeared from sight amongst the meadows. There was to be no doubt about its period as there were fragments of 'Arretine' pottery in the ground. This was brought from Italy and its presence in English sites conclusively dates them to within three years of the invasion.

This fortress at Lake Farm may have housed the Second Legion during the winter of 43, and was its base during the following spring for the onslaught on Badbury Rings, Spetisbury Camp, and Hod and Hambledon Hills. These forts are strung along the Stour, and Spetisbury was in the process of reconstruction when the Roman forces attacked. Sections of its inner rampart are only half-built. Skeletons of 130 defenders of the hill-fort were unearthed by railway navvies in 1857 when the Somerset and Dorset line was sliced into the east side of the earthworks. Many of the bones were hacked with sword cuts, and others had been fractured. The bodies had been buried with their weapons, and had been clothed as there were many pieces of personal jewellery.

There are Roman marching camps on the other side of the

River Stour, at Crab Farm, Shapwick, and near Tarrant Keynston. Earthworks are abundant in this area and many have revealed relics of the invasion. Scrub clearance in 1964, a quarter of a mile from Badbury Rings hill-fort, turned up human bones and a previously unknown enclosure. Excavation the following year revealed that its ditch dated from the late Iron Age and had been deepened from five and a half feet to thirteen and a half feet "shortly before the Roman invasion". Soil that had washed from the top of the bank contained a Roman ballista bolt-head.

These artillery machines were decisive in the capture of another Stour hill-fort, on Hod Hill to the north-west of Blandford. It is an isolated hillside rising sheer from the east banks of the river and curving upwards across a dome-shaped down. Slopes protect the hilltop on all sides, but it is flat enough on top for buildings and farming, and sufficiently high to command the valley pass and much more. The defences of Hod Hill are still immense. There are two main ramparts in a large square, with curved corners and fortified gateways. The inner-most of the ramparts is fifty feet wide and fifteen feet high but looks, and is, much higher because deep quarry pits lie behind the defences and a twenty-foot ditch plummets on the outside.

Inside, the area curtained by the ramparts is the largest of any hill-fort in Dorset. Hod Hill has an internal area of 55 acres, compared with 45 at Maiden Castle; 34 at Hambledon Hill; 25 at Eggardon Hill; 18 at Badbury Rings. It was built, probably, in the third century BC, and became a powerful tribal centre, being refortified before the Roman invasion. This rebuilding was in progress when the Romans arrived, as can be seen at the south-east corner where the new outer ditch stops abruptly and the spoil heap remains uncleared.

The more recent history of Hod is that it was ploughed for the first time about 1830. Celtic and Roman antiquities were soon being found in quantity and collected locally, the principal hoard now having passed to the British Museum though the finest objects are still in private hands. William Cowell, one of the older men in the district when Sir Ian Richmond came to excavate the hill-fort in the 1950s, told the archaeologist: "When I was young and wanted some money for baccy, I used to walk up Hod and see what I could find in the plough. If it was something metal, I knew that I could take it to Mr (Henry) Durden at Blandford; and I would always get sixpence, or sometimes a shilling for it."

Ploughing was resumed this century, under the pressures of the last war, and destroyed much of the archaeology. It has ceased now but only the southern part of the eastern section of the hill has been completely spared from disturbance. Here the Royal Commission on Historical Monuments has found visible signs of the staggering total of 240 structures in an area only 620 by 800 feet. Most of these are huts, enclosures, and pits. At least 53 circular depressions, many of them showing clearly on the ground, mark the sites of the huts.

Richmond's excavations, from 1951–58 published in the British Museum's two volumes on *Hod Hill*, revealed that the community relied for defence on catapulted slingstones rather than hand-thrown weapons like spears. Arsenals of a total of 1,322 pebbles were found in three separate heaps. There was also evidence that a twentieth of the fort's area was given over to the accommodation of chariots and horses. These were the shock-troops of Celtic warfare, skilled in the type of battle that Caesar and Tacitus described.

One of the huts was the chieftain's, its status being assumed by the excavators because a main track led directly to it from one of the gates. Inside, they found iron spears rather than slingstones. Puddled clay for pot-making was kept in a storage pit, cut into the chalk, in one of the outbuildings.

More significantly, Richmond found a "systematic scatter of iron heads of Roman ballista-bolts. Eleven of these murderous

Bolt-firing ballista machine, the artillery piece of the Roman conquest. It was used to devastating effect against the southern hill-forts. This replica is at Chesterholm, Northumberland. *Photograph: Roland Gant*

tips were found, each some three and a half inches long, with a socket for the wooden shaft and a solid four-sided head brought to a sharp point and projecting at the base".

He noted the position of each and compiled a unique record of the spread of missiles from Roman artillery. The arc of fire was calculated at about ten degrees. The source of the fire was a short distance outside the defences. Sighting shots and wides were also found.

The conclusion was that a movable siege-tower more than fifty feet high and housing the ballista machine acted as lookout to correct the line and angle of fire. Only the chieftain's hut was attacked. Blitzkrieg was Richmond's word for it, and the outcome was that the act of intimidation had succeeded in showing the "deadly and devastating precision" of the Roman military machines.

The excavator summed up: "The lack of evidence for an assault of the hill-fort, or for subsequent devastation within it, would strongly suggest that capitulation was there and then induced, by showing dramatically what concentrated fire could do."

Unconditional surrender followed and the defences were slighted and the huts demolished. All the inhabitants were moved away, probably into one of the defenceless settlements on the valley side.

What followed was unusual. The Second Legion commandeered the hilltop and built their own fort inside the north-west corner of the Iron Age defences, utilising existing ramparts for two sides with additional Roman ditches to protect the garrison from the remainder of the hill. It is 753 feet across from north to south and 587 feet wide in the east-west direction. The north side is a double rampart of the native fort, which was then topped with a breastwork of flints to make a stout parapet, though this was pulled down and used for building in the valley villages during the Middle Ages. On the next side, the west, there was just a single rampart of the old fort to be utilised. Neither the victors nor the vanquished needed more: it stands above a 350-foot near-sheer drop to the Stour. For the other two sides of the fort, the Roman engineers had to do their own building, across the virtually open top of the hill. They cut a line of defences where now the rare frog orchids grow, through the scattering of native huts and into solid chalk.

The entrance to the Roman fort on Hod Hill, overlooking the Stour valley in central Dorset. *Photograph: John Pitfield*

This work was based upon a simple but lethal ditch system overlooked by an inner rampart. It was a ten foot high wall with a walk along the top, timber reinforcements, and sides made from stacks of turf. The ditches lie on the outside and take up a level strip ninety feet wide, starting at the far end with an initial ditch twenty feet wide and five feet deep. It started with a vertical drop but then offered a gentle rise towards the fort. This was a trap – the intruder was offered an unhindered run across 55 feet of open ground.

Suddenly, he came to a previously unnoticed ditch, intended to throw an attacker on to the rocks and break his leg. This, and another ditch, lay directly under the shadow of the wall and escape would have been impossible for any who fell. Those who turned to run back to the outermost ditch were also in a trap. The first ditch they had leapt effortlessly was impossible to jump back across. Escape was blocked by a vertical outer face, within the thirty-yard killing range of hand-thrown missiles from the fort wall. As the enemy tried to scramble up the rock face their backs would have been open targets for spears thrown from the rampart.

The defences encouraged the approach and confidence of the attacker, and then kept him in a field of fire from which there was no retreat. It was the intellectual side of warfare, compared with the sheer bulk of their prehistoric predecessors. Intricate causeways also protected the entrances and all three Roman gateways were heavily timbered and provided with ballista ramps, two of which can still be seen. The artillery was set up as directed by the military manual on "towers with three posts at the front and two at the back" – to give a wider arc of fire – and positioned to shoot into the right side of an approaching enemy. That side, against right-handed opponents, would have been unshielded. These missiles would have had an effective range of about two hundred yards, outdistancing the thirty-yard killing limit of hand-thrown weapons by seven times. The attackers would not have been able to retaliate. This gave the legionaries the opportunity to break a massed attack before it reached the ditches of the fort.

Water storage and sanitation problems influenced the siting of a Roman fort. In the case of Hod Hill the horses would have been taken down to the river and watered, but large reservoirs had to be maintained on the hill for everyday use and emergencies. One of these water tanks originally held over 1,500 gallons. Leather water-carriers were probably hauled by pulleys, directly up the three hundred feet high one-in-one gradient from the river bank. The corner in the original ramparts of the Iron Age fort was breached for a water-gate, the route the horses were taken to the river.

Sewage, on the other hand, had to be disposed of downstream of the fort, and this accounts for the latrine and ablutions block being built immediately inside the southern gate. It was 34 feet long and had separate compartments opening onto a passage. Each latrine had an open front and would have held a tub. Adjoining the latrine block were two rooms in which rinsing troughs would have been installed. The Romans used Mediterranean sponges as we use toilet paper and these had to be cleaned after use. One room was probably for the cavalry troopers and the other for legionaries.

Richmond's excavators also found the stable blocks, grooms' quarters, granary, cookhouse, legionary barracks, and – in the centre of the fort – the principia, or headquarters building. There were separate houses for the legionary and cavalry commanders. The latter lived in far more sumptuous surroundings and this reflected the higher class-status of the trooper in the Roman army.

Evidence that the army here had a fighting rôle was to be unearthed from its hospital. The size and provision made inside this building indicated that Hod Hill – as a forward post on the new frontier – had to expect high casualties. The hospital was four times larger than its equivalent in garrisons defending peaceful areas and had about a hundred beds.

Detailed figures were calculated for the strength of the garrison. It had an estimated total of 718 men, including four hundred legionaries; 234 troopers with 252 horses; 84 grooms. Hod Hill sent out mounted patrols to police the Celtic peasantry of the densely populated Dorset downlands during the first six years of Roman rule. It was occupied, like most of the early forts in the West Country, from about 44 to 50. The hilltop was then abandoned and never reoccupied.

The strong military presence on the edge of Cranborne Chase had been necessary to ensure the pacification and subjugation of the tribes that had resisted Roman rule. The hillforts had only been taken after a struggle. Lieutenant General Augustus Pitt-Rivers found some clues to the activities of the Hod garrisons when he excavated the native farm at Rotherley Down, near Tollard Royal, towards the end of the last century. He found that as an Iron Age settlement it had functioned with about fifty grain storage pits. With the coming of Roman rule, however, this number had declined to only twenty – although the same number of houses were occupied. The only satisfactory explanation was that two-thirds of their corn was seized immediately after the harvest by Roman officials.

Another way of impressing the might of Rome upon the minds and bodies of the defeated natives was in using forced labour from the native settlements to build the causeway of Ackling Dyke, the Roman road from Badbury Rings to Salisbury. It is unnecessarily high for its entire course along the edge of Cranborne Chase.

The road is raised on an embankment forty feet wide and six feet high for its passage across the driest countryside in Dorset. There was no need for any elaborate causeway, as a paved track would have been sufficient. It was to be a permanent monument to the enslavement of Britain and cuts through ancient burial mounds, ceremonial earthworks, and field systems with complete contempt for the old way of life. Each mile contains a million cubic feet of chalk, and would have taken the hard labour of a thousand people working for a month. It is built on this scale for fifteen miles.

Military roads, by contrast, were of minimal construction. The one to Hod Hill leads from Badbury Rings and, in places, its pebbled surface has been adopted for later parish boundaries. It was only embanked where the terrain made this necessary. An excavation at Lazerton Farm, Stourpaine, in 1972–73 revealed the approach road to Hod. A clearly visible two-foot high causeway led across the meadow beside the Iwerne Brook – and had to be ancient as it coincided with a mediaeval manorial boundary. It was also in a direct line with the Ashfield Gate, eleven hundred feet away, which the Romans cut through the eastern ramparts of the Iron Age fortifications to reach their own fort. The dig confirmed that this bank across the Iwerne valley was originally sixteen feet wide with a base of flints resting on the former ground surface. There was a parallel side-ditch, three and a half feet wide, a short distance to the south.

After the initial seizure of Hod Hill and the containment of the Stour valley, the main legionary force went westward. It may well have gone by sea, and anyway that was how it would be supplied, as Vespasian built another shore base at Weymouth. A road was driven inland, similar to the pattern at Selsey Bill and Hamworthy. These parallel lines of advance were clearly defined for the convenience and safety of the fleet, each being on, or close to, a promontory that could be easily spotted from a distance.

A similar coastal depot was established at Lepe, on the Solent shore beside the Beaulieu estuary, for the crossing to the Isle of Wight. From another, at Southampton, a long arm of the sea brought the highly populated Hampshire downlands within

The four great banks of the Iron Age hill-fort of Maiden Castle, Dorset, which was stormed by the Second Legion. Its lines were etched in snow at the beginning of 1963.

Photograph: Frederick G. Masters

marching distance. These forward bases may have been built later in the campaign, after the decisive battles in the west, when the hold on the region could be consolidated.

It was on the other side of the hill from Weymouth that the Second Legion had its strongest taste of blood for which archaeological evidence has so far been found. To the north of the coastal ridgeway are the great, complex fortifications of Maiden Castle. Triple ramparts with huge ditches between were revetted with timber and limestone. Complicated outworks protected the entrances, to ensure that all who approached had to pass through a long passageway during which time they were observed and overlooked. The formalities of entry were carried out at sentry boxes at the inner end of a forecourt, the two gateways suggesting 'in' and 'out'.

The ramparts of the fortification were engineered with one weapon in mind – the slingstone. The defences had been designed with mathematical precision, taking into account a combination of distance and height, to ensure that the advantage was with the defender. Those firing slingstones from the inner bank had their attackers just within catapult range but for the intruders the uphill line of fire would have lessened the effect of the return shots. Mortimer Wheeler's excavations at Maiden Castle in the 1930s uncovered hoards of thousands of sling-stones, a consistent size having been achieved by collecting beach pebbles from the Chesil Bank where they are graded by nature.

The assault on Maiden Castle was in 44. Wheeler's excavators found hollows filled with earth, ash, and ballista-bolts. Then the skeletons began to emerge "in all manner of contortions and orientations, with all the semblance of having been slung carelessly into their crude graves".

Wheeler wrote in his autobiography, *Still Digging*, that the dead had met a savagely violent end: "The skulls of many of them had been hacked viciously at the time of death; one of them bore no less than nine deep cuts. The victims had been struck variously on the top, front or back of the head – in other words, the wounds were battle-wounds, as indeed their repetition suggested, rather than the mark of methodical execution."

The fallen Celt – a Roman bronze of the moment of defeat.

Photograph: Colin Graham

One of the defenders of Maiden Castle, slaughtered by the Romans and uncovered during Mortimer Wheeler's excavations in 1937. *Photograph: Frederick G. Maste*

One skull had a square hole punched through it, in the quadrangular shape of a Roman ballista-bolt. Another skeleton had an iron arrow-head embedded in its vertebrae. Even that had not killed him, for his head had later received a lethal sword-cut. In all, the pieces of twenty-three men and eleven women were discovered.

It was a massacre, but there were surviving friends or associates who came forward to give the dead a few token comforts for the other world. Most were provided with bowls, and one a mug, for food and drink. In two cases there were joints of lamb pushed into their hands. Rigor mortis had set in, so the dead had probably been retrieved the following night.

The initial Roman assault was with a barrage of ballista-bolts from a cart-mounted artillery machine – as devastating as spraying the area with an M60 machine gun. Flares were also fired from the machine into the huts and gateway buildings. Each century of the legion had a ten-man unit specialising in ballista operations. This gives a figure of sixty ballista machines per legion, though one Celtic hill-fort is unlikely to have required artillery deployment on this scale.

After the firing of the bolts, auxiliaries and the legionaries climbed the walls and stormed through the smoke into the fort.

The wounded were slaughtered. When opposition had been cut down the gates were torn away and the surrounding stone walls levered into ruins. It was an action that must have typified a Roman attack on a hill-fort. Prehistoric hill-forts are ancient monuments on the grand scale and even with famous examples like Maiden Castle only a small percentage of the total area has been excavated.

In most cases the extent of scientific excavation is nil and the archaeological record stands on chance finds. Eggardon Hill, the most westerly escarpment of the main Wessex chalklands, is another of the great defended hilltops that Vespasian must have attacked. It would be fitting for there to be an extensive excavation there, if only for the combination of great earthworks with superb scenery, but such investigations are now unlikely. The undisturbed half of the hill has been bought by the National Trust and is now safeguarded. Archaeological priorities have to be directed towards sites that are threatened with destruction. Eggardon, one still feels, must offer something worthwhile. It has a view to Start Point and Dartmoor – and a Roman marching camp placed menacingly on its Roman approach road, above Winterbourne Abbas. The temptation is to visualise it as the last bastion of Celtic resistance to the main thrust of the Roman invasion. Once Eggardon had fallen the entire rich chalklands of Wessex would have been under effective Roman control, leaving Vespasian only to mop up isolated patches of local dissent.

One may have been the great earthworks of Pilsdon Pen, the highest point of Dorset, where a nine hundred foot gravel plateau stands above the Marshwood Vale. A Roman ballista-bolt was discovered at the centre of the fort during excavations in the 1960s. Waddon Hill, a Roman fort on a nearby hilltop, has revealed that Roman soldiers had their heroes: a gem-stone from there shows Ajax lifting the body of Achilles, a scene from the Trojan war.

A highly important chain of Roman signal posts and forts can be traced across the south-western peninsula in a straight line from Waddon Hill fort to a fort at Wiveliscombe, Somerset, and a signal station on the north Devon coast at Old Burrow. Waddon Hill remained in commission until about 79, and a replacement for Old Burrow was also retained into the 70s.

Precisely along this same line lie three lofty points – Combe Beacon, the ridge of the Blackdown Hills, and Dunkery Beacon. The last is the 1705-foot high point of Exmoor.

The Romans seem to have come to terms with the realities of West Country weather, in that Old Burrow was soon abandoned in favour of a site further west at Martinhoe, which was lower by three hundred feet and less often shrouded by hill fog and sea mists. Graham Webster suggested in volume one of *Britannia* that "one might expect more stations of this kind to keep the whole of the Bristol Channel under observation".

One strong contender is Steep Holm, a 250-foot high limestone island midway between the Mendip Hills and Wales. There is a mound of stones at its western point, above Rudder Rock, which was incorporated into a Victorian gun battery in 1866. It, and other spots on the island, have yielded first century artefacts. The view from the island embraces the whole of the Bristol Channel from Ilfracombe to Berkeley, or at least its present nuclear power station.

Towards the far west of the peninsula, there was a Roman fort at Nanstallon, near Bodmin, which was occupied from about 50 to 80. A Roman signal station at Stoke Hill, above Exeter, formerly thought to be later, is now also considered to belong to the first century system.

The fort twelve miles south-east at High Peak, a wooded 514-foot clifftop to the west of Sidmouth, also appears to be a first century signal station.

At Waddon Hill, where it was the author's delight to have dug in the excavations for one day, were found large quantities of hare bones. It was symbolic of the changing order. For its part, the animal sacred to the Celts had taken advantage of the taboo and proliferated. For their part, the Romans were only too happy to kill them for sport and food.

This was to be the last invasion of Britain by peoples more advanced than the existing occupants, and the first that had been undertaken for a political purpose by a continental power. Previous newcomers had fought for space, for homes and farms, rather than a principal of annexation. The pace of the occupation was, however, to be slower than the new administration had intended. For when Claudius landed in Kent in 43 – having left Lucius Vitellius in control in Rome – he reviewed the progress of the invasion and received envoys from the Orkneys. That was over optimistic. It was to take another forty years for the Romans to reach Cape Wrath, and even then their passage was only by courtesy of the northern peoples.

Of more practical use to Claudius were the envoys who brought submissions from the Regni, Iceni and the Dobunni. These three hard-pressed native Iron Age tribes had directly faced the spread of the Gallic frontier. For them, Rome was salvation – and an end to their retreat in the path of an earlier colonisation. The Iceni in Norfolk, and the Dobunni of the Cotswolds, were not of immediate use, but the acquiescence of the Regni of the Sussex Downs was important in enabling the Romans to push forward their western onslaught. It had assured Vespasian of a safe anchorage, food, supplies, a civilian labour force, and freedom from harassment.

The meeting between Claudius and his entourage with the British chiefs may have taken place at Chelmsford, Essex, J G F Hind has postulated in *Greece and Rome* volume 21, on the ground of its uniquely imperial name, Caesaromagus. Early military occupation there, apparently a fort, has been dated between 43 and 49. Graham Webster, on the other hand, says in *The Roman Invasion of Britain* that "this would surely have been

Claudius, the emperor who brought Britain into the empire. This bronze head was found at Saxmundham, Suffolk, where it had been thrown into a river during the Boudican insurrection.

Courtesy: British Museum

at the British capital", Colchester. There was, however, another capital, in the sense of wherever the army council met and the headquarters buildings were sited. It was certainly not in London. A military base, such as Chelmsford, may have been politically neutral and therefore more acceptable than one of the old tribal capitals. It would also have offered infinitely tighter security, for the benefit of all concerned. Claudius would have visited the great British tribal centre of

Camulodunum – Colchester, in north-east Essex – but that does not preclude the tribal submissions having taken place elsewhere.

Although twice nearly shipwrecked (first off the Ligurian shore and then in rounding the Côte d'Azur), the whole exercise went so smoothly that Claudius, anticipating total victory, was able to set off back to Rome after only sixteen days in Britain.

This was his greatest achievement. He returned to glory. The decoration of the headless spear – signifying a disarmed enemy – was awarded to the soldiers who had fought in Britain. Claudius also made the award to Posides, the eunuch, who was his favourite ex-slave.

Plaques were erected by local councillors in Italy in honour of the leading participants of the British conquest. One, found at Turin, was to Gaius Gavius, a centurion of the Eighth Legion in 43, and its chief centurion by about 60. It records that he was "decorated in the British war with necklets, armlets and medals, and with a golden crown".

Vespasian was awarded the decree of *triumphalia ornamenta* in 44 in recognition of his achievements in the campaign, though it does not follow that he would have been recalled to Rome for the erection of his triumphal statue. Aulus Plautius, the leader of the invasion, became the new province's first governor. He was a commander of consular rank.

Three objectives had been secured. The emperor's prestige had been boosted, particularly by securing an objective which Caesar himself had only visited; there would no longer be the possibility of a strong Celtic nation rising to rival Rome on the rich hills of southern Britain; and there were indications from amongst the loot of the mineral wealth of the new province. Few could have foreseen a mere island becoming instead a burden on the Roman empire for the next four hundred years. The place was never to lose its independent spirit.

The lasting effect of the events of AD 43 had been the stemming of the tide of Gallic advancement and the fossilising of the sub-divisions of lowland Britain for the next five centuries. To a great extent this same geography of populations continued unchanged in the Saxon period, and the pattern can be followed through the Middle Ages and the Industrial Revolution to the present day.

The archaeologist, Tom Lethbridge, in *The Painted Men*, noticed that the Saxon kingdoms in Britain basically occupied the same divisions as the pre-Roman tribes – and indicated that the tribal areas not only stayed intact through the Roman period but that "the old British cantons had come under the rule of Anglo-Saxon families and that much of the former British stock remained in them".

Lethbridge put forward the theory, novel for the mid-1950s but accepted now, that the British stock is far from being Germanic, as used to be assumed, but is basically a Celtic-Gaulish mixture. The Gallic influence was intensifying up to 43, as the grip of the Belgic settlers strengthened, and but for Roman intervention, would have been destined for greater things.

"Had the Belgae been given time enough to extend their conquests to the whole of the lowland zone of Britain, and to weld the country into one unit, it is improbable that the Roman army could ever have subdued it. Tacitus, who is very fair in his estimates, bluntly ascribes the success of the Roman army to dissension among the Britons."

Archaeologists have still to locate Britain's first capital, or to identify it as such. Excavations in the 1970s finally demolished the smug assumption that London was founded as a military supply base and bridgehead in the initial Claudian conquest of 43. Nothing has been found in Roman Londinium that indicates a settlement pre-dating 50, and the coin evidence points to its foundation between 53 and 55.

The Roman roads that converged at the south end of London Bridge were constructed between 50 and 65 – a programme interrupted by Boudica in 60. Little pottery has been found in London that can be dated earlier than the rebellion, and it has no claim to being the capital of Britannia before the building of a palace and a forum after the destruction of 60. Canterbury, Richborough, Lympne, and even Chichester – garrisoned until about 70 – are more likely candidates for the seat of provincial command in the first two decades of Roman rule. Villas to the west of Chichester are amongst the earliest in Britain and show high levels of Romanisation.

Invasion gives way to insurrection

THE ARCH OF Claudius in Rome honoured the emperor's achievement in these islands. The inscription has been reconstructed in a courtyard wall of the Conservatori Museum in the Capitol, Rome. Its words, like any that have to be cut in stone, are a simplification. He is acclaimed "because he received the surrender of eleven tribes of Britain, defeated without any loss, and because he was the first to have brought the barbarian peoples across the ocean under the influence of the Roman people".

Eleven kings had been bought or defeated, but problems remained. A people bred on the sides of some of the most inhospitable mountains in Europe – some of which would literally burst into flame – had to come to terms with the fiery temperaments and indented geography of a modest little island at the edge of the world.

Even the British lowlands could present difficulties, as with the Iceni revolt of 47–48, after which the Romans postponed the idea of bringing the turbulent area into the province and instead installed a client king, Prasutagus, whose wife was Boudica, which is the current spelling of Boadicea.

The discovery at Gallows Hill, Thetford, of the first stronghold of the Iceni that can be dated to the client-state period of Prasutagus and Boudica from 48 to 60 was described by Norman Hammond in *The Times* on 11 August 1981. The

Full-face Roman helmet with visor mask, of probable first century date, from Ribchester, Lancashire.

Photograph: Colin Graham

fortified enclosure had been spotted the previous year, showing as three rectangular ditches, with openings towards the east, on an aerial photograph. The site lies close to the point where Ickneild Way enters from the north into the Little Ouse valley, and archaeological interest in the area had been sharpened by the metal-detector discovery in 1979 of a fourth century treasure of gold and silver less than a hundred yards from the Iceni enclosure.

Excavations by Norfolk Archaeological Unit revealed that this had a middle ditch 488 feet by 260 feet, enclosing three large circular houses. These were about forty feet in diameter – giving a floor area of 1,134 square feet – and faced the eastern entrance. The inner and outer ditches were added later, at which time the northern two houses appear to have been rebuilt. Gallo-Belgic and imported Roman pottery from the

41

mid-first century pointed to a date after the first Iceni revolt of 47–48 but before the devastating second uprising of 60.

The outer and middle ditches had a depth of four feet, but the inner one was eight feet deep. It enclosed about an acre. Between the middle ditch and the new outer one there was a barrier of seven circuits of postholes, each holding timbers about four inches in diameter and four inches apart. These may have been normal palisades "set vertically in stockades", Hammond writes, "or slanted outwards in a chevaux-de-frise arrangement of bristling pointed stakes".

Tony Gregory, director of the dig for Norfolk Archaeological Unit, summed up the implications of the discovery: "We estimate that if each timber was six feet long then seventy miles of running feet of lumber would have been needed to build these defences. This, together with the manpower needed to dig the ditches and move away thousands of tons of soil, was a colossal investment simply to defend a one-acre site. The person who had the defences built was clearly of high social rank. The defences were planned by experienced people. Perhaps we can see them as being erected by native labour with Roman planning and advice."

The Romans in Britain were always to have their troubles from the hill country, which led to the decisions to conquer Wales (successfully) and Scotland (unsuccessfully). For many years, however, these were options to be avoided, the early orders from Rome demanding a beneficial province with the least expense; the wild peoples were to be left to their hills.

After five years of armed truce following the invasion, the Romans took the weapons from the lowland tribes in 48. Tacitus says that the new governor, Ostorius Scapula, "disarmed all those suspected on the Roman side of the Trent and the Severn". This shows that the Fosse Way marked the division between civilian and military areas by 48. It was not the actual frontier, but was built as a secure line of communications – a straightening of miles of prehistoric trackway that already followed the Cotswold escarpment, being known to archaeologists (because of the geology) as the Jurassic Way – which linked support facilities well behind the potentially unsettled regions.

The Fosse was a military road defining and giving access to what was intended as a forward fighting zone. The country on the lowland side of the Fosse had to be guaranteed secure from penetration by insurgents. The problem for the military was to achieve the necessary depth of defences on the other side of the road. This was simple in the south-western sector where the Romans utilised the Bristol Channel and its adjoining marshes as the front line.

In the west Midlands, on the other hand, the terrain worked against Roman ideas of security. The results on the ground show the magnitude of the threat. The military corridor of the south-west spread into a huge bulge, with twenty forts scattered across 2,500 square miles. Wales was kept from England by fifty miles of defences, from Wroxeter in the borderland to High Cross at the centre of the Fosse.

Military coverage on this scale had become both necessary and permanent. Forts intended for short-term use were turned into a series of garrisons. The financial strains of the provincial government were spread by taxation to the subject peoples of the east. Refugees from the occupied lowlands found in the Welsh mountains the spiritual support of the Druid priesthood, who realised that this was going to be the final chance to save the last strongholds of their faith.

Caradoc (or Caractacus in its Latinised form, though Caradawg, the Welsh version, is preferable) after his initial defeat on home territory in East Anglia in 43, was welcomed in the west and found acceptance as an overall commander of the united Welsh tribes. He carried the war from Silurian territory to the country of the Ordovices. He was the son of Cunobelin, the great Catuvellaunian ruler of Colchester.

In about 49 the Twentieth Legion moved west to Kingsholm, Gloucester, from Colchester it seems. It brought its own Belgic potters. Their output in Gloucestershire was considerable, and the work is similar in style to that of the Savernake kilns in Wiltshire.

Three miles west of these an overgrown mound on the north side of Martinsell Camp at Oare, was described by its excavators in 1908 as a "Late Celtic rubbish heap" but re-investigations by Vivien G Swan in 1975, for volume six of *Britannia*, showed it to be a kiln waste heap dating to the middle of the first century. The dump had also been used as a convenient tip for domestic and other rubbish, including iron slag and a lead-glazed sherd that was imported into Britain after the Roman invasion. Other pottery was pre-conquest but can be confidently said to be ex-military stores from Sussex, the huge stocks that had been shipped into Fishbourne and other supply bases. Vivien Swan suggests that much of this had been requisitioned for Augustus's campaigns in Germany and put in store on his retreat: "When Claudius's massive undertaking to conquer Britain was planned, these stores may have been released to help overcome any initial supply difficulties. Old weapons, armour, and other military equipment certainly seem to have been stored and recirculated by the Roman quartermasters; and even today, government requisitions are stockpiled for decades until they are released under emergency circumstances."

The other point is that there is no other way of explaining how a miscellaneous assortment of early first century Italian army-ordered stores can turn up in the middle of Wiltshire.

The products of the Oare pottery itself are also unusual, being of the Gallo-Belgic type produced in Essex and Hertfordshire. They are unlike any pre-Roman pottery in Wiltshire, which makes it clear that the potters were imported.

Probably they were employed by the Roman army, or relied upon it for their sales.

The walled town of Cunetione (derived from Cunetio, the Celtic river name for the Kennet), now deserted at Mildenhall, lies four miles north-east from Oare. It seems to have had military origins as a Claudian fort – and an early well there contained wares of between 50 to 60. It had been abandoned whilst still usable – and its use then as a convenient rubbish pit has all the marks of the Roman army breaking camp, possibly when the phoney victory was brought abruptly to an end.

Nine years after the invasion, however, to the Roman authorities at least, the western rising must have seemed all but over. Ostorius Scapula, the governor of the new province of Britain, had achieved a sharp and spectacular example of Roman campaigning skills in AD 52.

Caradoc who, in the words of Tacitus "had defied our power for so many years" had been defeated in Shropshire by a Roman army advancing under a tortoise of locked shields to pull down the wall of his stronghold.

"It was a great victory," Tacitus says. Caradoc's wife and daughter were captured and his brother surrendered. Caradoc himself "sought sanctuary with Cartismandua, queen of the Brigantes. But the defeated have no refuge. He was arrested, and handed over to the conquerors."

They realised the political value of their prize and Caradoc was sent to Rome, accompanied by his family. He is said to have made a speech pleading for his life, though in defiant terms as he pointed out that his downfall and their triumph were famous only because he had not surrendered.

"If you want to rule the world," he asked, "does it follow that everyone else welcomes enslavement?" Claudius responded by pardoning Caradoc and his family, releasing them from their chains.

They gave similar homage to Agrippina, who was seated

before Roman standards – which for Rome was a break with tradition, though the Celts understood respect for the female line – and provided the spectacle with a moment of "unprecedented novelty". It was a theatrical climax to an expedition, but it achieved little.

Cornelius Tacitus, writing in *The Annals of Rome*, records that "the people were curious to see the man who had defied our power for so many years" and describes the rapture of the Senate: "It devoted numerous complimentary speeches to the capture of Caradoc. This was hailed as equal in glory to any previous Roman general's exhibition of a captured king. They cited the display of Syphax by Publius Cornelius Scipio Africanus (203 BC) and of Perseus by Lucius Aemilius Paulus (168 BC). Ostorius received an honorary Triumph. But now his success, hitherto unblemished, began to waver. Possibly the elimination of Caradoc had caused a slackening of energy, in the belief that the war was over. Or perhaps the enemy's sympathy with their great king had whetted their appetite for revenge." As for the *triumphalia ornamenta* to Ostorius Scapula – a triumphal statue – Claudius did not recall him to Rome to enjoy his moment of pride; instead, he was to face a messy campaign against the Silures, during which he died.

Captives and martyrs can be emotive stimulants in the Celtic world. The resentment of the Cornovii, Ordovices, and Silures spilled across the Welsh marches to threaten the survival of the Roman state. Effective guerilla action by the Silures during Ostorius Scapula's years as governor (47–52) had brought the conflict to the Roman side of the Severn. In that the Rhine and the Danube were no barrier to the Roman army, they can hardly have believed that the Britons would be stopped by their country's longest river. They had been crossing it for generations, and continued to do so. The state was in chaos. It was taking the continuous efforts of more than fifty thousand Roman soldiers to maintain the province.

By 54 the position was desperate. With the assassination of the emperor, Claudius – poisoned by his niece and spouse, Agrippina – the great psychological obstacle to disengagement was weakened. For the conquest of Britain was the achievement of Claudius's reign. He had carried out what Caesar had found impossible. He had also made Mauretania a province of empire, but a desert state lacks the glamour of a northern isle. Claudius had no personal doubts as to which was the most prestigious, for he named his son Britannicus.

Britannicus would have succeeded him as emperor, but Agrippina persuaded Claudius to set him aside and choose her own son, Nero, as his heir. Britain figured in the reappraisal of commitments at the beginning of Nero's reign. As the military and economic cost of holding Britain increased, Rome was forced to consider the possibility of withdrawal. That this option was discussed is revealed by the historian Gaius Suetonius Tranquillus, writing some sixty years later but from full access to the Roman archives: "Nero felt no ambition or hope to extend or enlarge the Roman empire, and even considered withdrawing his forces from Britain: yet kept them there because such a decision might have reflected on the glory won by his adoptive father Claudius."

A major Romanised cult centre was established at an early date – probably around 55 – on Hayling Island in the pro-Roman territory of the Hampshire Atrebates. The last ruler of this tribe, Cogidubnus, was probably directly involved in the building of a large circular shrine or cella, constructed in stone, 45 feet in diameter and about seventy feet high. Its style was Gallic, very similar to the cella which survives at Périgueux in France. All that remains on Hayling Island, however, is a crop-mark in the barley. Dedications of similar circular temples in France point to Augustus and Mars Mullo, or some Celtic merging of classical and native beliefs. There had been an Iron Age temple on the Hayling Island site, possibly founded by

Commios, king of the Atrebates, who had acted as a British envoy to Caesar's Rome before 55 BC. The indications are that his descendant, Cogidubnus, was equally out of line with the general mood of the nation a century later.

Aulus Didius Gallus, the governor in Britain from 52 to 58, was managing little more than a holding operation. Tacitus remarks that he established "a few forts in more advanced positions, so that he could claim the credit of making some annexations". He held his job for four years under Nero, being replaced by Quintius Veranius in 58. Veranius had mountain warfare experience but lived only a few months more, dying in office later in the year. The province continued to founder.

Britain's third governor of 58 was a hardline choice with an impeccable military pedigree. Suetonius Paulinus had been the first governor, in 42, of Mauretania – that other addition to empire. There he had fought and conquered the mountain peoples of the High Atlas, where success had largely been a matter of cutting off the tribesmen in the hills from their oases supply lines.

He realised that there could be no peace in lowland Britain without the pacification of the Welsh. The campaign went ahead in the year 60. Half the Roman forces in Britain pushed forward, on two fronts, with the Fourteenth Legion operating from Wroxeter and the Twentieth Legion from Chester. The Fourteenth marched towards the strongholds of the Silures in the southern hills. Suetonius led the Twentieth himself, into the territory of the Ordovices, along the North Wales seaboard. He replayed his African tactics, by moving along the line of least difficulty and separating the hill people from the island of Anglesey which, says Tacitus, "was feeding the native resistance".

Anglesey was a bastion of Druidic culture, and from across the water it had attracted a stream of refugees. Their wailing curses on the Menai beaches were insufficient to hold back the legionary landings. The cavalry waded ashore to hack to pieces the Druids and their groves. It should have been a time of bay-leaved dispatches, to announce the victory in Rome. But the autumn news of AD 60 was travelling in reverse, with a message to Suetonius that rebellion had engulfed Colchester, the country's second largest Roman colony.

He had won the mountains but was nearly to lose the province. The flashpoint for the troubles was at the other side of the country, in the farmlands of East Anglia, and had its roots in an arrangement that pre-dated Suetonius Paulinus and Nero. For Prasutagus, the king of the Iceni, had negotiated a cash grant in the time of Claudius. The terms of this were redefined in 60, reducing it to a loan. It has been suggested that this was due to sharp practice on the part of the provincial procurator, but more likely it was a direct result of Prasutagus's death that same year, with the treaty valid only whilst he lived, and a reversion of property to the Romans after his death. The effects were going to be disastrous, but they were not illegal.

With the governor preoccupied in farthest Wales, the pay-master, like any civil servant, went by the rules and proceeded to enforce the default clause. Catus Decianus, the procurator of the province – the title of its chief treasury official – ruled that the royal estates were forfeit. The Celts respected the female line and Boudica, Prasutagus's widow, had become monarch. Boudicca was the form of her name recently in favour, though in Victorian times it was Boadicea. More correctly, she was Boudica or Buddeg, and the name meant (as does *buddug* in modern Welsh) 'victory', which was to be hers for a month.

After the death of Prasutagus, Boudica had been seized, whipped, and evicted from her household. Her two teenage daughters, princesses of the Iceni, were raped. Together these were the ingredients of revolution – outrage to unify a cause, an obvious leader, and the opportunity for immediate action.

Boudica's speech must have been a little more rousing than that put into her mouth by Dio Cassius, but his description of

Boudica in her chariot, rearing opposite the Houses of Parliament in London – a Victorian imperial celebration of the insurrection that cost 70,000 Roman lives.
Photograph: Colin Graham

the lady is convincing enough: "A great mass of bright red hair fell to her knees. She wore a great twisted golden necklace and a tunic of many colours, over which was a thick mantle, fastened by a brooch."

She led a peasant army that was straining for revenge. The population of Iron Age England was extensive and dense by contemporary Roman and European standards. Tacitus says that Boudica fielded an incredible multitude. On its own that statement might be subject to question – reasons might be needed to explain how a woman and her supporters were successful in firing three new Roman cities – but there were enough Roman families with direct knowledge of the rebellion to make a cover-up difficult. Caesar had also remarked on the number of people inhabiting Britain: "The population is immense; homesteads closely resembling those of the Gauls are met with at every turn, and cattle are very numerous."

These hordes had an irresistible target within easy distance of their Norfolk and Suffolk farmsteads. It was symbolically offensive and pseudo-military. The Romans had established a large colonia for legionary veterans and their dependents at

Colchester, to the south-east of the site of Cunobelin's royal court. It may have been built as a counterweight to these native traditions, but probably the spot was chosen because it was already a flourishing port and one of the most cosmopolitan places in the province.

Veterans are not likely to have been popular with the natives. They had earned their pensions by killing such people, and in Vergil's *Eclogues* the ex-soldiers who returned to their Italian homeland are presented as being arrogantly vulgar in their relationship with the rest of the population.

Even the very architecture of the colonia was alien; there were no mortared buildings in the Celtic world – the first did not appear in Ireland for another seven hundred years – and it must have been regarded as an obscenity by those who remembered the great age of Cunobelin who had minted something in the region of a million gold coins in the three decades preceding the Roman invasion.

A little of the wealth of Cunobelin – a handful of the million gold coins minted at Colchester, Essex, in the three decades preceding the Roman invasion. They carry the emblem of the prancing horse, some with the chieftain's abbreviated name "CVNO" and others with that of the city, "CAMV" (Camulodunum). *Photograph: Colin Graham*

Colchester pottery urn of about AD 61, when such wares were in considerable demand. *Photograph: John Pitfield*

Colchester, to the Britons, writes Tacitus, was "the citadel of servitude". They spent two days there reducing it to burnt ruins. The great temple of Claudius was smashed down to its huge vaulted podium. This core of the building was to survive through Dark Age and Saxon times, being utilised by the Normans for the foundations of their castle. The other symbolic relic of the destruction of the colonia is a life-sized bronze head of Claudius, torn from a public statue, that was thrown into a river near Saxmundham. The temple of *divus Claudius*, incidentally, has been shown by Professor Duncan Fishwick, in volumes three and four of *Britannia*, to have been dedicated to the deified Claudius, and not to the living emperor as was once assumed.

From Colchester the revolution spread to St Albans and London, the other two major cities of the province. St Albans was still largely a native town, but that may not have spared its occupants as they were probably regarded as collaborators with the regime. The newly built town of London was already the principal port for the country, functioning as a kind of miniature Hong Kong – a waterfront market-place that handled most of the province's imports and exports, commerce, travellers, and administration. It must have been an exhilarating place to burn. Buildings collapsed and bricks powdered. Samian pottery, the imported table-ware of the foreign classes, was turned from red to black by the heat. Glass and metal melted and trickled across the debris. Boudica's achievement is a band of charred soil, a few inches thick, lying twenty feet down between the basements of the city of London. It was more than Hitler was to manage. Hundreds of bodies were thrown in the Wall Brook, and probably even more in the Thames, where the tide floated them beyond the reach of archaeology. In all, from the three destroyed towns, there were 70,000 massacred.

As this figure is given by Tacitus, who specifically states that it is "established", it can be assumed that it is from official statistics. These, in a state which instigated a five-yearly census, can be taken as correct. But they may be only the total of Roman and other non-British subjects, their wives and children, who were killed in the rebellion. It is quite likely that it excludes the British quislings for whom there must have been equally barbaric treatment. The figure is almost what one might expect, for a Roman army in Britain of nearly 60,000 would have had a civilian accompaniment of at least an equal number of adminis-trators, suppliers, spouses, and pensioners. It shows the level of Roman involvement, particularly if compared with a later example of colonialism – the British in India were able to rule 450 million people for an outlay of ten thousand. The British, like the Romans, perfected the technique of policing the natives with their own people, or subject peoples from elsewhere in the empire.

Slaughter on the scale of events in AD 60 is inevitably

followed by stories of atrocity, and Dio Cassius records that the insurgents brought captured women to the groves of Andrasta, a goddess known also from Gaul, where "their breasts were cut off and stuffed in their mouths, so that they seemed to be eating them, and their bodies were then skewered lengthwise on pointed stakes".

London, though in existence for only half a decade, and "not dignified by the name of a colony, but crowded with merchants and provisions", was already the largest city in the country. Of the three sacked towns it was the only one where there was a slim chance of escape. Fleeing Romans poured on to the boats along the waterfront, though there were nothing like enough ships. Boarding them must have been a similar matter of privilege or luck as it was with the helicopters attending the fall of Saigon. Catus Decianus and his treasury staff successfully escaped overseas.

So the news sailed towards Rome. It was the biggest military disaster in the Roman empire for two generations, since Publius Quintilius Varus lost three legions at Teutoburger Wald in the failed attempt to conquer Germany in AD 9. Varus committed suicide, but Suetonius Paulinus still had the bulk of his army, and the duty to redeem himself. Petilius Cerialis tried to intervene from the north, by leading a relief force of the Ninth Legion from the legionary fortress at Lincoln, but was ambushed in the Fen Country. His infantry were hacked to pieces and only the horsemen made it back to Lincoln.

This left just the Second Legion in a position to come to the aid of Suetonius, from its western bases at Gloucester and, possibly, Wimborne and Exeter. These were two, three and four days march, respectively, from a link-up with Suetonius at High Cross, the hub of the fort system between the Severn and the Trent. This had the advantage of being at the crossroads of England, where Watling Street met the Fosse; it was also a major provisioning centre on the route to the army in Wales –

and therefore in a position to supply the same army in the reverse direction.

Poenius Posthumous, the commander of the Second Legion, misinterpreted the situation. He received Suetonius's order to march his men, but took no action. By staying at his own defences he may have had quite valid reasons for fearing that the south-west would otherwise become a bloodbath. On the other hand he had disobeyed the most important order of his life and left the future of the province in the balance. When he realised the full implications of his decision he did the honourable thing according to the custom of his time and fell upon his sword.

Boudica was given one month of uninterrupted revolution. News of the disaster would have taken four days to reach North Wales. Suetonius then marched his army to within sight of London. That would have taken him a week, given that Harold's Saxon army in 1066 was able to troop – also straight from the exhaustion of battle – from Yorkshire to Sussex at the speed of nearly forty miles a day. But when they arrived to scenes of unimaginable devastation, Suetonius Paulinus realised that the scale of the uprising was beyond immediate suppression. He decided against committing his men to a burning city. Probably he was wise, given that today police commanders are equally unsure whether to throw their men into the uncertainties of a riot, or withdraw until the morning after. Suetonius had an additional problem – nowhere to go. He marched back to High Cross, to avoid the chance of the hordes descending upon him prematurely, and decided to draw the enemy to a battleground of his professional choosing.

The rebellion had now been burning for at least a fortnight; given some slippage in the timetable it was probably three weeks. Boudica had growing difficulties. She knew there was an undefeated Roman army waiting in the wings, and that she had neither the food nor the organisation to turn her looters into a coherent force that could play the same kind of waiting game. After a month there would have been a constant danger of the rebels dispersing homewards. Boudica's achievement was that she was able to round up her confederates and lead them along Watling Street towards Suetonius.

Classical accounts tell us the kind of country where the battle took place. Donald Dudley and Graham Webster have suggested in *The Rebellion of Boudicca* that Suetonius could well have selected the wooded ridge at Mancetter, near Atherstone, Warwickshire, as the point where "the rearward protection he needed" would have enabled his army to "face Watling Street and oppose a further British advance". He had to safeguard his rear, and for the Romans in that position there would have been no turning back from the fearsome hordes.

Tacitus describes ferocious Celtic charges up the slope. These were halted by two volleys of Roman javelins, and the legionaries and auxiliaries plunged into the mêlée with their short stabbing swords. Cavalry charges finally broke the British ranks.

Dio Cassius gives a different version, of a close-run battle with continued onslaughts by both sides. The fight was carried at times by the British chariots, until they drew all the fire of the Roman archers. Both agree that at the end, after the Britons had turned to run, their escape was blocked by hundreds of wagons and oxen at the rear. Thousands of men were cut down, Tacitus giving casualty figures (for what they are worth) of eighty thousand slaughtered Britons, for a loss of four hundred on the Roman side. He says: "It was a famous victory, equal to those of ancient times."

Some escaped, including Boudica herself. She appears to have returned to the land of the Iceni in Norfolk, but did not wait for the Roman retribution and clearances to catch up with her. Tacitus says she took poison, though Dio Cassius says she was killed by a disease. Dio adds that the "Britons mourned her deeply, and gave her a rich burial". Its site is unknown, if it still exists. The Romans who ravaged Iceni territory in the spring of 61 would probably have tortured to discover its whereabouts, and plundered and destroyed any lasting symbol of insurrection.

Numerous hoards of Iceni silver coins were buried in Norfolk but not recovered. Their owners were presumably killed, though at least they had the pleasure of denying the Romans some loot. Tribal names are rare on Celtic coins, but some of these were stamped ECEN or ECENI. It is a pity we insist on calling them the Iceni if they knew themselves as the Eceni, and that a stubborn insistence upon anglicising every foreign-sounding name has to start with our own ancestors.

Reinforcements were sent to Britain from the Rhineland. Two thousand legionaries were needed to bring the Ninth Legion back to strength. Eight cohorts of auxiliaries also arrived, together with a thousand élite cavalrymen of an emergency rapid deployment force; a cohort, incidentally, consisted of 480 men. The army was established in tented camps throughout the troubled countryside. A first century Roman fort at Great Chesterford, beside the River Cam in the north-west corner of Essex, was investigated in 1971 when construction of a motor-way, the M11, threatened the site. Strategically it cuts off any break-out from the Icenian lands towards London. Dating evidence revealed nothing to suggest an earlier, Claudian, occupation. The pottery was of the Neronian and early Flavian periods, making it almost certain that it was a fort constructed during the aftermath of Boudica's revolt, possibly as the winter-quarters for the auxiliaries of the Ninth Legion. There were battle honours for the victors, the Twentieth Legion Valeria and the Fourteenth Legion Gemina, which received the right to include the appellation Victrix in their titles, becoming respectively the *Legio Vicesima Valeria, Victrix* and the *Legio (XIV) Gemina Martia, Victrix*.

In the months that followed Boudica's defeat, Tacitus says,

"the territory of every single state that had been disloyal or unreliable was laid to waste by fire and the sword."

When all else failed, the Romans reached for a political solution. Tacitus reports that "many of the rebels did not lay down their arms, conscious of their guilt and with special reasons for dreading what the governor might do. Excellent officer though he was, they feared he would abuse their surrender, and punish every offence with undue severity, taking it as a personal injury. The government therefore replaced him, by Petronius Turpilianus. They hoped he would be more inclined to listen to pleas of mitigation or protestations of repentance, since he had not witnessed the enemy crimes. He dealt with the existing troubles, but risked no further move before handing over his post to Trebellius Maximus."

That is from the *Agricola*, but in *The Annals of Imperial Rome* Tacitus says Suetonius Paulinus was recalled from Britain for refusing to terminate the war: "His successor, the recent consul Publius Petronius Turpilianus, neither provoking the enemy nor provoked, called this ignoble inactivity peace with honour." He might have allowed that it was an advancement on the general military practice of creating a desert and calling it peace.

The arrival in Britain of Trebellius Maximus was probably in the summer or autumn of 62. "Trebellius," Tacitus continues in the *Agricola*, "was deficient in energy and lacking military experience, but he kept control of the province by an easy-going kind of administration. The barbarians learned, like the Romans, to accept seductive vices, and the intervention of the civil wars provided him with a valid excuse for inactivity."

Trebellius Maximus found that an inactive army is a danger rather than a support to the fabric of the state. Tacitus describes "a serious mutiny; for the troops, accustomed to campaigns, got out of hand when they had nothing to do. Trebellius fled and hid to escape his angry army. He compromised his honour and dignity and commanded merely on sufferance. By a kind of tacit bargain the troops had licence to do as they pleased, and the general had his life, so the mutiny stopped short of bloodshed."

The 60s saw the creation of one of the first fully Romanised parts of the British countryside, on the chalklands beside the tidal reaches of the Medway, downstream from Maidstone, Kent. A villa near Eccles had a corridor-length house with masonry foundations, tessellated floors, and painted wall plaster. It had a separate bath building. The date of this villa was about 65, and that at Cobham Park near Rochester was also probably built soon after the year 70. The impressive main buildings at Fishbourne, Sussex, built to palace standards, date from 75.

The great marble tomb of Julius Alpinus Classicianus, procurator of Roman Britain from AD 60 to about 65, reconstructed in the British Museum from inscribed blocks discovered in the foundation course of a bastion of London Wall at Trinity House Square in 1935.

Courtesy: British Museum

In other parts of Britain the pace of change was slower. Circular timber huts were still being erected within the town wall at Silchester, Hampshire, in the 70s and the 80s. Only in the first years of the next century were some of them pulled down and the site redeveloped with rectangular timbered houses under tiled roofs. Stone-built houses were almost entirely restricted to the countryside and there was to be little use of stone in urban domestic architecture before 160. The countryside, with more space and wealth, led with styles of building that were later copied in the towns. Town architecture was self-assertive on the continent but in Britain it was always derivative and lagged behind that in the countryside. Creeping Romanisation was the pattern of the sixties, and its exponents made for quietly effective rulers.

Trebellius was able to rule, undramatically and with pragmatism, until 69. Tacitus was to denounce him for "the cowardly inactivity he called peace", though perhaps we can today recognise it as a style of government sophisticated for its time, and hope he kept a decent cellar of Falernian wine.

Of equal importance to the restoration of the British province after Boudica's rebellion had been the arrival from the Rhineland of Julius Alpinus Classicianus in the winter of 60. He was appointed procurator, the province's chief treasury officer, with absolute powers over the state's moneys. A man of provincial roots, with a tribal-born wife, he named his daughter Pacata, child of peace, and advocated mercy and reconciliation. Classicianus was a benevolent tax inspector and he understood that peace had its price. The denarius was stronger than the sword.

Rolling back the frontier

THE COMPARATIVE PEACE of the sixties failed to last the decade. Whilst Roman rule in the lowland south was consolidated, discontent remained on the borders, and the general northward spread of Roman influence brought tension to the Pennines. Britain was also destabilised by the civil wars that raged across the empire. The governor, Trebellius, departed to support Aulus Vitellius who had been announced as emperor in 68 by the German legions. Vitellius, with Valens and Caecira, defeated Marcus Salvius Otho, who had previously been proclaimed by his troops. Then Vitellius was defeated by Vespasian's army, under Antonius Primus. In Britain there was a mutiny led by Roscius Coelius, the commander of the Twentieth Legion. Part of the protest seems to have been caused by constraints on their traditional practices of corruption.

In 69, when Vespasian became the new emperor in Rome, Venutius and the Brigantes went into open revolt from the rock-cut fortress at Stanwick in Yorkshire. Venutius had opposed the Romans since 51 but the tribal response had been muted and divided. His queen, Cartismandua, received Roman support. She had betrayed the fleeing hero Caradoc to the Romans after his defeat in Shropshire. By 69, however, opinion hardened behind the king and it was Cartismandua who was exiled from her kingdom.

Venutius marshalled the rising tide of resentment into rapid

61

expansion of his 150-acre stronghold at Stanwick – based on an earlier hill-fort on the Tofts, which became a central command centre – by a further 700 acres to create the largest fortified enclosure of prehistoric Britain.

The uprising was not crushed until 74, by Petillius Cerealis who was governor of Britain from 71 to 74, and the founder of York. He was related to Vespasian, and as consul in 70 he had suppressed the revolt of the Civilis, which prepared him for his British experiences.

The forward garrison advanced from Lincoln. Tacitus writes in the *Agricola*: "Petillius Cerealis at once struck terror into their hearts by attacking the state of the Brigantes, which is said to be the most populous in the whole province. After a series of battles, some of them by no means bloodless, Petillius had overrun, if not actually conquered, the major part of their territory."

These events were incorporated by Juvenal into a line of his satires: "Destroy the tents of the Moors, the forts of the Brigantes."

Stanwick was unfinished when it fell, the entrance on the southern side – in the middle of a rampart which is a mile and a half long – being incomplete. It was hastily made unusable by digging a continuous ditch. Such a fort would have needed the manpower of the most numerous of the country's peoples to engineer and hold its defences, but equally it looks to have been a death-trap on a monumental scale. Some refugees from Brigantian territory never returned to collect their money, Coritanian coin hoards having been found at Honley and Lightcliffe, Yorkshire.

Sextus Julius Frontinus was the governor of Britain from 75 to 78, and Tacitus says he "was equal to shouldering the heavy burden, and rose as high as a man then could rise. He subdued by force of arms the strong and warlike nation of the Silures, after a hard struggle, not only against the valour of his enemy, but against the difficulties of the terrain."

The native hill-fort at South Cadbury, Somerset, was not stormed until three decades after the Roman invasion.

Photograph: Colin Graham

Those difficulties, in southern Wales, must have been considerable: they necessitated the establishment of a legionary fortress of great size, covering 50 acres at the tidal limits of the Usk estuary. It is Caerleon, the Castle of the Legions.

The conquest was completed in 76. Frontinus was highly accomplished in other fields and, in later life, in 97, he was appointed superintendent of Rome's water supply. He died in about 106, leaving writings on aqueducts, and *Strategematica*, a compilation of the sayings and tactics of antiquity's great commanders.

There was also trouble in the West Country. The Iron Age fort above South Cadbury, Somerset, had remained in native occupation and its defences were intact. This, however, was brought to an end in the 70s. The excavators on the hilltop in 1966–70, looking for the tribal capital that might have been Arthur's fabled Camelot of the sixth century, found the evidence of a massacre that had taken place four hundred years earlier. The ground at the site of the fort's south-west gate was littered

63

with the dismembered fragments of thirty men, women and children. One only showed any trace of a battle injury – with his forearm chipped by a sword blow. Around them were iron pikes and javelins and a hundred brooches that were all that was left of the defenders' clothing.

Leslie Alcock, the excavator, writing in *By South Cadbury is that Camelot* (words of John Selden in the seventeenth century) speculated that after the battle and the massacre the corpses had been left to the wolves. A Roman detachment then returned to wreck the defences "and the timber-work of the gate was burned down over the pitiful remains".

At first the excavators thought they had found another of the twenty Wessex strongholds overthrown by Vespasian after the Claudian invasion of 43. They then realised that the bulk of imported Samian table-ware found at the site, left by the troops who had slighted the defences, had been made in Gaul during the reign of Nero, 54 to 68. The fragments of pottery found at the same level as the bodies looked to be native Durotrigian grey ware, but microscopic examination revealed subtle differences and confirmed an early Roman date. The attack had not taken place earlier than 70, and it had proved that one at least of the native forts had remained in use for a generation after the Roman invasion. This is an indication that the outlying parts of the Durotrigic region had come to terms after the storming of the fortresses on the Dorset Downs.

The appearance of the South Cadbury devastation suggests the fort eventually fell in a punitive raid. Its people may have received the blame for some atrocity against local Roman settlers, or been held responsible for mugging travellers on the nearby Fosse Way; at this point the road crosses the Somerset levels only five miles to the north-west.

Archaeologically, the discoveries are important as a reminder that the generalities of invasion and occupation are blurred at the edges. The Romans may have been brutal at Maiden Castle in 44 but they were sufficiently pragmatic to know when to leave alone. South Cadbury was regarded as tolerable for three decades. It stands within sight of the country's major military road and could easily have been cleared out at the first sign of any trouble, which is probably precisely what happened.

Continuity at Cadbury contrasted with the rapid economic exploitation that was taking place in the range of hills to the north. There, lead mining had become a Roman nationalised industry. It had its beginnings in the Iron Age, producing weights for fish-nets used in the Somerset wetlands. Roman lead and silver mining in the Mendip Hills was on a greatly increased scale and most of the information about its development has come from the stampings on various pigs of lead that have been found. Several appear to have been stolen and hidden, but never recovered. They show that the mines were in production under Roman control in 49. Claudian pigs have been found at Blagdon and Wookey. On them appears the name of the Charterhouse district, contracted to Veb(. . .) and once as Vetp, which may together suggest a form along the lines of Veb-t-p.

The procurator in control of the mines in Vespasian's reign was Tiberius Claudius Trifolius, or some variant upon that. He seems to have been too successful. Output was high because the veins of Mendip ore come to the surface at Charterhouse whereas the existing Roman mines in Spain and Gaul extracted their lead with far more difficulty from deep underground. Pliny records in his *Historia Naturalis*, written before 77, that a law was enacted restricting the production of British lead, to relieve competition with the Spanish mines. The bureaucrats of the European Economic Community would have felt at home in first century Rome.

The pigs have their own story. About 24 ladles, each of twenty cubic inches and weighing eight pounds, went into a standard lead pig of 200 librae. These were then weighed and stamped with their excess, above the standard 200 librae – one from Stockbridge, Hampshire, having XXX as its stamping, and a weight of 230 librae (166 pounds).

Four pigs of lead constituted a Roman cart-load (which has been ascertained because four pigs have been found together at Brough-on-Humber, at Pulborough, and Green Ore on Mendip) giving a maximum load of 1,000 librae. In practice, the average weight of a pig was 195 librae (140½ pounds) and twenty times this weight yielded the miner's fodder of 2,820 pounds which survived into recent times in Derbyshire and Yorkshire. The word had its origin in the Latin fodere, to dig up or mine. In Derbyshire the Roman engineers installed wooden piston-pumps which enabled the miners to extract all the lead down to the level of the permanent water table.

Silver was the highly important by-product of the industry. The lead ore – known as galena – of the Mendip Hills contains 0.04 per cent silver. In the event, there were facilities to re-process only half the lead to extract its silver. Some pigs of Mendip lead contain only minute traces of silver, indicating that it had been removed. Others, however, still contain 0.04 to 0.05 per cent silver. This means that the Romans were finding ore with a silver content of thirteen ounces to eighteen ounces per ton. Comparisons with Roman pigs from other parts of Britain show that with levels like this the Mendip ores were uniquely rich. The content of silver in the pigs from elsewhere is very low, varying between about one ounce to three ounces per ton.

BRIT EX ARG stamped on pigs is "Britannicum ex argentariis" – from Britain's lead-silver works – and does not indicate that the silver has been removed ("ex argento") as used to be thought. Many pigs with the inscription contain more silver than those without.

Lead from the Mendips carried the capital's water-supply, and accumulated in their bodies, where it may have had much the same effect as present-day urban airborne lead fallout from car exhausts – reducing brilliant minds to average, and the average to dullards. There was a major lead problem in Roman Britain, though it may not have been recognised as such. "*Cave: plumbum*" was the heading in *The Times* to a report on 27 October 1982 disclosing that excavations on a Roman cemetery at Cirencester, Gloucestershire, had revealed high levels of lead in the skeletons, in some cases enough to have killed children. Dr H A Waldron concludes in his account of the excavations that the amount of lead in the bodies was ten times higher than modern levels, which are themselves a thousand times greater than prehistoric exposures. Lead water pipes would be a simple explanation but none has yet been found in Roman Cirencester.

The lead from Britain was accompanied by large quantities of smelted iron. It was probably shipped to Boulogne, the head-quarters of the British fleet, in returning supply vessels that maintained the ferry service of empire. Caesar mentioned the iron industry of the Weald of Sussex and Kent in his *Conquest of Gaul*. The nodules of carbonate ore found in the Wadhurst clays – lumps from a couple of inches to well over a foot across – have a forty to fifty per cent iron content. The clays also supported a high-canopy forest cover, providing charcoal for the reduction of the ore which required upwards of 1,200 degrees centigrade. It was also convenient that the clay was suitable for furnace building. The ore was taken from open pits, many of which survive as ponds.

Expansion of the Wealden industry in the Roman period was under the direction of *Classis Britannica*, the British fleet, which was in line with Roman thinking on the need for a state monopoly in strategic minerals, and logical as the fleet had to arrange the shipping. The output from the Weald was on a scale virtually unparalleled in the Roman empire, it being apparently a larger producer of iron than any other area, except for Steiermark in Austria.

Other British exports appealed directly to Roman taste. They had found in the province one of the rarest of the world's

One of the earliest burials in style in Roman Britain,
a porphyry cinerary urn found at Warwick Square,
London. It contained a coin of Claudius.

Courtesy: British Museum

semi-precious stones. From the area of Castleton, Derbyshire,
the Romans quarried an outstanding blue-veined fluorspar
known today as Blue John. It was carved into vases, two of
which have been found in a firmly first century context, under
the ashes of Pompeii which was overwhelmed in 79. The Duke
of Devonshire had one of them brought back from Italy, to his
great Derbyshire mansion at Chatsworth.

There is no known source of the crystalline stone away from
a limited part of Derbyshire and its appeal to collectors was still
causing problems in 1981. Two men were fined for digging a
trench on National Trust land at Winnats Pass and a Peak
national park planning spokesman commented: "Blue John is
produced in only two caverns in the Winnats Pass area of
Castleton. There is not a great deal left, though I believe there is

one pillar of Blue John which is said to be worth a quarter of a million pounds."

Fluorspar, calcium fluoride, is colourless and transparent. Impurities give it colour. The additive in the case of Blue John was said to be manganese by the textbooks but George Osborn, an industrial chemist now living at Wimborne, Dorset, remembers putting this to the test.

"We had some samples from the Hope mine, and failed to find any manganese in them. What gave it colour was later found to be element europium, present as one part per hundred million. It then meant nothing to us, and had no applications, but now it is mined in its own right in Sweden and has made it possible to create spectrum in colour television sets."

Purbeck marble and Bath freestone were both being extensively quarried from the early years of the Roman occupation. The marble was used for monumental inscriptions, turning up on sites from Exeter – which has produced a life-sized eagle – to Colchester. Bath oolite had reached Colchester by 60. Brick, tile and pottery kilns had also been established, an Imperial tilery of Nero's time, 54 to 68, having been claimed at Little London, near Silchester, Hampshire.

The products of two pottery kilns at East End, Corfe Mullen, Dorset, included bead-rimmed pots of native style, together with a wide range of flagons, jars and bowls. These kilns

Samian pottery, the dinner service of the best households, was imported from Gaul. *Photograph: John Pitfield*

Early Romano-British pottery, from Alice Holt Forest, Hampshire.

Photograph: John Pitfield

functioned in the first decade or so of Roman rule and would have supplied the Second Legion's garrison at Lake Farm, half a mile away.

Apart from the north Italian 'Arretine' pottery brought across with the invasion, and the import of Gaulish Samian red-ware of dinner service quality, the country remained self-sufficient in pottery production, as it had been in the Iron Age.

Tableware for the Roman army had at first been turned out by potters attached to the units (as at Lake Farm) but a wider industry was developing. Kilns at Alice Holt Forest, Hampshire, produced bead-rim cooking pots of hard grey ware, from about the year 60. It was a continuation or resumption of pottery production on a site that had operated there in Belgic times.

Major A G Wade, who commanded the forest's Home Guard, heard in 1944 from one of his men, Private Disney, of an old pottery site known to the soldier's grandfather. Only grass would grow there, Wade notes in *Alice Holt Forest*, because the ground was five feet deep in broken pots – kiln wasters – and ashes. These "most extensive ancient potteries covering many acres" were discovered by D L Long in 1839 but in the true tradition of British archaeology "no one took any notice of Long's report".

Except, that is, for the owner of Goose Green Farm who found enough sherds in one of the mounds to make himself a driveway. Wade proceeded to excavate the kiln sites, finding hundreds of pots: "The earliest types recovered to date are bead-rim, lathe-burnished vessels of which I recovered hundreds of specimens, the carinated keel-shaped pots, the pure Belgic bead-rim with the high flange on the shoulder, and the oil bottles."

Britain had become a functioning Roman state, rather than the military adventure of previous decades, but its stability remained in doubt. In the early summer of 78 there was another setback for the Romans. A cavalry squadron stationed in North Wales had been virtually wiped out by the Ordovices; the arrival of the province's new governor, Gnaeus Julius Agricola, coincided with the opportunity for a new war. Agricola took the chance to prove himself to his men, and to establish a style of action that was to characterise his governorship. Tacitus, his son-in-law and biographer, says that Agricola "decided to go and meet the peril. He concentrated the legionaries serving on detachment duties and a small force of auxiliaries. As the Ordovices did not venture to descend into the plain, he led his men up into the hills, marching in front himself so as to impart his own courage to the rest by sharing their danger, and cut to pieces almost the whole fighting force of the tribe."

Horse's eye-masks, its protection in battle, from Ribchester, Lancashire.

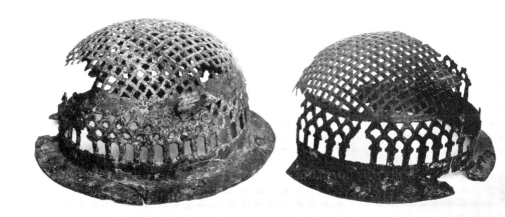

First, however, the new governor had to have a secure base in the capital. Urbanisation and a major waterfront development were changing the look of London. A quay for merchant ships, built about 79, was excavated in 1981 on the north side of Lower Thames Street, near London Bridge. Its timbers were two feet thick. Behind the quay there was a road and ware-houses, with more imposing buildings on a second terrace beyond. This was the beginning of the port of London. The expansion of the capital was followed by pacification in the country. A lead waterpipe discovered beneath a shop at Eastgate Street, Chester, in 1899 has an inscription dating its manufacture to when "Vespasian was consul for the ninth time and Titus for the seventh time and when Gnaeus Julius Agricola was governor of Britain". That was 79, when the garrison was being prepared for the arrival of the Second Legion Adiutrix from Lincoln for the campaign in North Wales.

Agricola had decided to repeat, and complete, Suetonius Paulinus's conquest of Anglesey. This he managed with a theatrical gesture rather than bloodshed, by sending a detach-ment of auxiliaries to swim the Menai Straits – Anglesey, "whose strait is its rampart", to quote from the *Book of Taliesin* – bringing peace talks in the wake of a surprise attack.

Anglesey was known to the Welsh as Môn, and no longer would it fully live up to its lines by the bard Taliesin: "There will come men to Môn/to be initiated in the ways of wizards". Tacitus describes the arrival of the men from Rome in almost the last (there was, still, Ireland) bastion of the Celtic world: "The enemy army was ranged along the shore like a forest of weapons and soldiers among which women ran ceaselessly about like furies, shrieking imprecations, with black robes and dishevelled hair and torches in their hands. All around stood druids with their hands raised to the sky, howling wild curses. At this sight our soldiers were gripped by fear."

The party was over, but the same wailing women, attendant upon the dying, were recorded from the Highlands of Scotland in 1690 by James Garden, professor of divinity at Aberdeen, in his letters to the antiquary John Aubrey, published in *Monumenta Britannica*. North Wales was under military occupation and a fort was built at Caernarfon for two cohorts, of horsemen and infantry, amounting to a thousand men.

Having brought the province back under Roman control, Agricola is credited by Tacitus with perceptive political management. He tried to lessen the causes of discontent and rebellion, by removing some of the excesses of patronage, and the resentment caused by severe penalties inflicted for minor offences. Slaves and ex-slaves were no longer used for official business. He smoothed the processes of taxation, grain tithes and tributes, so that the burden could be discharged without the complications of attendant corruption and petty regulations. It had been "the tricks of profiteers, which were more bitterly resented than the tax itself". By curtailing these abuses "Agricola made the Britons appreciate the advantages of peace, which, through the negligence or arbitrariness of previous governors, had been as much feared as war". The translations are from the Harold Mattingly and S A Handford edition of *The Agricola and the Germania* in Penguin Classics.

Tribal submissions and the building of more garrisons strengthened the security of the province in 79. There was also a concerted programme of Romanisation, with incentives for private and official provision of temples, public squares, and decent houses.

Agricola also attempted to influence the leadership of the next generation, providing an education in the Roman arts for the sons of chiefs. Language was the other barrier that was attacked.

Tacitus writes: "The result was that instead of loathing the Latin tongue they became eager to speak it effectively. In the same way, our national dress came into favour and the toga was everywhere to be seen. And so the population was gradually led into the demoralising temptations of arcades, baths, and sumptuous banquets. The unsuspecting Britons spoke of such novelties as 'civilisation', when in fact they were only a feature of their enslavement."

In the third and fourth summers of Agricola's campaigns the Roman armies moved steadily northward. Forts were built in northern England and southern Scotland, and Tacitus says: "It has been observed by experts that no general ever showed a better eye for ground than Agricola. No fort on a site of his choosing was ever taken by storm, ever capitulated, or was ever abandoned."

His advance was checked by geography, when he found himself at the foothills of the Scottish Highlands: "The Clyde and the Forth, carried inland to a great depth on the tides of opposite seas, are separated only by a narrow neck of land. This isthmus was now firmly held by garrisons, and the whole expanse of country to the south was safely in our hands. The enemy had been pushed into what was virtually another island."

Agricola's innovations, or those of his engineers, have been noticed by excavators. Castlecary, a Stirlingshire fort later incorporated into the Antonine Wall, was one of his frontier posts. He built forts of about eight to ten acres. Terracing of the rampart foundations and inturned gateways are among their distinguishing features. At Cardean in Scotland there was experimentation with the ditch system.

Michael J Jones writes in *Roman Fort Defences*: "How much Agricola himself was responsible, or how much he owed to his officers, we cannot know. The occurrence of these characteristics does seem, however, to fit in with Tacitus's statement about Agricola's energy in choosing sites for himself."

The operations in the Scottish Highlands depended upon flexibility, achieved by using the fleet to hit at harbours and coastal settlements northwards from the Tay, well ahead of the advancing legions.

Tacitus writes: "The war was pushed forward simultaneously by land and sea: and infantry, cavalry, and marines, often meeting in the same camp, would mess and make merry together."

The immediate result was a general uprising throughout the mountains and glens, leading to Roman consideration of a withdrawal of forces to the secure fort system between the Forth and the Clyde. Agricola's response, however, was a forward thrust with three divisions.

The camp of the Ninth Legion was attacked at night and nearly fell during the savage fighting that followed, being saved at dawn by the arrival of Roman reinforcements. The native opposition was then squeezed between the two Roman armies, and dispersed into marshes and woods, surviving to fight another day. Their spirits were revived by rites and sacrifices.

An entertaining diversion was provided by a cohort of German squaddies, from the Usipi tribe, who had been transferred to the Scottish campaign. In 83 they mutinied, killing a centurion and some soldiers. They then appropriated three small warships and sailed around the north of Scotland, raiding coastal communities for food and then eating each other when this failed and they were reduced to starvation – picking first the weakest and then by drawing lots. They were finally defeated by a general lack of maritime skills, accentuated by some of the most difficult waters in Europe. After losing their boats the pirates were taken by the Suebi and the Frissi, two northern tribes, and sold as slaves. Some passed back into the Roman world, and reached their home territory on the Rhine where, Tacitus says, they "gained notoriety by telling the story of their wonderful adventure". It does not sound wonderful, but it was not an wholly inappropriate way for the Roman army to have first reached the farthest north of mainland Britain.

Tacitus builds up his story of the Scottish campaign into a climax. Agricola, whose year-old son had just died, occupied his mind with plans to bring the war to its conclusion. The fleet continued to harry the northern coast and Romanised Britons from the south were enlisted into the army.

Tacitus describes a gathering of the clans, with more than 30,000 flocking to Mount Graupius, in the Grampian Mountains, where their thoughts are put into a set-piece speech attributed to the leader Calgacus. The site of the battle must lie at the end of Agricola's line of marching camps, on the south side of the Moray Firth, probably near Elgin where the mountains close in on the coastal belt along which the Romans advanced. The Romans had reached "the most distant dwellers upon earth, the last of the free". The words are an artificial and stilted device for balancing the narrative, but the sentiments are real enough: "A rich enemy excites their cupidity; a poor one their lust for power. East and West alike have failed to satisfy them. They are the only people on earth to whose covetousness both riches and poverty are equally tempting. To robbery, butchery, and rapine, they give the lying name of 'government'; they create a desolation and call it peace.

"We Britons," Calgacus is given to say, "are sold into slavery anew every day: we have to pay the purchase price ourselves and feed our masters into the bargain."

It was a battle into which Agricola committed 8,000 infantry and 3,000 cavalry. The legions were kept to the rear, in front of the rampart of a marching camp, and the brunt of the battle was to be met by the auxiliaries. Tacitus, say his Penguin translators, "finds it 'glorious' that Roman legions should stand safely in reserve while their brave auxiliaries bear the brunt of battle". This, however, is to underestimate Tacitus's talent. What he says – "victory would be vastly more glorious if it cost no Roman blood" – is heavily sarcastic and means the opposite. A victory, for public consumption in Rome, had to be an overwhelming success, and not offset by a high Roman death toll. If there had to be losses, then it would be more acceptable if these took place amongst the mercenaries.

The Roman auxiliaries were heavily outnumbered in the Grampians and faced the manoeuvring of charioteers. Agricola refused to bring the Roman legions to the front, keeping them in reserve in positions where they could react to events. It was in keeping with Agricola's character, optimistic and resolute in the face of difficulties, as his son-in-law puts it.

The battle opened with an exchange of spears, successfully parried by the North Britons with their great swords and trim shields. The results were unspectacular and Agricola sent in four cohorts of Batavians and two of Tungrians to fight it out at sword-point. Here the drilled skills of the Romans, and the fast stabbing of their short swords, were brutally effective against the clumsy slashing movements of the British weapons. The cohorts advanced across flat ground to the foot of a hillside. Roman cavalry had overturned the war chariots. But as the infantry plunged further into the British ranks the battle was enveloped in confusion.

The Tacitus account gives the Romans victory from perseverance and methodical and co-ordinated responses. They surrounded the Britons and came upon the more complacent warriors at the rear. Prisoners were accepted as a matter of course, but slaughtered as soon as their captors felt threatened by a new wave of opposition. The battle ended as had most other conflicts in the British campaigns.

"Equipment, bodies, and mangled limbs lay all around on the bloodstained earth: and even the vanquished now and then recovered their fury and their courage. When they reached the woods, they rallied and profited by their local knowledge to ambush the first rash of pursuers."

This was another Roman victory, but the mountain landscape had become a bandit country for the kind of continual warfare in which the Celts excelled.

Agricola later received the formal surrender of the territory of the Boresti, taking hostages as its guarantee of good behaviour. To symbolise the presumed completion of Roman conquest in mainland Britain, Agricola requested his admiral to repeat the exploits of the mutinous Usipi pirates and sail around the northern coast of Britain. Meanwhile the infantry and cavalry were placed in their hibernia, winter quarters. Agricola was then recalled by the emperor, Domitian, in 84, and faced retirement in Rome, where he died in 93.

The inroads through the far north had been punitive rather than an occupation, and, as Tacitus says, Britain was "completely conquered and then immediately let go". The legions were pulled back from the barren mountains and forward positions were abandoned. Some Perthshire forts, which had been intended as permanent, were demolished, though others lasted until the reign of Trajan at the start of the second century.

The legionaries demolishing the fort at Inchtuthil, Perthshire, buried twelve tons of bent nails. That they did not remove them is hardly surprising, given that it is unlikely smelting and reprocessing facilities existed within three hundred miles. Similar iron relics of empire have since been left by the British on islands all over the world. A reason for burying the nails – rather than simply abandoning them in heaps – was, as Herodian observed, that the natives of the Highlands valued iron as highly as gold. In this, the inhabitants of Scotland were as practical as their successors, in that it was iron rather than gold which one day enabled the British to conquer their way round the globe. The Roman empire, like all others in history, was wasteful in withdrawal. The imperative was to bring back men rather than materials.

Troops were needed in 84 to defend the empire in vital positions much closer to its heart, on the Rhine and the Danube, as Harold Mattingly, the translator of Tacitus, pointed out. By about 87 the latest legion to be posted to Britain, the Second Legion Adiutrix – which had replaced the Fourteenth Legion in 71 – was on its way to the Danube. Agricola had been given a chance to sort out the British problem, but he might have been too committed to the view that warfare has a military solution.

The palace on the south coast

THE EARLIEST ROMAN palace in Britain, indeed anywhere outside Italy, was discovered at Fishbourne, near Chichester, in 1960. A mechanical digger preparing a trench for a trunk water-main smashed through a mosaic of black-and-white geometric patterns that were quickly identified as dating from the first century AD and being absolutely unique.

Local action to save the site was taken with commendable speed and success. Ivan Margary, with the support of the excavation committee of Chichester Civic Society, was able to buy out the farmer and by December 1962 the land was in the ownership of Sussex Archaeological Trust.

Excavations that followed showed that in about AD 75 a deep-water channel was constructed from Chichester Channel to the site. A wharf of timber and stone was built on the north side of this cutting. Work then started on a ten-acre palace, or proto-palace, as no other is known, under the direction of continental craftsmen. Squared blocks of Bracklesham limestone, from the now submerged Mixen Reef off Selsey Bill, were used to face the west side. Four wings, with colonnades, surrounded a formal garden; half of this has been restored and replanted, but most of the main living rooms lie under the busy south-coast road, the A27, and the houses beside it. Watercress beds south of the village are in the former Roman harbour.

Two more black-and-white mosaic floors from the first

Geometric black and white pattern of one of the earliest mosaic floors that has been discovered in Britain, dating from about AD 75, at Fishbourne, Sussex.   *Photograph: John Pitfield*

century were found during excavations. One has a surround of rosettes and vine-leaves with vases at the corner. They had survived despite extensive rebuilding of the villa during the second century and its continued lengthy occupation.

The impressive west wing was the area where visitors were officially received, in a room of fine painted plasterwork. Guests could arrive by road or by sea, and if they came by water they would find the approaches from the wharf landscaped and gardened.

A display in the museum adjoining the foundations of the palace at Fishbourne shows the scale of the original quantity surveying for its construction. Levelling of the two building platforms required the shifting of 10,000 cubic yards of clay. The buildings themselves covered 250,000 square feet – a modern bungalow has a floor space less than a thousand square feet. The materials included stone sufficient for one and a half miles of walling, 550 gutter blocks, 160 columns, 43,000 roof tiles and 1,000 water pipes.

It was a building fit to receive an emperor, but its location has tended to encourage speculation that it was a retirement home for the ageing king Cogidubnus of the Regni. It has been argued that the palace was too close to his tribal capital, Chichester, to be politically acceptable as the home of a member of the Roman administration.

This, however, overlooks the fact that Chichester was a Roman creation, and that the tribal centre is now under the sea off Selsey Bill. Numerous quarter-staters, typical Celtic coins with a revolving cross and birds' heads on one side and a horse-and-wheel on the other, have been washed up from this submerged town. Chichester was its Romanised transplant, with a name, Noviomagus Regnensium, that announced new-ness. Sea-worn boulders from the beach at Selsey were used in the foundations of its forum. The government of Britain could have been carried out in style from Fishbourne and Chichester, and far more securely than from the recently troubled lands of East Anglia or the Thames Valley. It would have been dangerous and provocative to provide too easy an opportunity for the settling of old scores. The prospect of moving the clerkly baggage of government into a region where Romans had been hacked to death fifteen years earlier and their homes burnt to the ground, might not seem unnatural to a governor steeped in the traditions of the army but it was not likely to appeal to his family, officials and their wives. Old Cogidubnus may well have earned himself a few favours from the Roman administration; but this is not likely to have included the most palatial and richly-ornamented living quarters north of the Alps, together with a shipload of Mediterranean craftsmen and numerous servants (whose extensive quarters have yet to be found) – and all just to keep him in a fashion to which he was previously unaccustomed. It is more likely that Fishbourne was the family home of the governor of the province of Britain, and that it was constructed for Frontinus or Agricola. Campaigning governors needed to leave their wives and children and servants in comfort and safety, and the more equable (and survivable) climate of the south coast made it an ideal place for the reunion of the family in winter. The palace lay in secure treaty territory. No battles had been fought over it, and the sea at the bottom of the garden stretched all the way to Rome.

Fishbourne is so totally exceptional that it needs to be stressed that Britain generally did not produce such buildings until the great estates of the fourth century. Roman Britain was a predominantly rural society and many of the towns were slow to develop. Dorchester, in Dorset, lies in an area of densely-packed native settlements, and is close to the quarries of Ham Hill and Purbeck. Conditions, however, were not conducive to its growth. So far, there is no evidence of any stone building in the town that is earlier than the year 200, and by the end of the Roman period there were still a number of vacant plots inside its town walls on which nothing had ever been built.

Some consideration should be given to the population of Roman Britain. This has long been regarded as something in the order of one or two millions, but these figures are underestimates. There is every indication that the total lay between three and four millions, not so far short of the general five million estimate for England in the Middle Ages. The reasons for a substantial upward revision are compelling. Caesar observed that it was a highly populated island, and in Roman times most of the people were in the countryside. The towns housed only a twentieth of the population. Huge numbers of native peoples farmed the chalklands of Wessex with an intensity that was not matched until the 1950s with the aid of government subsidies, full mechanisation, and mountains of fertilisers. Aerial photography has shown similar concentrations of settlements and ancient fields across the gravel plains of the river valleys and vales, areas historians once thought were smothered with forests two thousand years ago. Construction of each new mile of motorway adds to the burden of archaeological teams, scurrying to keep pace with the ever-mounting succession of previously unknown sites.

We now know, for example, that the Fenlands were drained, rich, and highly settled in Roman times.

Even in Wiltshire, which has been at the receiving end of continuous documentation and fieldwork since John Aubrey "discovered" Avebury in the seventeenth century, the re-opening of the Littlecote Park mosaic led to a total revision of Roman settlement patterns. When it was first investigated there were only four known villas in the area of the Roman town of Cunetione, near Marlborough. By the time the mosaic was put on view to the public this total had been pushed to thirty-three.

To convert this into a numbers game is inevitably to invite error; however, it is likely that the total population of town and country in Roman Britain might not have been much less than the non-suburban village and farmstead population of twentieth century rural England and Wales. This is a figure of around four million, well within the resources of the land, even on Roman terms. The marginal soils and high pastures of the farthest hill country were also far from being vacant lands.

In the western Celtic fringes of Britain in Roman times the most common type of settlement was the rath, or round. There are many in Cornwall, Devon, south-west Wales, and across the Irish Sea. Ireland has in excess of forty thousand raths, dating from the second or first century BC and then through the entire millennium up to the year 1100. They are oval or circular hilltop enclosures, ranging in size from less than half an acre to three acres, fortified by a ditch and a bank.

Only one has been totally excavated: Walesland Rath in

Fine-featured limestone carving from Cirencester, Gloucestershire, which was one of the largest towns in Roman Britain. It shows signs of gilding. *Photograph: John Pitfield*

Pembroke, in 1968. It enclosed half an acre, which had been intensively occupied with huts, which had left 560 postholes, and a rectangular Roman building. There were wooden spear-tips preserved in a waterlogged ditch but otherwise finds were sparse. Future hopes of finding useful material depends on selecting a site with a suitably damp ditch. Those living in Walesland Rath, and everyone else in rath country, had ample reason to devise stormwater gullies.

Coin evidence is precious to the archaeologist but it is useless as an indicator of population, even in the larger towns. Richard Reece, taking Cirencester as his example, estimates in *Roman Coinage in the Western Empire*, in volume four of *Britannia*, that "what survives is probably not one hundred-thousandth part of the money in circulation in Corinium at any one time". The six thousand coins found there that date from the period 41 to 138

Imported Roman glass, used mainly for perfumes and spices.

Photograph: John Pitfield

represent a century of losses but "would only make up the takings of one prosperous shopkeeper during one week of life in the Roman town". Ten times that number of coins might be recovered from a total excavation of Cirencester, but even this would have to be considered in relative terms: "It is inconceivable that the number could reach two hundred thousand coins. This means that we can never approach the turnover of one prosperous shopkeeper for one year."

Exhibits in a museum, like a visit to the palace at Fishbourne, can often distort expectations of ordinary Roman living. The Romans made fine glass, with flasks and jars of an infinite variety of shapes and colours – some portraying human faces – but little, if any, was wasted on windows. Natural alternatives included mare's placenta (the semi-transparent afterbirth) which was still commonly found in Ireland into the nineteenth century and said to be impervious to British bayonets.

Shutters and half-doors would be opened to provide light.

Half-doors survive in crofting communities and, universally, in stable-blocks, as well as in the less likely setting of Durham miners' cottages, though they must once have been widespread. They are the simplest way of admitting light and controlling ventilation without the simultaneous invasion of the house by animals. Those who have never kept stock (or found a horse in their lounge) may find it hard to appreciate the nagging persistence of the threat of animal invasion. The problem is alleviated in the western world today by strict segregation, but in poorer societies, and in earlier times, such separation would have been impractical.

Roman pets were not so different from our own. Dogs, of the hound and working type, were kept along with cats. These were domesticated in Britain in Iron Age and Roman times. A native settlement excavated at Gussage All Saints, Dorset, in the 1970s, produced the bones of a litter of five new-born kittens. This important find effectively demolished the convenient assertion that the domestic cat was brought to Britain by the Romans, with excavator Geoffrey Wainwright cautioning in *Gussage All Saints*: "Even if, as could be claimed, the kittens

Paw-print of a cat, on a tile found at St Paul's, London. *Courtesy: British Museum*

Romano-Celtic horse-and-rider brooch from Suffolk, one of the more powerful portrayals of the national spirit, is more a reflection of the shape of their breeds than stylistic exaggeration. *Photograph: Colin Graham*

were the litter of a wild cat there would seem to be little point in bringing them back to the settlement and indeed not much point in killing them at all." If they were wild and to be killed it would have been done where they were found.

Problems of over-population amongst tame cats must have been commonplace in Roman times. Four out of twenty-five pieces of brick found in a posthole at Bothwellhaugh Roman fort, Lanarkshire, in 1968 bore the clear pad impressions of a cat. The offending animal may have been lifted clear as in three of the fragments it had clawed the drying clay – many cats refuse to retract their claws when picked up.

But for the Celts the superior domesticated animal was the horse. Romano-Celtic drawings of horses have often been described as exaggerated or stylised. They are often nothing of the kind, but are realistic representations of how horses used to look. They closely resembled Exmoor and Shetland ponies of the present day, which are very different from the standard lines of the streamlined modern horse. Celtic horses had a low body, big head, shaggy mane, and a spreading tail that trailed the ground. They are featured on horse-and-rider brooches which fell to the ground in cremation pyres, as at the funeral temple on Cold Kitchen Hill, near Mere, Wiltshire, and a Celtic horseman is carved on a stone frieze from Kingscote, Gloucestershire. The Romans imported a larger draught-horse into Britain, for transport use, though for a time the available breed would have coped.

The Celtic horse at its most stylised and streamlined, more so than on pre-Roman coins, is the Uffington chalk-cut figure on the hillside of an Iron Age fort in Oxfordshire. It gives its name to the Vale of the White Horse. As it appears today, the 365-feet long animal is being ridden hard and fast – its head straining forwards – though reins, if they existed, have grassed over.

Created by a warrior culture which included some of the best horsemen in Europe, the Uffington carving is unlikely to have lacked that vital component – its rider. In fact, there were still traces of a saddle on its back when drawings were sketched for *The Gentleman's Magazine* in 1796 and for Daniel Lysons' *Berkshire* (the county boundaries changed in 1974) in 1813.

G W B Huntingford, in his 1957 paper *The Scouring of the White Horse*, gives a contemporary parallel to the Uffington White Horse: namely, the finding by Christopher Hawkes in the 1930s of a similar horse (with rider) scratched in outline on the lid of a third century water-jar from a pottery at Linwood, near Ringwood, in Hampshire. Huntingford was confident enough to claim that the lid drawing was "surely made by someone who was familiar with the White Horse". If this is so then the matter may be taken a stage further, as such an accurate artist is unlikely to have imagined the rider.

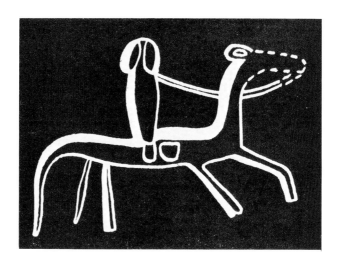

Horse and phallic rider scratching on a pot-lid from Ringwood, Hampshire.

Courtesy: Dorset County Magazine

The horse-rider of the Linwood jar is not a person but a phallus. If it is a portrayal of the Uffington hill carving, then a phallus fifty feet high might arise from the middle of its back if the turf is ever stripped. It will have shortened with time – remarkable though this may seem. Tradition is that the horse has crept up the hill and aerial photography confirms this. There is a darker area of grass, a strip fifteen feet below its belly-line, which reveals the original shape. The movement came about because with each successive recutting the top and bottom of the animal would have been sliced back equally. Between times, however, the grass encroached from the base at a faster rate than it came down from the top. As the top line suffered erosion, the silt would collect in the groove along the base. These changes were then consolidated by the grass, which prefers to grow upwards.

One relevant parallel, for the symbolism, is that a clay representation of a four-horse chariot, found in the Romano-Celtic temple at Wroxeter, is also driven by a phallic emblem.

Thirty foot phallus of the Cerne Giant hill-figure, enlarged early in the twentieth century by the incorporation of the navel into the penis.

Photograph: Colin Graham

The other parallel is the first century Romano-Celtic hill figure of a naked man at Cerne Abbas, Dorset. The Cerne Giant has a phallus of thirty feet, though the navel has now become incorporated in the penis, which means its present length is an

Scale drawing of the chalk-cut Cerne Giant.

Courtesy: Dorset County Magazine

exaggeration by five feet. Gerald Pitman was the first to record this change, in a letter to the *Dorset County Magazine* in 1978, and showed that it had happened between 1764 and 1926. The alteration seems to have occurred early in the twentieth century for, as Pitman points out, the owner of the Cerne Giant at its 1887 recutting was the famous archaeologist, Augustus Pitt-Rivers, who would have been aware of the navel from anti-quarian literature.

The fact that these imperceptible changes are taking place to hill figures, even those owned by the National Trust or the Environment Department, shows that we must have a much more open mind about their original shapes. In 1979, Yorkshire Television discovered a lion-skin trailing from the outstretched arm of the Cerne Giant. They painted it onto the grass – it lasted until the rains – for the filming of a documentary, Arthur C Clarke's *Mysterious World*.

Researchers had probed the steep hillside with resistivity meters, and fed the results into a computer. The printouts revealed a forty-feet wide lionskin draped over the figure's elbow. Its outline was cut into the chalk rock of the escarpment.

This trench was neglected during the scourings of the Middle Ages, when the outline of the 180-foot high figure was recut and grassed over. It was left out because it had become meaningless to post-Roman generations, and was therefore

The Cerne Giant, a Romano-Celtic chalk-cut figure of Hercules on the Dorset Downs, pictured in 1979 when its lionskin was discovered by electronic probing and painted upon the grass below the outstretched arm.

Photograph: Colin Graham

Typical Gallo-Roman bronze of Hercules, naked with a club and a lionskin over the other arm.

Courtesy: Dorset County Magazine

abandoned to the grass. It survives under the turf as a channel of damper, softer soil, which is not visible from the surface.

The finding of the lost trench confirmed that the Giant is probably a native Celtic version of the Roman god Hercules. He was portrayed naked in Gallo-Roman bronzes of the first century AD, with a club in his right hand and a skin draped over his left.

Efforts should now be made to find out whether the Cerne Giant was originally accompanied by other figures. Further north along the Cerne hillside, beginning about 115 feet from his right leg (the left, as you look at him) the faint lines of a terrier – in length about one hundred and fifty feet and standing on the same contour as the Giant – were observed in low-angle winter sun in January 1969 and again during the drought of July 1976.

These details I recorded in the *Dorset County Magazine* in

1978: "Though grass covered, its outline appears as a slightly darker shape than the surrounding hillside. The dog, like the Giant, is cut in full proportions, without any allowance for perspective or the foreshortening caused by this medium. Its shape has a precedent, in that a Roman bronze of a terrier was dropped as an offering into a Celtic sacred well at the temple to Coventina near Carrawburgh, Northumberland."

Votive representations of dogs were also found in the temple of Nodons at Lydney Park, Gloucestershire. One was carved on a funnel-shaped piece of pottery and held an offering of twenty-one coins: "Cernunnos too, in a silver cauldron found at Gundestrup, Denmark, is depicted surrounded by animals, though they are wild and not domesticated. One is a wolf, though that would be stretching the shape of the Cerne beast impossibly far. It may be more relevant that a belief in huge, supernatural black dogs is one of the most persistent elements in British folklore."

Traditional archaeology, on the other hand, has always found a refuge in the safety of monumental artefacts that can be moulded to our own view of society's needs. The obvious Roman legacy was the road system, the basis of the pre-motorway British road system, circa AD 60 to 1960. Sir Christopher Wren noticed in the seventeenth century (according to a note John Aubrey made for his *Monumenta Britannica*), that the main deviations from this pattern occurred in the vicinity of the great monastic houses, which were the only post-Roman institutions in the countryside powerful enough to generate their own roads.

Straight roads into towns have always been self-perpetuating; it is only in the last twenty years that planners have begun to accept that heavy traffic is destroying the structure and quality of life in these communities. But we must beware that our supposed needs do not condition us to a blind acceptance of the primacy of road transport.

Strabo emphasised the economic importance of the navigable waterways in Roman Gaul. Freight in Britain was also moved by water, by river, canal and coastal shipping as far as was possible, the costs being a twentieth of those for carriage by road. Transport overland was also slower. Making maximum use of the waterways was a natural extension of Britain's external trading methods. Boulogne was the ferry port of Europe but there were other, longer sea-links, including one from Bordeaux to York.

Inland, Britain had its canal system which included the Car Dyke, around the Fens to Lincoln, and the Foss Dike, which ran from there to the River Trent.

On the borders of the province there were simmerings of unrest at those points where the Roman world came into direct contact with unconquered Celtic peoples. Britain was strongly fortified by Trajan, emperor between 98 and 117, and the decision to reinforce the northern frontier region was put into action by his first governor, Titus Avidius Quietus.

Agricola's road into the Borders, the Stanegate, was used to link a line of forts built at the end of the first century at Carlisle, Nether Denton, Chesterholm, and Corbridge. Short sections

Stanegate Roman road, the supply line for the northern forts – and later for Hadrian's Wall – at Barcombe, Northumberland.

of this military way are preserved beside the modern road into High Crosby, five miles east of Carlisle, and on the fringes of Naworth Park. It is much more easily seen at the rear of the later Hadrian's Wall at Greenhead and the descent to its crossing of Haltwhistle Burn. The fortlet defending this gradient was constructed about the year 100 and remained in use for some time. Its eastern gate was then blocked and the walls were later pulled down to the foundations. The stone was reused for the building of the Roman wall, and one of its quarries cuts into the eastern side of Haltwhistle Burn fortlet.

Other forts were discovered in 1933–34, by Gerald Simpson, at Boothby Bank precipice above the River Irthing, and at Old Church. The first site had the field name Castle Hill on an estate map and Simpson proved its accuracy with a six foot trench which revealed a Roman rampart of beaten clay. The other site, on which stands St Martin's church, was of cohort size, housing 480 men. It was stone-built but had been levelled in Roman times and its masonry incorporated into the great wall.

There were alterations too, for the Fishbourne palace. At the start of the second century it was partially rebuilt and could then well have passed into domestic ownership as government in Britain became increasingly London orientated. The supremacy of the capital became absolute about the year 105, probably during the governorship of Lucius Neratius Marcellus, when a stone-walled fort, enclosing twelve acres, was built at Cripplegate on the northern edge of Roman London. The city forum, beneath the modern banks in Gracechurch Street, quadrupled in size about the same time. London was now a city.

The province's second city was York. Its first stone-walled fortress was built in 107, replacing a clay and timber construction of Agricola's time.

Plants of the Roman garden

THE ROMANS INTRODUCED a number of plants to Britain, the descendants of which still survive two thousand years later as part of our natural flora. Other, more sensitive, species they attempted to establish would have been killed off long ago by cold winters and the intense competition from other plants when the formal gardening stopped.

Recent interest in the Roman garden was stimulated by the unique experiment at Fishbourne Palace in Sussex where bedding-trenches for hedges and borders were traced in the mid-1960s. This made possible a reconstruction of the original garden, plus trimmed box hedging, with advice from *The Sunday Times* gardening correspondent, Lanning Roper.

Determining just what plants the Romans brought with them is more difficult, but the following list has been compiled mainly from the archaeological reports catalogued by Sir Harry Godwin for his *History of the British Flora*. It is necessarily incomplete for it relies on the fact that only under certain conditions can microscopic pollen grains resist decomposition and be brought from antiquity to the laboratory. Unfortunately, there are very few botanical scholars available to conduct pollen analysis – and, consequently, they are extremely hard pressed – neither are there many archaeological sites with acidic soils or waterlogged hollows (even an abandoned well will do) that are necessary for the survival of these spores.

Introduction of the electron microscope, and other advances, meant that between the two editions of Godwin's work, published in 1956 and 1975, the total of historical plant records had multiplied ten-fold. Despite this there are obvious gaps, of choice Mediterranean flowering plants like the peony, which the Romans must have attempted to establish in the climatically less hostile southern coastal districts. Also missing is the bay, though it is susceptible to frost. This was the emblem of victory and its leaves were the laurel wreaths of the poets, quite apart from being used medicinally and as a food flavouring. For a specimen tree that evoked the landscape of home the obvious choice would be the cypress, the columnar conifer of the olive groves.

What follows is a list of known Roman introductions, but omitting records such as those for larch and silver-fir which occur as writing tablets found in a well at Chew Magna, Avon, and which were almost certainly imported. Of these two examples, however, the silver-fir qualifies under other criteria, being confirmed by pollen analysis as growing in Britain from Roman times. The Romans are responsible for the following non-native additions to the British flora.

Alexanders	Pot-herb and vegetable: like celery, imported from the Mediterranean and grown at Caerwent (nearest prolific present-day location is Steep Holm island in the Bristol Channel). Only tolerates unfrosted coastal regions.
Apple	Fruit: the earliest of the domesticated varieties were cultivated by the Romans and imported into Britain.
Box	Hedging shrub: Roman-grown but probably already native in Britain.
Broad Bean	Pulse: introduced by the Romans and cultivated in Britain, as now.

Buckwater	Flour-producing nuts: the flowers of the plant also attracted honeybees. An Asiatic species brought to Britain by the Romans.
Celery	Stem vegetable: probably both imported by the Romans and cultivated here as well.
Cherry	Fruit: imported and also cultivated here, readily germinating from spat stones. Grown also as an ornamental tree.
Coriander	Herb: imported and possibly cultivated, being capable of surviving on its own in East Anglia.
Crab Apple	Fruit: hard and small wild apples, used for wine-making and food flavouring.
Damson	Fruit: small dark plums, probably already established in Britain in Iron Age times.
Deadly Nightshade	Medicine and lotion: cultivated at first and then also thriving in the wild on lime-rich southern soils.
Dill	Herb and medicine: introduced by the Romans and cultivated in Britain.
Fennel	Herb: imported and also cultivated here, being capable of naturalising itself in coastal areas.
Fig	Fruit: imported by the Romans, and probably grown in Britain as an ornamental tree.
Flax	Netting-fibre and oil-seed: grown here by the Romans and re-introduced in 1940 for the same purpose, and for linen, its blue fields being the colour of southern England at war.
Grape Vine	Fruit: mainly imported but probably also cultivated here, Britain south of York being within the climatic range of vine-growing which was carried on commercially in mediaeval times.
Ground Elder	Pot-herb: brought by the Romans and escaped from cultivation to survive as a weed.
Hemlock	Killer drug: used for euthanasia, suicide and

execution. Turned up on cultivated ground in Roman times, though probably mainly just as a weed.

Hemp — Netting-fibre: imported and also cultivated in Britain. It is also a medicine and hallucinogen, though perhaps it might not have been recognised as such.

Henbane — Medicine: introduced by the Romans and escaped into the wild in the disturbed soils of coastal cliffs, where the seeds can survive for decades until conditions are right for germination.

Lentil — Pulse: imported to Britain by the Romans and possibly also cultivated here, though it seems unlikely.

Medlar — Fruit: imported and also cultivated here by the Romans, being eaten when rotten. The tree is ornamental.

Mulberry — Fruit: imported, being popular at Roman feast-times, and cultivated in southern Britain as an ornamental tree.

Mustard — Herb: cultivated by the Romans, and also spread as a weed.

Opium Poppy — Flower and drug: introduced by the Romans, and seeded itself onto disturbed and arable ground.

Pea — Pulse: both imported by the Romans and cultivated here, as it is now.

Plum — Fruit: imported and cultivated, probably becoming established by mid-Roman times.

Radish — Vegetable: domestic root-crop, imported and cultivated. It can only be perpetuated by gardening.

Silver Fir — Timber tree: imported and also grown here

	ornamentally, though not without problems in the British climate. It is encouraged by cool and moist conditions but then devastated by spring frosts.
Spruce	Timber tree: a softwood introduced and cultivated, otherwise it would not have regenerated itself on the scale that seems to have occurred in the Roman period.
Stone Pine	Timber tree: possibly also a gardened specimen tree, but it may only turn up on British sites as a result of extensive imports of wood, particularly by the military to build forts.
Sweet Chestnut	Nut and timber tree: both products were imported by the Romans, and it was also cultivated in southern Britain.
Vervain	Ritual plant: of druidic Celtic name, though also cultivated as an altar plant by the Romans.
Walnut	Nut and timber tree: imported as nuts and furniture wood, and it was cultivated in gardens and small orchards as now.
Woad	Dye-plant: the colour of Celtic war-paint, grown also as a fabric colouring and perpetuated itself as a weed in the Roman cornfields.

Exotic birds were also introduced into the new British gardens. The largest and most spectacular were the peafowl, which had been brought to Europe with the return of Alexander the Great's armies from Persia in the fourth century BC. They were regarded as a great delicacy, being reconstituted for their final appearance on the dining table in a dressing of their own feathers. No bones from such a feast have been recovered in Britain, and their rarity in these islands must make any such discoveries highly improbable, but as a highly ornamental addition to the country's drab native bird life they made a vivid

The peacock brooch from Lulworth, Dorset – an unmistakable portrayal, in the Romano-Celtic idiom.
Photograph: Colin Graham

impression on one Celtic craftsman. A Romano-British brooch found near Lulworth Cove, Dorset, is in the unmistakable form of a peacock.

To the gourmets also can be attributed the introduction into Britain of the large continental edible snail, *Helix pomatia*. This is about two inches in diameter. On the other side of the Channel it has a widespread distribution from eastern France – where it is a pest in the vineyards – to the Baltic, and southwards up to the 7,000 feet contour in the Alps. In Britain, however, it has an exceedingly patchy distribution, which appears to be the result of random escapes or introductions into the wild, and which often coincides with the presence nearby of Roman settlements. The snail, which is known as the Roman snail, shows a better ability to survive on chalk soils, perhaps because the *pomatia* of its Latin name refers to the chalky excretion with which it seals itself on hibernation, the word being from the Greek *poma*, a pot-lid. It has a localised range along the North Downs of Kent and Surrey and on the Chiltern Hills to the north-west of London, with isolated colonies in Gloucestershire, Wiltshire and Sussex. They are usually found in hedgerows.

As well as enriching the native flora and wildlife the Romans left distinctive marks upon the fabric of the English countryside, though these were reduced from the obvious to the obscure by the post-mediaeval creation of small enclosed fields all across lowland Britain. Further traces have ironically been swept away with the destruction of those same small fields, ripped apart to provide the great cereal acreages of the farming revolution that has taken place since 1955. The subject is now relegated to the world of aerial photography. Similar blows have removed the visual impact of the Roman road system. For more than a thousand years the efforts of the Roman surveyors survived as the ribbons of the national road network, a monument to rigid planning mentality in a centralised society. It was the same all across Europe, Saint Paul being able to write of the unhindered rights of travel from the Atlantic to Asia, the benefit of being "a citizen of no mean city".

In Britain the overall pattern of the Roman road system was unchallenged until the introduction of turnpike roads in the eighteenth century and even then it retained widespread dominance until the curving lines of 1920s motor race tracks were made available to all and unleashed to whip great weals across the landscape in the post-1959 motorway programme. The Roman roads were laid out by graphics with a general indifference to the contours, the calculations being set out on a plane-table, a drawing-board marked off in degrees from the centre. This was also the methodology of town planning and where land was shared out in parcels, say to communities of veterans, the divisions were undertaken with the same straight-edged repetition.

There are Roman field layouts still surviving in use in East Anglia, particularly convincing examples being those between Holme and Brancaster in Norfolk, and those at Ripe in Suffolk. A map of the Holme area in 1609 shows that the same boundaries existed then and were even more complete, which means they must pre-date the age of the enclosures. These fields have produced average present-day hedge lengths of 410 yards and a Roman *stadium*, the unit of land measure, was equal to 202½ yards. The Holme hedges, therefore, are in effect two *stadia* and the odd surplus five feet are probably the boundaries which were presumably excluded from the calculations. On the other hand, English hedge lengths are based upon post-mediaeval imperial chain measures with the three commonest lengths being 220 yards (ten chains), 264 yards (twelve chains) and 176 yards (eight chains). The shortest common unit of hedgerow length is two chains (forty-four yards). All these combinations produce square measures in acres, but the Roman fields in East Anglia do not round off into any of the English, Scottish or Irish variants of the acre.

Hedges can be an aid to archaeological dating, a fact which is now being accepted and expressed as a scientific equation. Hedges can be accurately dated from the quantity of their shrub species. This new aid to archaeology, via natural history, was first suggested by Dr Max Hooper of the Nature Conservancy Research Centre at Monks Wood, Hertfordshire, who was studying the effects of toxic chemicals on bird populations at the time. Simply, Hooper's rule is that the more shrub species there are in a hedgerow, the older it is.

"It can be said, using a statistical measure, that ninety-five per cent of hedges with ten species in a thirty yard length will be between eight hundred and 1,150 years old." One or more additional species will have found their way into the hedge at intervals of less than thirty yards during each hundred years. The underlying assumption is that you are dealing with what was once a one-species hedge – and luckily most were. In the calculations only the established trees and shrubs (ignore seed-lings) must be counted and such plants as brambles, honey-suckle, nettles, flowers and ivy must not be included.

It takes a century for a hedge to lose its initial vigour and allow the first interloping species to root at reasonably regular intervals. This diversification continues at the same slow pace through the centuries. The first new species is unlikely to be the Field Maple (*Acer campestre*), as this on average takes four hundred years to arrive, and the Spindle Tree (*Euonymus europaeus*) seldom appears in less than six hundred years. Elder (*Sambucus nigra*) is much more likely to be the first coloniser with Hawthorn forming the original component of the hedge; but of this there are two species: the common Hawthorn, or May-tree (*Crataegus monogyna*) is the one normally seen, but the other, *Crataegus laevigata* (the so-called Midland Hawthorn) – distinguished by less indented, rounded, glassy and darker leaves – occurs only in its pure form in hedges that are at least a thousand years old. In hedges of lesser years you find hybrids between the two species.

An indicator of pre-Roman woodland is the Wild Service Tree, *Sorbus torminalis*, which has virtually never been planted by man either as a forest or specimen tree. It exists only as a rarity in southern England and Wales at the extremity of its European range. It was a tree of the primaeval forest canopy, and it is safe to assume that where it occurs there has been continuity of woodland through at least two thousand years.

The clinching factor that a wood existed in Roman times is the presence on the ground of a dense growth of Dog's Mercury, *Mercurialis perennis*. With a spread rate of less than eight inches a year it is a very slow coloniser of newer forests. G F Peterken and Margaret Game of the Nature Conservancy conclude in their study of the plant in the *Journal of Ecology*: "Ancient woods are sites where Dog's Mercury could have remained on the same patch of ground for hundreds or thousands of years. It seems reasonable to interpret the existing scatter of Mercury in such woods as relict fragments of an original more extensive population in primaeval woodland."

Housing, sex and food

THE PEOPLE OF Roman Britain have twentieth century counterparts in the African state of Zimbabwe; here, though landlocked, the inhabitants exhibit a similar range of lifestyles, extremes of wealth, and standards of accommodation, and therefore provide an ideal comparison.

To begin with, both states were artificial colonial creations incorporating a variety of passive and warrior tribes whose total population was around four million. In Roman Britain about ninety per cent lived in the countryside in huts of mud, timber and straw – dramatically recreated by Peter Reynolds on a Hampshire hilltop in his Butser Ancient Farm experiment – and about one per cent were the farming elite who lived in rich villas; five per cent occupied houses in towns, and the remaining four per cent lived in and around the army garrisons.

The picture was locally influenced, as with Zimbabwe, by sporadic pockets of mineral wealth.

The staple crop in Zimbabwe is maize, rather than the traditional British grains such as wheat, barley, and oats, and it is a food-exporting state. This comparison can be taken further, for it provides the key to how Roman Britain survived for four centuries; there can be no other reason why the empire should have clung on to this prestigious but troublesome island through a score of crises. After all, as Reynolds reminds us in *Iron-Age Farm*, it was no tropical paradise; the weather was similar to that of today, and was even described by Tacitus as being quite foul.

The one crucial commodity in which Roman Britain was always self-sufficient was food. Continental harvests fluctuate between glut and disaster but the maritime influence on the British climate ensures consistent and dependable yields with a tendency to peak at the very times when the country is close to conditions that cause a grain failure in Europe. For example, in 1982 British agriculture produced twenty-two million tons of grain which amounts to a third of a ton per person, enough to feed the entire population twice over if the nation suddenly went completely vegetarian. The Roman invasion itself led to a great jump in production because it introduced the rotary quern which was far more efficient than the Celtic method of grinding wheat by rubbing two stones together.

The national need for grain in Roman Britain was about a pound per head per day, or 650,000 tons a year for a four million population. As now, considerably more would be required for the feeding of stock in winter, though hay would have been used for as long as possible. Overall consumption must have been between one-and-a-half and two million tons. This was readily obtainable given the known extent of the Roman grainlands, even after allowing for poor yields, infestation by the weed charlock, general wastage, and lack of modern chemical fertilisers with the consequent need for crop rotation. Although the yield per plant was low by comparison with twentieth-century strains, the ancient varieties were far more concentrated in their protein – they had twice the food value of today's bread wheat. And with this kind of surplus there would have been no need to slaughter stock as winter approached because they could not be fed. This is a widespread myth manufactured by archaeologists and historians who fail to notice how farming works, and to wonder what a society without freezers and a canning industry did with a mountain of mutton and beef. Salting requires impractically large quantities of the mineral for its application on a national scale.

It is likely that the province's minimum grain requirements were exceeded by at least fifty per cent in dry summers. Despite the fact that the Butser experiment has shown the bearded wheats – Einkorn, Emmer, and Spelt – were difficult to thresh, and that there was loss in collection as well as mould in the storage pits and granaries, there was still sufficient surplus for a regular export trade. Then, as now, there was intensive culti-vation of the Wessex downlands, in East Anglia, and on the drained Fens.

In areas of low rainfall such as eastern England which receives less than twenty-five inches a year, the basic require-ment for high yield corn-growing is a soil that retains what little moisture it can get. In central southern England where the annual rainfall is thirty to forty inches (and more in Dorset), a well-drained chalk or sandy soil is essential to dispose of the excessive dampness. Grain storage pits were sterilised with fire and reusable indefinitely; many settlements had hundreds of them. One of the largest imperial grain-producing estates, Professor C F C Hawkes has suggested, was at Castor in Lincolnshire.

There is literary evidence that suggests Britain was the granary of Europe. In the year 359 Julian, then Caesar and heir to the empire, sorted out the mess in the Rhineland and negotiated the return of Roman soldiers who had been taken prisoner-of-war. Food was desperately short, both for the army and those living in the cities, and he organised an armada of eight hundred transport vessels to ferry sufficient grain from Britain to relieve the crisis. The boats would each have been capable of carrying at least twelve tons, and it is reasonable to assume they went backwards and forwards ten times or more. For eight hundred of them to have been used indicates a massive urgent requirement, as well as a considerable long term supply afterwards. The total amount that Britain was able to provide cannot therefore have been less than a hundred thousand tons of grain, and may well have been closer to a quarter of a million. Although some of it probably came from the army's granaries there is compelling evidence that the province was already well established as a major food-exporting state.

Each grain field was rotated annually with the Celtic Bean, *Vicia faba minor*, which was the alternative staple crop of the Iron Age and of Roman Britain. As well as its harvest of beans, the stems and foliage provided fodder for the stock. But the greatest benefit to agriculture came from the nitrogen nodules on the roots of the beans which enriched the soil in an age when the only other available additives were manure and compost.

Ploughing was done with a simple implement known as an ard which was dragged across the field by a pair of animals; these were usually cows, as they gave milk as a bonus. The work of Reynolds and his Butser team over the past decade has shown that the ard "stirs up the soil rather than inverts it. In effect only the topsoil is cultivated, which accords exactly with the most modern methods of farming." In fact, the ard has also left its score-marks on the ancient sub-soil, but only where the ground was thin in the first place.

The Butser project has shown the native diet was at least as nutritious as ours – and considerably healthier in its fibre content.

Re-construction at Butser of exposed cone-roofed round houses has shown them to have been capable of withstanding hurricane-force winds and severe storms; four feet of rain in six months did not spring leaks, and they have subsequently proved to need minimal maintenance and to be as water and draught proof as our own. The secret of their structural strength lies in the curvature, for no flat surface is ever presented to the power of the weather. Roofs were steeply pitched and made principally of thatch, or even grass. As theory was developed into practice at Butser, it became clear that a central roof support is a figment of archaeological assumption – and that none is necessary.

Roman bronze lamps range from the elaborate, with a scallop-shell lid, to the utterly plain. *Photograph: John Pitfield*

Houses really come into their own during the evening and, of course, at night and one of the assets of the Roman invasion was the general introduction of the oil lamp. Scallop shells were used at first and their shape was copied by the first pre-Roman pottery lamps, the shell motif then recurring in lamp designs for centuries afterwards.

The standard Roman lamp was a palm-shaped circular dish with a covered top, the discus around the inlet hole being used for designs; these reached their most intricate stage in the second half of the first century, and depicted all aspects of life from boats and chariots to temples and gods. Many that were imported into Britain from southern Italy must have widened Celtic horizons: animal subjects, for instance, embrace the entire range of domestic, wild and exotic – one even shows a mongoose enchanting a cobra. Another subject, from the warmer climate of Mediterranean mythology, shows a boy on

Bronze lamp of the first century on a pricket-stand of fourth century date, with lion-claw feet.

Photograph: John Pitfield

An amphora. Ships trading with Britain had racks of these, bringing wine and olive oil into the province.

Photograph: John Pitfield

a dolphin. Gladiators were popular, and one is shown battling with an ostrich. Ethnic peoples, too, are included and some of the designs are fine studies of negroes.

The lamps were fuelled with olive oil and burnt for several hours though the light they gave was only the equivalent of half candle power and insufficient for little more than allowing movement about a room. In Britain, where imported olive oil was at a premium, the locally made substitute was produced from flax seed.

There are frequent reminders that lamps were for use at bedtime. All sexual life is represented, from any variety of activity between couples, plus masturbation by both sexes, oral intercourse, and old men in bed with boys. Grotesque actors are shown in potentially painful situations and one of them is

110

Roman lamp with a night scene – intercourse from the rear between boy and girl. There are so many representations of this position that it must be regarded as the standard method in the Roman world.

Photograph: John Pitfield

fleeing from a pelican which is showing particular interest in his erection. Another has a satyrical head sprouting from the back of a panther with a detached phallus to one side, whilst others are totally phallic in their own right.

Roman pottery oil lamp in the shape of a face. *Photograph: John Pitfield*

Old man taking some exercise in bed with a boy. *Photograph: John Pitfield*

Priapus had his resurrection when the southern Italian villas were emptied of volcanic ash. One beautiful wall painting, in pastel colour, shows a woman unveiling a three-foot high phallus at the centre of a room. Lucius Caelius Firmianus Lactantius, a Christian writer who went to Gaul in about 306 to teach Constantine's son Crispus, noted that "brides seat themselves on this god's genital member in order to make the first offering of their virginity to the god". And later in the third century, the philosopher Aurelius Augustinus wrote that the phallus of the god Janus was likewise used "in order to open the way for the conception of the seed". In ancient Rome the gods had a hand in everything; even Saturn, primarily responsible for seeding and sowing, assisted with the progress of the semen.

For genuine sexual contact the wealthy Roman could turn to his male and female slaves. Horace cheerfully proclaimed in one of his satires: "And when your lust is hot, surely if a maid or pageboy is handy, to attack instanter, you won't choose to grin and bear it? I won't. I like a cheap and easy love!"

Oral intercourse depicted on a Roman pottery lamp.

Photograph: John Pitfield

A more conventional view of a pair of
lovers.

Photograph: John Pitfield

Roman theatre – the actor and
the pelican.

Photograph: John Pitfield

Elsewhere, Platus consoles his daughter, who is complaining
of her spouse's infidelity, and sternly reminds her: "He keeps
you well jewelled and dressed, and he gives you your food and
your maids. Better come to your senses." Post-Roman British
law followed some of these precepts in a refined way, but the
effect was still the same. Until the partial liberation brought
about by the First World War a woman without private means
who chose not to enter the marriage stakes made an alternative
commitment to lifelong poverty. Aulus Gellius, in his *Noctes
Atticae* of the second century, expressed the official Roman line:
"The state cannot be safe unless marriages are frequent."

Conversely, the state had no interest in outlawing prostitution; in fact, through the army, it actually owned a chain of
brothels around the frontiers of the empire. This ambiguity

Grotesque actor with a problem of priapic proportions. *Photograph: John Pitfield*

over the status of prostitution is equally reflected in English law where it has never been illegal for a man to pay a woman to have sex with him, only for her to offend by asking for money. Augustinus, in *De Civitate Dei*, reflects the dilemma of Christianity in its desire to control sexual relationships: "Banish prostitution from society and you reduce it to chaos through unsatisfied lust."

The activities of Roman emperors, however, were never expected to set any kind of example to the common people; in fact, it was frequently the reverse. Tiberius, in the early part of the first century, is said to have enjoyed swimming in his pool with a number of small boys; he called them his 'minnows', on account of the delicate way they kept darting to and fro

114

between his legs. Hypocritically, he was prepared to act to strengthen the institution of marriage and revived the family council system of jurisdiction to punish women accused of improprieties.

Marriages in the Roman world were customarily arranged when the prospective partners were still children (as is still the practice in many eastern countries) and finally took place when the boy reached fifteen or sixteen and the girl twelve. This also accords with Islamic law, where prospective brides must have reached menstruation and are therefore examined when they are between twelve and thirteen. As the average age for the onset of menstruation in Britain today is about thirteen, this casts doubt on the commonly held assumption that sexual maturity now arrives earlier than at any other time in human history. It is certainly no different from that recorded in the *De passionibus mulierum* of the thirteenth century, and it is worth bearing in mind that Tacitus, when in his twenties, married a girl of thirteen and later wrote: "The true Romans married without love and loved without refinement or reverence."

Ancient marriage customs recorded from insular parts of the

Debauchery, represented by a marble statuette of Bacchus, the god of wine, from Winchcombe, Gloucestershire.
Courtesy: British Museum

British Isles, such as Portland in Dorset, suggest the Celtic practice was for couples to live together over a trial period until there was a pregnancy to ensure that the pair were fertile. If they failed to conceive they would then part without any stigma or obstacle to the forming of new relationships. Given the Celtic enjoyment of drunken festivities it can be assumed that the marriage, when it took place, would be accompanied by extended rituals as lively as any in the Roman empire.

There was also far more sexual equality in Celtic Britain, where a woman could become queen, than under Roman rule where all rights of ownership, property and inheritance belonged to the male.

In native homes, wood was the principal material used by the ordinary Britons for their hut furnishings and, consequently, these have not survived; but the trendy sophistication of Roman villa-life led to the production of elaborate stone copies of many of these items, some of which are still occasionally found. A large industry developed, for instance, around Kimmeridge in Dorset where beds of blackstone shale form ledges running into the sea; this material was also worked in the Iron Age and Roman periods for lathe-turned bracelets. The use of shale in furniture making resulted in superb levels of craftsmanship as the up-market versions of wooden prototypes evolved into tables of stone supported on legs carved with claw-feet and sea-lion shoulders.

But the shale was also useful in other ways. It is naturally oil-bearing – it actually supports oil-wells in the 1980s – and gives a shining polish. However, oiling is essential for its maintenance and although this would have been no problem in a household with servants and slaves, it does present problems for its long-term preservation. If left untreated for any length of time and exposed to the air, such as in a house or even a cupboard, the shale eventually crumbles to dust. This process can sometimes be averted by various conservation techniques applied to those pieces retrieved damp from the ground, but this general instability of untreated shale means that very few such Roman objects have survived to go on show in museums. The Kimmeridge industry was prolific in its output of panels, floor tiles, flat dishes, spindle whorls, and small carvings.

The sea-lion table legs are also an indication of the way exotic animals fascinated the Roman mind. And this, in turn, led a number of contemporary writers to dismiss the British fauna as far too boring for their taste. One of the panegyrical authors, espousing the virtues of Britain, says however that its forests have no giant beasts, nor "poisonous creeping things, but rather an incalculable number of flocks and herds full of milk and laden with fleeces". Though the wildlife was tame by international standards, the Romans themselves were partly to blame. Bears, for instance, were killed at Colchester and at Richmond in Yorkshire; reindeer were becoming scarce due to the warming of the climate, though John Aubrey records that in the early part of the seventeenth century they were still known to be present in North Wales and Cumbria. The three common mammals that are now extinct in Britain are the beaver, the wolf and the wild boar. The latter was one of the symbols of the Celts and featured variously on the coinage of Cunobelin, the Iceni, and the Coritani; in Gaul, too, it represented privilege and power.

Literary records are the best means of determining what the Britons wore, for it is only in the warmer, drier parts of the Roman empire such as Egypt that the actual materials them-selves have occasionally survived. Clothing mattered consider-ably in a damp and cold climate. Tiberius Claudius Paulinus, governor in 220 of the York-ruled province Britannia Inferior, gave one of his assessors some clothes: "Though you deserve more," he told Sennius Sollemnis, "yet I hope you will be pleased to accept these few gifts, since they are offered to you in compliment: a wrap of Canusine wool, an embroidered

Laodicean dalmatic, a gold brooch with gems, two thick rugs, a British tossia" – a cloak or rug – "and a seal-skin."

There is a fragment of British cloth in the British Museum: it is wool yarn with a striped pattern and came from the late fourth century signal station at Huntcliff in Yorkshire.

By comparison, there is a relative abundance of ancient footwear, much of it having been found in the muddy banks of the Thames in London. The leather shoes are flat-soled and often hob-nailed, and the styles include pointed toes that would not have looked unfashionable in a mediaeval court.

Cult of the 'stiff and deformed' heads

TOTEM-POLE HEADS were on general display outside domestic huts and public temples throughout both the Iron Age and Roman periods in Britain. There is evidence that the making of wooden idols had come down from the end of the Neolithic period, about 2,500 BC. A large post-hole, which probably held a totem-pole, was discovered on Thickthorn Down, Cranborne Chase, on the border of Dorset and Wiltshire, in the 1930s, at the east end of an oval cenotaph barrow of the intermediate period between the Neolithic and the Bronze Age.

An impaled skull was found during excavations of the vast Iron Age fortress of the Brigantian peoples at Stanwick, Yorkshire. It had stood at the entrance. Such displays were to be the British way with traitors down the ages, culminating in the bloody aftermath of the Monmouth Rebellion in 1685.

There was also nothing new in the Iron Age veneration of the head. A chalk-cut carving of a circular highly-stylised face, constructed on a curvilinear and maze-like premise, was picked up from the ramparts of Maiden Castle hill-fort, Dorset, in 1971. It dates probably from before the Roman invasion. But its wide eyes are similar to those on a drum-shaped object two thousand years older, found in a burial mound at Folkton Wold, Yorkshire. The only minor difference is that the Folkton eyes are represented by concentric circles, and those of the Maiden Castle carving are spirals. As for the representations of the hair

Chalk-cut stylised face from Maiden Castle, Dorset.

Photograph: Colin Graham

and mouth – the only two other features depicted on either – the styles of Folkton and Maiden Castle are the same. Both use three-sided, asymmetrical curvilinear forms.

The same artistic forms found expression in a different medium in the Roman period. A late first century AD Roman disc brooch found at Kirmington, Humberside, displays the same symbolism as the Maiden Castle face and the Folkton drum. Its eyes are also big and wide, comprising two double concentric circles with traces of red enamel, with curvilinear indentations above and below. The brooch is discussed in Richard Hattatt's *Ancient and Romano-British Brooches*, the first full study of this fascinating group of artefacts.

These longstanding native forms of artistic representation were supplemented, and eventually supplanted, by a more

Romano-Celtic disc brooch, with wide eyes and curvilinear enamelled indentations, from Kirmington, South Humberside.

Courtesy: Dorset County Magazine

naturalistic style of art, brought across the Channel in the late Iron Age with the increasing waves of Celtic migrants coming into Britain. In Europe the cult of the head was already strongly established, with coins of the Osismi in Gaul showing severed heads, and it was to dominate native art in Britain throughout the Roman period.

Professor Jean Markale writes in *Celtic Civilisation* that: "Celtic legend is the legend of blood and of death." He quotes an Irish example: "Two girls entered bearing a large platter with a man's head covered in blood." And a Welsh hero whose head was preserved: "I carry at my side the head of Uryen, the generous chief of the army."

Diodorus Siculus, the Greek historian of the first century BC, recorded these practices of the Celtic peoples: "They cut the heads from fallen enemies and attach them to their horses' necks. They give bloodstained spoils to their servants to carry and sing the chant of death and the hymn of victory. They nail these trophies to the doors of their houses. The heads of the most distinguished enemies they embalm in cedar oil and preserve like relics, and display them with pride to strangers."

Posidonius, a philosopher of the same period, says that these heads were mounted like hunting trophies on the walls of houses. British, or Gallic, auxiliaries featured on Trajan's column in Rome are offering the emperor the long-haired severed heads of vanquished Dacians.

Veneration of the human head formed the basis for some of the strongest cults in northern Europe. Skulls are still preserved in niches cut into pillars in the third century Celtic sanctuary at Roquepertuse in France.

Evidence that such heads were kept in a British public building during the Roman period has come from the city of Viroconium Cornoviorum at Wroxeter, Shropshire. Excavations in 1980 uncovered nine skulls, mostly of young men in their early twenties. Two had been cut with a knife, apparently after death. No other bones were found in the vicinity, making it unlikely that these could have been burials.

Confirmation that they were in fact trophies, or *memento mori*, came from subsequent forensic examination. Dr J L Wilkinson of University College, Cardiff, noted a general presence of linoleic acid. The skulls had been immersed, or regularly rubbed, with linseed or a similar yellowish vegetable oil. They had been oiled, like English cricket bats, to prevent them from cracking. Their preservation at Wroxeter was no lingering relic of an earlier cult. For they were discovered in the rubble above the ruins of the basilica, an indoor sports hall, and put there at the end of the Roman era, between AD 450 and 500.

Substitutes for the real thing were mass-produced in wood, though few have survived. These have been preserved in bogs

Unusual Romano–Celtic limestone carving of totem-pole type with sexual symbolism transferred to the head.

Photograph: Colin Graham

and other deoxygenated waterlogged places, hardly the settings where such objects might have been prolific. The earlier wooden heads, and sometimes their counterparts in stone, tend to have extremely long faces, probably arising from the practical reason that wood is easiest worked in this fashion – as in African carvings – and lends itself to totem poles.

Stone heads are the durable form of the art but their occurrence, as might be expected, coincides with the availability of suitable rock and cannot be taken as proof of exceptionally strong head-cult feelings in those areas. They are particularly common in the region of Hadrian's Wall, and localised distribution in lowland Britain, southwards to Somerset and Dorset, generally follows the stone belts.

Some stone heads have been found many miles from where they were manufactured, and may well have been sold as cult objects at such places as temple shops, where wooden versions are likely to have been marketed in a similar way. Being lighter

123

**The simplest form of the Celtic head, showing
only the nose and eyes with a slight depression for
the mouth, in sandstone from Thetford, Norfolk.**

Photograph: Colin Graham

they could have been distributed much more widely, and might
even have been sold by travelling salesmen from their carts.
Heads of the three types – real, wood and stone – were on
general display in the late Iron Age and throughout the four
centuries of Roman Britain.

In the classical world there had been the Greek herms at
gateways and other entrances, but the Celtic stone heads of the
late Iron Age were simplistic in their design, often showing only
the nose and eyes in any detail, with the merest depressions to
indicate the mouth and ears. The form of the nose and eyes is
frequently phallic, the nose representing an inverted penis, with
the eyes as testicles. Their look is always discomforting, unset-
tling or menacing.

After the Roman invasion the style of the heads gradually

124

Fusion of styles, native carved but strongly Roman in appearance: a limestone carving at Bath.

Photograph: John Pitfield

changed. Although the head continued to be the principal cult object in Britain and Celtic Europe, the form of its representation became increasingly influenced by the complexity and total realism of Roman sculpture. The appearance of these later heads tends to veer as before from the disturbing to the tortured, but the carvings show far greater facial detail.

The eyes and nose once more occupied a disproportionate and oversized area of the head but the remaining space was used to depict features such as the hair, beard and moustache as well as fully developed mouth and ears. The hair is characteristically shown in swept-back waves, being limed in real life into such ridges. If the subject is a death mask, it is shown with bulging rounded eyes. A head representing life has articulated pupils and a slight curve to the lips.

Some heads were phalloid in shape. One, found at Eype on the Dorset coast, shows a circular face inscribed on the side of the glans. The shaft is broken, though enough survives to show the nature of the shape, and this is decorated with interlaced

Striking carving from Roman Bath, in the Roman mode but with Celtic vigour. *Photograph: John Pitfield*

compass-drawn circles to produce a series of curvilinear triangles.

Dr Anne Ross, in *Pagan Celtic Britain*, suggests that a severed human head, set on a pillar, was the original phallic symbol. This, she believes, is the meaning that the Eype head would have conveyed to contemporary onlookers. It is difficult, however, to back-date our views either of divinity or symbolism. Many of our churches have life-sized representations of a slaughtered man dripping blood. These could be open to the wildest misinterpretation by future cultures, who might reasonably assume that we practised human sacrifice.

Phallic head, in greensand, from Eype, Dorset.
Photograph: Colin Graham

One of the most remarkable Celtic representations of the head is on a small erotic knob attached to a sherd of black Romano-British pottery found in the ruins of a Roman town house at Dorchester, Dorset, in the 1930s. This piece has been dismissed as a "crude female figure". It is, however, crude only in the prudish sense, and not in its workmanship. Though very small, the naked figure is perfectly detailed. Her face is the usual Celtic circle, with the prominent rounded eyes placed lower than usual. From between the eyes the nose rises upwards, instead of downwards as is normally the case. This nose is very different from the standard Celtic wedge-shape. It is absolutely phallic, both in the way it rises from the eyes – which become testicles – and in the accuracy of its styling, to the extent of having a bulbous tip to represent the glans.

127

Knob from a Dorset pot, with a pained face and phallic nose and eyes, found at Dorchester.
Photograph: Colin Graham

Overall, the impression given is that the figure is at the same time both a foetus and a pregnant woman. The legs are folded inwards to indicate a position for sex, or perhaps to put pressure on the stomach muscles as a preliminary to giving birth, and the vulva is wide open. The mouth slit is oval and horribly pained. There is a hand below the mouth that seems to show the throttling of the neck. This fragment of pot is of smooth black ware, of the burnished sort produced locally in kilns at Poole Harbour and Chickerell. It was found in household debris of the fourth century. Celtic art not only flourished in the Roman period but was to last into the Dark Ages; a statement for which there is contemporary documentary authority.

Gildas, the British monk who lived between about 516 to

Fermanagh basalt carving of a bishop clasping a crozier, one of the earliest Irish Christian stone carvings, probably of eighth century date but with all the typical "stiff and deformed" features of the earlier Celtic heads that Gildas had deplored.

Photograph: Colin Graham

570, confirms that the larger Celtic totem poles survived on public display into the middle of the sixth century. In *De Excidio Britanniae*, written about 545, he expresses disappointment at their quantity: "I shall not enumerate those diabolical idols of my country, which almost surpassed in number those of Egypt, and of which we still see some mouldering away within and without the deserted temples, with stiff and deformed features as was customary."

The phrase "stiff and deformed" is a perfect description of the typical Celtic head. In Ireland, which had been spared a Roman interlude, the transition from the pure Celtic world of the Iron Age into an outpost of Christian Europe was a more direct process. Not until the eighth century were there any solid buildings of mortared stone, and when the illuminator for the Book of Kells had to depict the Temple of Jerusalem he represented it in wooden Irish-style form.

The old art was to express the new visions. In the ruins of an early church at White Island, Fermanagh, is a line of long-faced effigies of bishops and other clerics. But an occasional crozier is the only clue to their ecclesiastical status. Without that refinement the figures would be dated far earlier than the eighth century.

A Celtic sub-culture was also perpetuated in England by the masons of the mediaeval churches. Grotesque masks and gargoyles are the clues to the pagan past. A frieze of Celtic style carvings decorates an arch of the Norman period in the church at Adel, Yorkshire. The cult of the head proved resilient and adaptable throughout these islands, spanning four epochs and more than a thousand years.

Language, indigenous and introduced

ROMAN RULE BROUGHT with it an official language, displacing the Celtic tongue which had itself been brought to southern Britain by immigrants from Gaul and the Low Countries over the previous 500 years. There were also traces of pre-Celtic speech, particularly in the least changing aspects of language, such as the names of rivers.

Deeply prehistoric names have survived to the present day in the names of the country's principal rivers – Severn, Thames, Ouse and Tees – which cannot be explained through Celtic or later etymologies. For the first at least, the Severn, the conquerors imposed their own name – Sabrina – but it failed to stick. Neither can it be assumed that Celtic disappeared from common use amongst the native peoples. An invasion that brings the dominance of an alien minority can only result in bilingualism, with words borrowed from each side turning up amongst monolinguals.

Tacitus noted that the Celts of Britain spoke a variant of the Gallic language. Given that Celtic speech has taken centuries in dying from the highland fringes of these islands, despite a cumulative succession of blows – English conquest, trade, literature, newspapers, radio and television – it must be assumed that Celtic managed to maintain a solid hold in many parts of the Roman province. In the far north, pre-Celtic was still being spoken by the Picts in the Scottish highlands. Picts, a cursory epithet for them in Latin, means "painted and tattooed". It is the language of the Roman trooper who faced the wild men. Scotland itself takes its name from intruders from Ulster, who made their first footholds in Argyll and the islands. These basic divisions, along cultural and tribal lines, gave the country four distinct languages.

Bede lists them as Latin, Bretti, Picti and Scotti. Scholars differ about how much Latin; some feel it was dominant, as it still is in the Logudorese dialect which survives in the hill country of central Sardinia, though no part of Britain can quite match that degree of remoteness.

The Bretti or Celtic tradition was oral and, at best, was only progressing in its written form towards primitive strokes. The position was so bad at the time of Caesar that the defenders of the Belgic forts sent their messages in Greek. Their own language, in its purest surviving form, is represented by the Breton regional tongue in France, which has been shown by analysis to have originated in the West Country. The philological similarities are with Cornish, though this is probably coincidental as the original exodus across the Channel is more likely to have taken place from Devon and Dorset, the latter county being in the front line of change, with extensive linear earthworks as evidence of the troubles and pressures of the fifth century. As a result of these, the Celtic language was taken back to the continent, where it survives in the Basse-Bretagne area of Brittany.

The language of the native Britons was highly inflected, though during the Roman period it became increasingly softened. The process is called lenition. *Abonā*, the Celtic word for river, is an example. By the close of the Roman era it had lost its case ending and was being rendered as *avon*, in which form it has survived as a specific name for several English rivers. Such is the decay of language that it was adopted in 1974 as the title for a new English county, and so a word that refers to water can end up describing a large area of dry land. The mutation of the language in late Roman times, of which this 'b' to 'v' (probably via 'f') is an instance, spread to several other consonants. A purer form of the Celtic language survived in Ireland, and was developing the Ogam style of inscriptions in the fourth century.

Latin, which originated as the dialect of Latium – the provincial centre of which was Rome – became the official language of empire. In Britain it was restricted by the limitation of conquest, with Cornwall, Wales, Cumbria, and Scotland being able to preserve the fabric (though not the monopoly) of their ancient speech into present times. Vulgar Latin, as distinct from literary Latin, was the common tongue of empire, and judging from the number of loan-words that have crept from Latin into Cornish, Welsh, and Briton it would seem to have been widespread in lowland England. It was certainly used on monumental inscriptions and for graffiti, though this was inevitable as British was a verbal language, with no alternative to Latin for the written word. But British survived, sufficiently for Bede to record Bretti as a tongue. It, or Cymraeg as the Welsh themselves call it, would probably have won through as the national language but for the Saxon advances. Latin remained élitist, the language of government and religion. It had its official and folk-spoken versions. There are clues to this, as Eric P Hamp says in volume six of *Britannia*: "An obvious example is the loss and partial restitution of 'n' before 's' (French *peser* and *penser*). In any part of the Empire the literal presence of these features marked a social (potter, infantryman) or situational (Quintilian at dinner) stratum of speech."

Christianity adopted the voices of the administration and preserved Latin as the official language of the church in Anglo-Saxon England. The Normans extended the Latin presence to the law and learning.

Latin was one of the legacies of Roman Britain – a cross-

133

cultural survival for one and a half thousand years. It did not cease to be the official language of the country for domestic records until removed by an Act of Parliament in 1650. By then a revolution had overthrown the monarchy and established a republic; and Latin belonged to the past. It was symbolically reinstated at the Restoration in 1660, but finally enacted out of the system in 1733.

The place-names of Roman Britain fell into disuse in the Saxon period, though a substantial number have been salvaged from classical sources and reapplied with varying degrees of likelihood to the country's principal Roman settlements. The Antonine Itinerary, Ptolemy's geography, and the Ravenna Cosmography have provided 113, 126, and over 300 names respectively of Britain's place-names, rivers, and islands.

Most of the major towns can be identified with certainty because they are corroborated by the appearance of the town's name on inscriptions. This can sometimes apply to minor settlements as well. The location, for instance, of Avalava was known to be in the region of Hadrian's Wall, since it appears along with other wall-forts on the Rudge cup. Its identification was clinched in the 1940s with the discovery of Avalava on a third century inscription at Burgh-by-Sands, on the Solway Firth. Avalava can also be perfectly defined as *aval* survives as 'apple' in Breton. The name means orchard.

Like most of the place-names of Roman Britain it is Celtic rather than Latin. In such cases the Romans, or Romanised Britons, described the local topography or adopted an existing name. Sometimes, however, the native population gave the lasting tag to Roman intrusion. Cesaromago, near Chelmsford, Essex, means 'Caesar's market'. Nemetotatio is an example of a name that links the two cultures. It was applied to a Roman fortified enclosure near the River Taw at North Tawton to the north of Dartmoor. The name combines Nemeto with Statio, the first element surviving in Irish as *nemed*, 'a sanctuary'. The other part gives away the purpose of the fort, which was a centre for tax collection, linked probably to granite or other mineral workings in the Dartmoor area. The names combine to say: "Tax collecting station by the sacred grove".

Modern placenames preserve the memory of that Celtic sanctuary among the landscape of small woods towards Crediton, with Nichols Nymet, Broadnymet, Nymet Tracey, Nymetwood, and East and West Nymph. There are a further four Nympton parishes to the south of South Molton.

Existing placenames can often provide clues to the location of their lost Latin equivalents. Velox was a Roman river name, shown by its place in a list in the Ravenna Cosmography as lying at the opposite end to a line of southern English waters that had opened with Dubris, Dover. Velox means 'swift'.

There is one river in southern England, the only one that flows from a mountain, to which the name is completely apt. This is a transliteration of the contemporary Celtic name for the Dart, which takes the highest rainfall in the south of England.

Eburacum was Roman York, and though it can be placed there with total certainty, it resists further explanation. It can be defined as the place of Eburos, or the place of yews, or even the place of cow-parsley if one prefers to look to its origins in the Welsh word *efwr*. But the inhabitants of Roman York would not have thought much of that choice. They had their own view – not accepted by modern etymologists – that the name meant 'Boar-town' and adopted a large boar on a pedestal as the allusive badge of York. It appeared on carvings and was adopted by the Saxons for their 'Eofor-Wic' version of the name.

Milestones, of which the remains of hundreds survive from Roman Britain, are generally a topographical disappointment. They often provide only a dedication to the emperor, and it is rare even to find distances marked. These, when they occur, are generally devoid of locational information, stating, say, "mille passus" (one mile) or "milia passum LIII" (53 miles) as the case requires. There are, however, some splendid exceptions.

One of the more rewarding is 88 inches high, and now in

Lincoln Museum. The Roman name for the settlements was Lindum, which in Celtic meant a mere, and refers to the Witham marshes. The stone praises Victorinus, soldier secessionist emperor of the Gallic sector of the empire – Gaul, Spain and Britain – during the time of Claudius the Second, 268 to 270: "For the emperor Caesar Marcus Piavonius Victorinus Pius Felix Invictus Augustus, pontifex maximus, with tribunician power, father of his country, from Lindum to Segelocum 14 miles." Segelocum is Littleborough, on the Trent. Several other milestones survive with inscriptions to Victorinus – who must have issued an edict for their erection as he ruled for only a year. He was assassinated by one of his own officers in Cologne in 270.

Navio was a Roman fort at Brough-on-Noe, Derbyshire. It is another Celtic word for water, running in this instance, and the Welsh *nofio* is to swim. A milestone found at Buxton announced "a Navione milia passum XI" (for Navio 11 miles). That is the correct distance in Roman miles from Buxton to Brough, and, as confirmation – thanks to the conservative nature of river names – the rapid flowing waters there are still known as the Noe.

Trimontium is another name that features on a milestone. It was the Roman fort at Newstead, Roxburghshire. Unlike the mainstream of Roman placenames in Britain, it has a purely Latin name, as was perhaps appropriate for a fortress of conquest. Trimontium means "place of the triple peaks" and is one of the most aptly named places in Roman Britain. The profile of the three tops of the Eildon Hills is the dominant landmark of south-east Scotland. Etymology is often an obscure intellectual game, but here is a gem that redeems the subject.

Relics of literacy

THE INVENTION OF the first books in the western world is generally credited to the early Christians, in the third century. In fact, they only copied a Roman practice. The technique of book-making was known and in use on the northern frontier of Britain in AD 100, fifteen years before the building of Hadrian's Wall. The method was to write in ink on tablets of wood and join them together in concertina fashion, with tie holes or hinges, so they opened in sequence – very much as a computer print-out unfolds today. More than a hundred such tablets were found in a Roman army rubbish dump at Vindolanda near Chesterholm, Northumberland, in 1973.

These hardly amount to a work of literature, being mostly from a legionary quartermaster's June stores list showing disbursements, apparently reaching a peak for the festival of Fors Fortuna on the 24th. Their content, however, usefully contradicted the accepted illusion that the Roman soldier subsisted on "porridge and sour wine and little or no meat".

Janet Watts of *The Guardian* newspaper reported the tablets as "listing the items of army fare like barley, venison, and wine opposite the quantities they consumed". Goat, pig, ham, and fish sauce, are mentioned as well, together with quantities of *ceruesa*, the Celtic beer, calculated by the *modius*, which it had been previously thought was only a dry measure. Items marked *per privatum* were purchases additional to a soldier's normal rations, deductions for his main keep being automatically made to his pay.

The accident which caused the preservation of these wooden tablets can only be ascribed to the cesspit into which they were tossed. As well as the rubbish there were quantities of straw, excreta, tannin and bryophytes – and urine, "the great preservative".

Dr Alan Bowman, working in the history department at Manchester University, described this "unsavoury process" as the reason for the survival of the writing tablets. The lettering barely lasted long enough to be read, being "so far from indelible that sometimes excavators can watch it disappear before their eyes as the new-found trophy hits the air". The wording is retrieved by immersing the wood in ether and methylated spirit to fix the imprint. Infra-red photography is then used to recover the image.

A more enduring category of personal messages preserve, ironically, the names of those who invoked intense feelings of hatred. Curses were usually inscribed into a piece of lead, which was then nailed, for divine effect, to the wall of a temple. Those quoted here are given in English, though they lose a little of their edge in translation from the Latin.

They are often phrased in the terminology of sympathetic magic, like this London inscription found at Telegraph Street, Moorgate, in 1934, and now in the British Museum: "I curse Tretia Maria and her life and mind and memory and liver and lungs mixed up together, and her words, thoughts and memory. . . ."

And, more colourfully, from the Roman reservoir at Bath, found in 1880: "May he who carried off Vilbia from me become as liquid as water, she who obscenely devoured her become dumb, whether Velvinna, Exsupereus, Severinus, Augustalis, Comitianus, Catusminianus, Germanilla, Jovina." It was left for the gods to identify the culprit, and for us to know of them all.

Often the venom was positively directed, as at an urn cemetery at Clothall, Hertfordshire: "Tacita, hereby accursed, is labelled old like putrid gore."

It is not unknown, in these *defixiones*, for father to curse son, or sons, as at the temple of Uley, Gloucestershire: "Canacus complains to the god Mercury about Vitalinus and Natalinus his sons concerning the stolen draught animal. He begs the god Mercury that they may neither have health . . . unless they repay me promptly for the animal they have stolen and the god the devotion which he himself has demanded of them."

A similar request for the restoration of stolen property is made on a bronze plate at the Romano-Celtic temple of Nodons at Lydney Park, Gloucestershire: "To the god Nodons. Silvianus has lost his ring and given half (a fee of half its value) to Nodons. Among those who are called Senicianus do not allow health until it is brought to the temple of Nodons." Silvianus had to return to renew the instructions, as an additional inscription is to the effect that "this curse comes into force again".

Nodons is unlikely to have earned the fees; certainly he failed if this particular object was the gold ring inscribed "Senicianus" that was excavated at Silchester, Hampshire.

An inscribed silver plate found at Stony Stratford, Buckinghamshire – forded by Watling Street – is confirmation of another payment for a vow: "To the god Jupiter and Volcanus, I Vassinus, hereby have provided six denarii when they might be pleased to bring me their votary, safe home, and on the fulfilment of my vow I have paid the money."

A lead plate from Caerleon, Gwent, has gladiatorial over-tones, in that confident fighters are known to have left their clothing in the cloakroom at the amphitheatre, on the assumption they would be fit enough to change back into it. Sometimes, in classical literature, this complacency was regarded as arrogance, which might help to explain this wording: "Lady Nemesis, I give thee a cloak and a pair of boots. Let he who wore them not redeem them, except with the life of his blood-red charger."

A clue to another favourite Roman pursuit is cut into a stone at Chedworth, Gloucestershire: "The green company". Green was one of the team colours of Roman chariot-racing, which appealed to the horse-skilled Belgic tribes and was highly popular in southern Britain.

An important function of notices on those outposts of united Europe was to remind the subjects that they were not excluded from the state bureaucracy. It might be a practical reassurance that buildings or courtyards were declared to be "Public Property" but the limits to such rights were marked by boundary stones with the word "Terminus".

There must have been many more reminders of the presence of the state on the kind of objects that have generally decayed to nothing. Wooden writing tablets found at Walbrook, London, are branded: "Issued by the Imperial Procurators of the Province of Britain." A procurator was a tax collector and a paymaster, fulfilling the aspirations of all the world's treasury ministers in that the money gatherer also controlled its spending.

Trade associations were also active, and worker participation in public life was directed towards such beneficial pastimes as the sponsoring of temples. A dedication slab found in the ruins of Roman Chichester has been built into the wall of the town's modern edifice of local power, the council chamber: "To Neptune and Minerva, for the welfare of the Divine House by the authority of Tiberius Claudius Cogidubnus, king and imperial legate in Britain, the Guild of Smiths and those therein gave this temple from their own resources . . ." Cogidubnus was a native client-king adopted by the Romans.

From an altar-shaped tombstone to one of the priests of the Roman hot-spring shrine at Bath, Avon, we learn that temple life could be compatible with a decent age. His position would have entailed little discomfort and few wants, though Bath was exceptional in that it provided, literally, the warmest job in

140

Britain: "To the spirits of the departed, Gaius Calpurnius Receptus, priest of the goddess Sulis, lived 75 years." That was exceptional old age for Roman Britain, half that being the general expectation.

It would be interesting to know the age which one of those Imperial Procurators of Provincia Britannia managed. Gaius Julius Alpinus Classicianus was Procurator of the province of Britain, succeeding Catus Decianus in that post in 60–61, just after Boudica's rebellion. Part of his tombstone survives in the British Museum, but lacks the part with his age. The stones were found smashed, and had been broken in Roman times, to be incorporated in a bastion of the Roman city wall to the north of Tower Hill. The man who came in the wake of one rebellion lost his memorial in the cause of bolstering the state against the next serious threat to its power. One feels he would have automatically approved.

The presence of the Governor of the British province filters through to us largely as a result of the abundance of his staff. Their graves include, from Irchester, Northamptonshire: "Anicius Saturninus, the Governor's officer in charge of horses, made this memorial to himself." Being in charge of the horses was a position with status, and remained so in every royal household until the opening of airports.

An altar from Dorchester, Oxfordshire, was dedicated: "To Jupiter best and greatest, and the deities of the emperors Marcus Varius Severus, the Governor's seconded officer, set up this altar with its screens, from his own funds." The last phrase implies that he had access to other moneys, or that people might assume that was the case.

There are clues to the control of the imperial estates in Britain, such as this early third century stone found near the extensive Combe Down quarries at Bath, Avon, which were worked in Roman times and have honeycombed the hillside to the present day.

"For the welfare of the Emperor Caesar Marcus Aurelius

Antoninus Pius, Felix Invictus Augustus, Naevius, imperial freedman and Procurator's assistant, restored from ground level these ruined headquarters." Bath oolite was used on a national scale, being found in Roman burial yards from Caerleon to Colchester.

One of the finest commemorative tablets of Roman Britain was found in about 1845 at the foot of the castle mound in Caerleon – literally "Castle of the Legions" – in Gwent. This was the greatest fortress in the West. The three-foot slab of sandstone is dated to around AD 258: "The Emperors Valerian and Gallienus, Augustis and Valerian, most noble Caesar, restored from ground levels these barrack blocks for the seventh cohort, through the agency of Desticus Juba, of senatorial rank and the emperor's propraetorial legate, and of Vitulasius Laetinianus, legate of the Second Legion Augusta, under the charge of Domitius Potentinus, prefect of the legion."

Tombstones are confirmation that the men of the legions came from other corners of the empire. A Cirencester inscription of the first half of the second century is set beneath a relief sculpture of a Roman trooper lancing a fallen enemy: "Sextus Valerius Genialis, trooper of the Cavalry Regiment of Thracians, a Frisian tribesman, from the troop of Genialis, aged 40, of 20 years' service, lies buried here."

Similarly, from Gloucester, is another reminder of the Thracian horsemen: "Rufus Sita, trooper of the sixth cohort of Thracians, aged 40 of 22 years' service, lies buried here. His heirs had this erected according to the terms of his will." He carried a royal name, for Sitas was a king of Thrace in pre-Roman times. Thrace never re-emerged as an independent kingdom, and is now the north-eastern province of Greece.

An inscription from the Roman cemetery at Wroxeter, Shropshire, gives one of the fullest military epitaphs: "Titus Flaminius, son of Titus, of the Pellian voting tribe from Faventia, aged 45, of 22 years' service, a soldier of the Fourteenth Legion

Gemina. I did my service, and now I am here. Read this and in your lifetime be more or less fortunate. When you enter Tartarus" – the dark abyss deep beneath the earth – "the gods prohibit you the grape-wine and water. Live honourably, while your star grants you time for life."

The legions had burial clubs, a six-foot gravestone being erected by one of these societies at Bath, Avon, to a young Belgic soldier who died at the end of the first century. His tribe had spread on both sides of the channel, so he could have been from Gaul, but we may prefer to regard him as one of the first Britons enlisted into the imperial army.

It reads: "Julius Vitalis, armourer of the Twentieth Legion Valeria Victrix, of nine years' service, aged 29, a Belgic tribes-man, with his funeral at the cost of the Guild of Armourers. He lies here."

Such quotations imply that the history of Roman Britain is written on its stones. In a way it is, but only a small proportion of such monuments have survived intact. There are less than 2,500 Romano-British inscriptions in the country's collections listed in R G Collingwood and R P Wright's *The Roman Inscriptions of Britain* and half of these amount to only odd letters or phrases. This is trivial when compared with Italy itself, the city of Rome alone having 20,000 funeral inscriptions.

Neither is the distribution of such monuments representative, being as much a matter of the accidents of subsequent history as their original presence. Many sites have only one surviving literary monument, and far more have none at all. The fort at Lympne, Kent, has one – but it is of the highest quality: "To Neptune, Lucius Aufidius Pantera, prefect of the British Fleet, set up this altar."

Richborough, on the other hand, another Kent fort, has an extensive collection comprising dozens of letters and figures. But they amount to nothing. None of them has any surviving meaning.

The other loss is often the object that was the purpose for the public statement, such as statue-bases found at Wroxeter, Shropshire, and Plumpton Wall, Cumbria. These have lost their subjects, but preserve one of the classical clichés in their inscriptions: "Born for the good of the state." It was a phrase applied to emperors in the fourth and fifth centuries, though not exclusively, and it is just possible that these might have displayed the features of governors of the British province.

Others had to work hard to preserve their own names. One citizen has come through where most governors failed and his name is now on display in the Clapham public library, London: "To the spirits of the departed, Titus Licinius Ascanius. He made this for himself in his lifetime."

Graffiti, however, are the common man's most effective way of balancing the record. A rectangular building stone from Maryport, Cumbria, shows in graphic outline what is proclaimed to be: "The phallus of Marcus Septimius." Just in case there should be any doubt why this merited public attention, Marcus's phallus is directed towards an accompanying drawing of the appropriate female organ.

144

The Romans build a wall

HADRIAN'S REIGN OPENED with insurrection amongst the Moors, amongst the Sarmatians in what is now Eastern Poland, and in Egypt. Libya and Palestine were approaching rebellion and, inevitably, "the Britons could not be kept under Roman control". Britannia, personifying the province, appears on an issue of Hadrian's coins in 119.

The sole literary evidence for what came next – the building of the Roman wall across Cumbria and Northumberland – is contained in the account of Hadrian's reign written anonymously by one calling himself Aelius Spartianus in the *Scriptores Historia Augustae* (available in Penguin translation as *Lives of the Later Caesars*): "Having completely transformed the soldiers, in royal fashion, he made for Britain," in 122, apparently, "where he set right many things and – the first to do so – drew a wall along the length of eighty miles to separate barbarians and Romans."

It was a visit for which Hadrian was not envied by intellectual society in Rome, as the poet Publius Annius Florus reminded him in a poem:

> I do not want to be Caesar
> To walk about among the Britons
> To endure the Scythian hoar-frosts

To which Hadrian retorted:

> I do not want to be Florus
> To walk about among taverns
> To lurk about among cook-shops
> To put up with the cockroaches

Hadrian's British wall broke with tradition and for the first time put the Roman empire within permanent borders. It probably won a certain amount of tacit administrative approval, if only because, in Ronald Reagan's word, it was "affordable".

From here on, however, there would be little but shrinkage; previous emperors had happily assumed that Rome knew no boundaries, but the lesson they were about to learn was that there has never been a defensible frontier in history. The very reason for the success of Roman forces in the previous five centuries, since the sack of Rome in 390 BC, was that they had eschewed the limitations of rigid lines of fixed positions. Theirs was a continental army of flexible mobility for which no bounds had been set. In troublesome territories they would string

Hadrian – life-size bronze head of the young emperor found in the Thames at London Bridge.

Photograph: Colin Graham

garrisons around the edges of conquered lands, and then push out further as the opportunities arose.

The problem with linear defences is that they all carry the same inherent weakness: they split and stretch the available manpower across dozens of miles, pinning down garrisons in a series of bunkers that then have to be defended in their own right. All initiative passes to the attacker, who has the freedom to select the weakest point knowing that only a small proportion of the army he is facing will be able to respond; the rest of the defending forces can be by-passed, and left as their own prisoners.

History's verdict on indefensible frontier fortifications is absolutely damning. Hadrian's Wall may be excused on the grounds that such an idea had not been tested before, but in our own time it has been tried repeatedly and invariably found wanting; notable failures include the Maginot Line, Vietnam's Demilitarized Zone, and Sinai's Bar Nev Line. The reason why fixed forward positions are built, even though each generation re-learns the drawbacks, is because they are psychologically comforting both for the army and the populace. They give apparent security to everyone, as they edge the perimeter of defended territory. Building them provides civilian work, and their occupation is a complex arrangement of manning which neatly ties down divisions of soldiers who might otherwise be a nuisance to normal community life. Politically, they are a sign to a watching outside world that the nation is armed and prepared, though, equally, they show it to be alarmed and beleagured. The alternative is to defend from the centre, being prepared to repel a raid and then counter-attack in force. A nation that is not committed to forward defences can meet an attacker on advantageous terms by deploying full forces at the time and place of the defender's choice.

Hadrian's Wall was unique in Europe, but its structure was by no means ill-considered or insubstantial, and the timing suggests the idea probably came from the East. The Great Wall of China had been constructed two hundred years earlier and descriptions of it may well have come via the Iranians or from the Indians who, on the other side of the Persian caravan route, frequently came west and fascinated the Romans. Dio Cassius records that they sent embassies to Rome in the time of Augustus and, "having partly proclaimed a treaty of alliance, concluded it now with the presentation of other gifts, of tigers, animals which the Romans and, if I mistake not the Greeks as well, saw then for the first time. They gave also a lad without arms, like the statues of Mercury one sees, but who made up for the want of hands by employing his feet, with which he could bend a bow, throw a dart, and play on the trumpet."

Immense amounts of information about India seeped into classical writings. It was such a different world that many of the accounts are inevitably highly coloured. Megasthenes could believe the tales of men without noses or mouths, of "people that sleep in their ears", of gold-mining ants, and the river Silas on which nothing would float. If this sort of exaggeration was reaching Rome it is certain that someone must have relayed travellers' tales of a Great Wall on the far frontier of India's neighbour.

A pedigree of this kind would explain why Hadrian's Wall was visualised and initially built on an extravagant scale. Its earliest parts are a ditch facing north and a wall ten Roman feet thick and fifteen feet high, which the Romans themselves realised was wasteful as later sections were reduced to a width of six feet – and could still have reached full height.

Timber prototypes, with wooden towers a third of a mile apart, had been tried on the German frontier, the Turk Wall of the Black Sea, and deep in Scotland, along the Gask Ridge, Perthshire. They are contemporary with the North African frontier barrier, the Fossatum Africae.

The British wall was based upon the Tyne estuary where

Replica of a stone turret and length of Hadrian's Wall built as part of a research project at Chesterholm, Northumberland, in 1974. The actual line of the Roman wall is a mile to the north.

Photograph: Roland Gant

the geopolitical possibilities were at their best. The rivers and sea defined a semi-natural boundary, coming in much more dramatically on the western seaboard with the Solway Firth and Eden estuary; it was already a form of border on the northern limits of Briganti territory, with established Roman forts on the Stanegate road. Although the seventy-five miles

The inhospitable landscape of Northumberland, west of Cawfields, crossed by Hadrian's Wall. The thin dry-stone wall to the right is a recent field boundary.

Photograph: Roland Gant

Turret and palisading of a reconstruction of the turf-walling of the western third of Hadrian's Wall, erected in 1973 at Chesterholm, Northumberland. *Photograph: Roland Gant*

between estuaries was crossed by deep-cut valleys, it was largely a landscape of great upland moors with limitless potential for quarrying. Strategically and ethnically, it was better than the mediaeval border between England and Scotland.

In all, the wall was 73 English miles (or eighty Roman ones) with an extension down the Solway Firth to prevent an amphibious detour around the end. Parts of the wall now carry an early nineteenth century road, and other sections show as a grassy hump across fields, but Hadrian's Wall for the modern tourist runs shoulder-high for miles across the outcrops and heather of the moors. Its permanent garrison would have originally required eight thousand men.

The wall ran across forty-five miles of Northumberland, to Gilsland on the River Irthing, and then for another thirty-six miles westward across Cumbria, where it was originally built of turf; this had to be twice the width of the stone section, and was twenty Roman feet thick. Turf-building was hardly part of the plan and must have been introduced to bring the wall to

150

completion when construction was falling behind schedule; this decision would have been taken by Britain's governor, Aulus Platorius Nepos, who before the year 122 was governor of Lower Germany from where – at the legionary base of Vetera – the Sixth Legion and first wall-builders were shipped into the Tyne. This temporary turf-wall was later rebuilt with stone, largely along the same course.

Accommodation for the soldiers, it was originally intended, would be provided by milecastles and watchtower turrets, and support from behind the lines would come from the series of earlier Roman forts on the Stanegate road, a mile or so to the south. Initially, it was an open frontier, with numerous gated crossing points. Access was subject to customs regulations, and evidence from the Rhine indicates that only unarmed passage was permissible, and then by payment of a toll.

The proliferation of gates also had a military purpose, to allow the Romans to mount swift and frequent patrols, and to that extent the wall was not quite the static frontier it appears. But the supervision of customs and population movement

By 1982 the reconstructed turf walling at Chesterholm, built by schoolchildren in 1973, was visibly tilting and showing the problems inherent with timber palisading. *Photograph: Roland Gant*

Housesteads, the best preserved of the Roman wall-forts, was built between AD 122 and 130. This is the granary, with a view to the Cheviots. Vercovicium, its Roman name, means "hilly place". *Courtesy: National Monuments Record*

bogged the Roman army down with administration and policing.

Because of its restricted space the wall was never much of a fighting platform, and observation and signalling for a patrol to intervene must have followed if a routine pattern of responses failed.

All this, however, was considered grossly inadequate, and at an early stage. Nepos tried to have the wall finished by 125 so its completion fell within his three-year period as governor, but complications arose from the emperor's inspection and his insistence upon revised specifications. Although each fort could accommodate eight hundred men, only thirty-two could be housed in a milecastle, and Hadrian regarded this as insufficient. It is possible the revised scheme was connected with the loss of the Ninth Legion Hispana which vanishes from history in about AD 130 and is never recorded again. Marcus Cornelius Fronto, the orator, writing about 162, mentions Roman legionary losses in Hadrian's time inflicted by the Jews and Britons. The former can take credit for the annihilation of the Twenty-Second Legion Deiotariana but the Ninth was the only British legion to vanish; this may not necessarily have happened in the province for, although it is last recorded in Britain shortly after 108 when it left York, its tile stamps have turned up at Nijmegen in the Netherlands and been dated to about 122. This suggests the Ninth was exchanged for the Sixth Legion which came to Britain with Platorius Nepos.

Major changes to the wall, including the decision to provide it with its own series of fifteen forts (though only one was

Bronze statue of the war god Mars found in the Foss Dike at Torksey, Lincolnshire. The inscription reads: "To the god Mars and the Imperial Divinities, the Colasuni, Bruccius, and Caratius offered one hundred sesterces from their own purse; Celatus the copper-smith made the figure and contributed a pound of bronze at a cost of three denarii."

Photograph: Colin Graham

definitely completed within the emperor's lifetime) came after Hadrian's intervention. The next problem was to safeguard the approaches to the rear of the wall – which in a lowering mist were as vulnerable as the open moors in front – and this was achieved by creating a security corridor. This vallum is on the English side. It is a flat-bottomed gouge into the rock, ten feet deep and twenty feet wide with banks of the same width that are set back thirty feet from its sides. Consequently, there was now less freedom of passage through the wall and although some causeways were provided the overall number of crossing points was reduced from about eighty to fifteen.

The legions known to be working on the building of the wall were the Second, Sixth and Twentieth; each was responsible for five miles at a stretch and sub-divided its sector between cohorts of 480 men. These, in turn, organised their work at centurial level, and all three units of organisation celebrated completion of each stage with ceremonies at which inscription stones were dedicated. On the other hand, some of the cohorts

The hooded deities of Housesteads. *Courtesy: National Monuments Record*

The ditch that accompanies Hadrian's Wall along its lowland sections. This is the country east from Gilsland, on the border of Northumberland and Cumbria, where the wall crosses the valley of the River Irthing.

would have been engaged in normal soldiering and it is likely that a major proportion of the actual workforce was British, paid or slave.

The fleet was brought in to help with some of the fort granaries – and "classis Britannicae" (British fleet) inscriptions have been found at Benwell, Newcastle, and in the wall itself near Birdoswald. Their engineers would also have been responsible for wharves and a bridge at the main Tyne supply base of Corbridge, and for another bridge which crossed the northern branch of the Tyne at Chesters.

Urban parts of the wall are still being discovered: in 1981, for instance, two or three courses of Roman masonry were found next to St Dominic's in the St Anne's district of Newcastle, and at the other end there has been a whole string of finds.

The summer of 1975, from May to July, was the driest since 1921 and provided the best patterns in archaeological crop marks since the advent of aerial photography. The differential coloration between ordinary parts of fields and the areas with ditches, holes and buried walls, became increasingly clear as heat drew all the moisture from the ground. Ancient ditches

Hercules: a gold-coated bronze statue nearly twenty inches high, from an estate near Birdoswald on Hadrian's Wall.

Photograph: Colin Graham

usually look the greenest as they provide plants with their optimum soil depth. Many sites took on a new clarity in 1975, and again in the drought-year of 1976. The major discovery of them all was that Hadrian's Wall does not stop at Bowness – ten miles north-west from Carlisle – but continues along the Solway Firth shoreline for a further five and a half miles. The parch marks were visible from the air and spotted by Professor Barri Jones of Manchester University: "I was doing a programme of work, involving air photography in Cumbria, and gradually realised what I had stumbled across."

Five fortlets, on the line of the wall, were already known to lie along this coast. Richard Bellhouse is an amateur archaeologist who uses an iron pole to prod the ground and establish the comparative resistance of different patches of soil: he discovered seven milecastles and twelve towers along the shore.

Great Chesters and the forts beside the extensive mudflats

of the north Cumbrian coast were built in the last decade of Hadrian's reign, 128 to 138. In his final two years the fort at Carvoran was converted from a timber and earthworks construction to one of stone.

There were many modifications in the layout and design of the forts and ancillary buildings which took place whilst the work was in progress. By the time the fort at Great Chesters was being pegged out it was decided there was no longer any advantage in having the defences projecting northward from the line of the wall. And now the older, western section of turf-wall was suffering chronic natural decay, speeded, no doubt, by the damp and hostile environment. By the year 138 the whole thing required perpetual renovation.

The Rudge cup, a bronze enamelled bowl four inches in diameter, was found in 1725 in one of the four villas on the Littlecote estate in the Kennet valley east of Marlborough, Wiltshire. It is encircled with a design showing a fortified wall with crenellated turrets and the inscription "A MAIS

Bronze bowl, showing western parts of Hadrian's Wall and listing its forts, probably issued to commemorate the completion of the frontier in about AD 138. It was found at Rudge, Wiltshire, in 1725. *Courtesy: Wimborne Bookshop*

ABALLAVA VXELODVM CABOGLANS BANNA". The fortification is obviously Hadrian's Wall and the placenames were identified by Ian Richmond as the Wall forts of Bowness, Burgh-by-Sands, Castlesteads, Birdoswald and Bewcastle. The shape suggests a date towards the middle of the second century and the subject matter indicates it is a commemorative mug to mark the completion of the western section of the stone wall and its forts, which were finished and manned in 139–40. It probably came south to the rich farmlands of Wiltshire with a retired army officer or civil servant who had left the bleak northern frontier for a more comfortable life in the valley beside the Bath road.

By its very existence, Hadrian's Wall caused a military sub-culture to evolve in Europe, ramifications from which remain embedded in the armed services, and further afield, to this day. Contemporary records were made on board smeared with wax and scratched with a wooden stylus. From them the word "underpants" made its way into the Latin-based languages.

The changing room of the bath-house in the wall-fort at Chesters, set in parkland beside the Tyne in Northumberland. These niches were probably clothes lockers. *Courtesy: National Monuments Record*

Diploma of the time of Hadrian, found at Stannington, Northumberland, in 1760. These bronze plates confirmed rights of citizenship and legal marriage given in return for military service. Duplicates of each were filed in Rome.

Courtesy: British Museum

The squaddies had the benefit of licensed brothels under army control and the supervision of medical officers. There were cult initiation ceremonies (with the painful use of stone and fire) into male-only brotherhoods similar to the officer élites of nineteenth-century Prussia. Medical units were installed in the auxiliary forts and some of the soldiers were personally visited in hospital by Hadrian himself.

In their forts the men had the same space per head as they might expect in the late twentieth century Royal Air Force – which means they did better than the equivalent British Army ranks. Forty people could be accommodated in a bath house, but that might not have been too uncomfortable as bathing was one of the passions of the Roman empire, even in the depths of Northumberland.

At the end of it all was freedom. A corroded bronze plaque discovered in the Chesterholm excavations in the 1970s – consigned to a box marked scrap and only spotted on cleaning – was the first discharge certificate to be found this century. Ten only have been found in Britain. The bronze was incised with a military diploma confirming twenty-five years of service and granting citizenship of Rome; it also legalised the recipient's wife and children. It would have been presented at a full parade and a duplicate reference copy sent to Rome to establish authenticity. The Roman army rewarded its auxiliary veterans with the rights of citizenship, although the men were almost entirely non-Roman by the second century; there were, however, still a few serving soldiers far from home in the island outposts of a continental empire.

One of the soldiers serving in the heart of Wales lost a touching reminder of the moment for which most of them were waiting: an intaglio found in a second century Roman fort near Brecon shows the reunion of the hero Ulysses with his hound, Argus.

Temporary return to Scotland

THE NEXT EMPEROR, Antoninus Pius, decided to abandon Hadrian's greatest creation. He chose a new governor for the province, Quintus Lollius Urbicus, to replace Publius Mummius Sisenna, who had come to the end of his three-year appointment.

Urbicus was told to evacuate the wall, or else reduce it to a few garrisoned forts with selected others which were to be maintained, and move the Roman army back into Scotland. This advance was to be halted a hundred miles north in the lowlands, between the Forth and the Clyde, where the distance between the east and west coasts is at its minimum, a mere thirty-five miles. This was well under half the width of country spanned by Hadrian's Wall and its landscape was studded by a number of small rounded hills on which forts could be built.

Under any other emperor the northward advance would have been considered an expansion of empire, a battling to quell turbulent peoples. But Antoninus Pius was different. His reign brought disarmament, an expansion of trade and the advancement of learning. Peace and prosperity were not marred by wars, revolts, or conspiracies. According to the contemporary Greek traveller Pausanias, author of *Periegis of Greece*, there were just two far-flung conflicts. These featured the Moors in North Africa and the Brigantes in Yorkshire, the Britons of the north Pennines.

Pausanias wrote: "The emperor deprived the Brigantes in

Heavy horseman and trampled North Briton, from a cavalryman's tomb at Kirkby Thore, Cumbria.

Courtesy: British Museum

Britain of most of their territories because they too (besides the Moors in North Africa) had entered into a war of aggression by invading the Genounian part, subjects of the Romans."

A problem here arises because Genounia is unknown, though there is every reason to believe that unrest among the Brigantes might have developed after the Roman army had marched away into the heart of Scotland. J G F Hind came up with an answer in 1977, in volume eight of *Britannia*. He suggests Pausanias confused the Brigantes of Yorkshire with the Brigantii of Austria; the latter had the Genauni of the Inn valley as their neighbours. This is such a beautifully simple explanation as it would be a ridiculously improbable coincidence to suggest the British Brigantes also had Genounian neighbours.

Hind also upset established archaeological thinking when he pointed out that the Brigantes were more likely to have looted the adjoining Romanised territories of the Cornovii in the Midlands or the Coritani in Leicestershire than bother with third-world tribes in Scotland.

As well as reducing forces round the wall, the new policy

involved withdrawing soldiers from the territory of the Brigantes. The Pennine forts at Brough-on-Noe and Slack were evacuated and it was left to one new garrison at Lanchester to patrol the area previously covered by the two forts at Binchester and Ebchester. Although the Brigantes had a history of revolt and might have been expected to take advantage of this new opportunity, it seems exposure to Roman civilisation had temporarily stilled the nationalist spirit in British peoples.

It is even possible that the move north came by invitation. There are many pointers to a largely stable and expanding second-century population in the area between the Borders and the Lowlands; this did not require policing from an extensive jigsaw of forts and was certainly not displaced by the post-139 Roman occupation. Elements of the population, the new bourgeoisie of southern Scotland, harassed perhaps by the anti-Roman Selgovae and Damnonii tribes, could have demanded imperial protection. Requests of this sort would have demolished the entire raison d'état for Hadrian's Wall: it was no longer of use to the state or its security if those beyond it were now calling for the province to be extended to incorporate them – the lure of successful capitalism through the ages.

The decision to pull out of Hadrian's costly monument may also have been a reaction to the resources it consumed, apart from the feeling that it was no longer in the right place. Although the military may have had a pride in their stone wall, its upkeep was exhausting, its situation bleak, and the tours of duty boring. They may have been pressing for this decision, or knew it would be pointless to suggest it till Hadrian departed.

In 139, the year after Hadrian's death, the supply base at Corbridge was rebuilt by the Second Legion. This point behind the Roman wall, where Dere Street bridged the River Tyne, was crucial for the support of all operations in north Britain. Along this road the Romans marched deep into Scotland, advancing to Strathmore.

Romano-Celtic relief of Hercules, part of a frieze in a military temple, at Corbridge, Northumberland. *Courtesy: National Monuments Record*

There was to be no repeat of Agricola's campaigns in the Highlands, but it remained clear that the hostility of the north Britons would inevitably spill south once again. The construction of the next defended frontier, the Antonine Wall between Grangepans of the Firth of Forth and Old Kilpatrick on the River Clyde was carried out under Lollius Urbicus and completed in 142 or 143. A string of forts was built before work proper started on the rampart; they began with a major garrison at Carriden, which overlooks the starting point for the wall, and had temporary camps at Muirhouses and Kinglass Park to protect the landward flank of the operations. The inland forts were Mumrills, Castlecary, and Balmuildy. Old Kilpatrick, on the Clyde, was the fort at the west end of the chosen line, and other forts were added every couple of miles as the wall was built. It was then handed over to Urbicus's successor, Gnaeus Papirius Aelianus.

Of Antoninus Pius the *Lives of the Later Caesars* says: "He conquered the Britons through his legate Lollius Urbicus and another wall was set up when the barbarians had been driven back."

The Antonine Wall was a refined version of Hadrian's Cumbrian turf-wall, with a ditch about forty feet wide and twelve feet deep, backed by a rampart of turf blocks on a stone foundation fourteen feet wide. Major differences between the two styles of building showed the Romans had learnt from their perpetual maintenance problems with the Cumbrian wall. This had stood only five feet from its ditch, and its weight led to slippage and subsidence, worsened by inadequate drainage. But with the new one this berm, a flat area of untouched ground between the ditch and bank, was increased to twenty feet in the eastern part of the wall and to almost thirty feet in the western sector. The supply lines of the Roman fleet ran up the east coast rather than the Atlantic seaboard and so the building, undertaken by the Second Legion, was begun at the Forth.

Behind the wall ran the Military Way, an army service road eighteen feet wide. Hadrian's Wall had utilised an earlier road, the Stanegate, but this lay too far from the wall and was another design flaw rectified in the building of the Antonine.

The best preserved section of the Antonine Wall, more than a mile in length, lies either side of Rough Castle, between Falkirk and Bonnybridge. Here, above the Forth and Clyde Canal, the ditch, wall and road remain clearly visible, as well as four beacon-platforms and the fort at Rough Castle. The beacons were signalling posts, set in pairs, and excavation of one of them on the west side of Rough Castle showed it to have been turf-built on stone foundations eighteen feet square. The surrounding ground was covered with charred wood.

Troops deployed along the new wall were mainly infantry,

with a few cavalry units, and the manpower was concentrated with twice the number of soldiers per mile as there had been on Hadrian's Wall. Although the number of troops employed was only slightly smaller than before, the distance fortified this time was less than half.

Manning was not evenly spaced, however, as about two-thirds of the total strength was garrisoned in the western sector where the Campsie Fells and Kilpatrick Hills rise from sea level to more than a thousand feet in less than a mile. These wet uplands must have troubled the Roman strategists. On the eastern end of the wall they were cushioned from potentially hostile landscape and peoples by a belt of friendly, or pacified, countryside in Fife, where Roman forts could give advance warning of incursions.

A bar which runs fifteen hundred feet into the Firth of Forth at Carriden formed a sheltered harbour less than a mile from the fort at Bridgeness and the end of the wall at Grangepans. It is now a triangle of silt, visible at low tide, which was then guarded by a fort on the top of the wooded cliffs above Burnfoot. Between the two forts were the wharves and supply depot for the Roman army in central Scotland. About ten miles eastwards along the Forth was an all-weather anchorage off the fort of Cramond in the mouth of the River Almond.

By the year 155 the Brigantes had revolted and Britannia appeared, droopy-faced, on a coin; that, however, is more likely a reflection on Celtic artistry as the coin was minted in London, than a comment upon the troubles. Coins were politically sensitive objects and no state deliberately publicises its reluctant peoples. It is just that the Celts did not mould happy faces.

The province at this time suffered a localised disaster, affecting some of its prosperous urbanised middle-classes. St Albans was devastated by fire in about 155, some fifty acres of the town being burnt to the ground. One site, at least, remained vacant for another century and was not redeveloped until about 275.

Such fires were the nightmares of British towns until the mid-eighteenth century when building practices changed and brick and tile finally replaced timber and thatch.

Back in the volatile areas of northern England, the Brigantian rebellion had the effect of drawing Roman troops south again, mainly from their reasonably secure area between the two walls. The fort at Newstead was temporarily evacuated and the surplus stores tipped into pits, along with a collection of head-trophies – the skulls of some of the North Britons who had fallen under the swords of auxiliaries.

The perpetual British war

WORK STARTED IN 158 in preparation for a major redisposition of British frontier forces. The fort at Newstead had been reoccupied and remained in use until after 180, but this was exceptional. Scotland, apart from Newstead and forts along Dere Street, was otherwise abandoned.

Preparations were in hand for an evacuation of the Antonine Wall – which took place in 163 and 164 – but first the previous border had to be reinstated. Hadrian's Wall was therefore reconstructed between the years 158 and 163. But there was not the manpower to occupy both frontiers simultaneously.

Troubles in the north would not be at the expense of prosperity in the south – a recurrent fact of British life. Changes were made in the rooms of the bathing area of the former palace at Fishbourne, Sussex, in about 160. Above the hypocaust heating system was set a magnificent and highly coloured mosaic floor, showing the latest fashion and state of the art. It contrasts with the drab black and white geometric patterns of the earlier floors, of about AD 75, in adjoining corridors. The new floor features cupid riding a dolphin, surrounded by sea horses and vases that have an elaborate Greek look. The artist appears to have signed his work with a little bird perched on one of the tendrils. This became the main room for the final period of the villa's occupation, from 160 until it was burnt to the ground during building alterations in the 280s. The floor has

Outstandingly high quality mosaic of cupid riding a dolphin, made in about AD 160, in the bathing area of the palace at Fishbourne, Sussex.

Photograph: John Pitfield

survived it all, perfectly preserved and restored despite problems of subsidence which has left the centre curving into a dip.

The trappings of the state moved out into the countryside in the wake of wealthy living. A *mansio* or inn of about 160, which would have been primarily an official lodging place for civil servants, has been discovered next to the later Orphic temple at Littlecote, Wiltshire. It has provided the only oak brewing vat to be discovered in Britain. The site is midway between London and Bath and its immediate area probably contained the full structure of a state establishment including a tax-collecting station and a fort.

At the beginning of the reign of Marcus Aurelius, 161 to 180, the *Lives of the Later Caesars* notes the "threat of a British war" and the dispatch of Sextus Calpurnicus Agricola to deal with the problem. By the autumn of 163 his name was in stone on the northern frontier in Britain, on a dedication slab seven feet wide in the Roman garrison town of Corbridge, beside the River Tyne, in Northumberland. It was the principal legionary supply base for the Roman wall. The new governor's name also appears on an inscription to "the Invincible Sun-god" found at Corbridge. His name has also been preserved at Ribchester, Chesterholm, and twice at Carvoran.

There was an inspection of troops on the wall by Marcus Aurelius and Lucius Verus towards the close of 163. But then something went wrong. Work stopped abruptly on a huge storehouse at Corbridge. The tools of the builders were left at

Standard Roman hypocaust, their cavity underfloor heating system with wall flues, at Fishbourne, Sussex. It was constructed in the 280s but never completed as the villa was then burnt to the ground. *Photograph: John Pitfield*

Sandstone relief of a wild man, a strongly Celtic carving of a Silenus-like figure, picked up from the burnt heather of a Northumberland moor near Stagshaw, between Corbridge and Hadrian's Wall.

Photograph: Colin Graham

their workplaces and no one ever bothered to steal them. The grass quickly grew round them. An officer buried his hoard of one hundred and sixty gold coins in a bronze jug beside a newly constructed gravel road; these were found at Corbridge in 1953. The latest of them dates to about 160 but it could easily have been another three or four years before they were paid out along the wall. Only a high-ranking officer could have accumulated this kind of surplus. But the only certainty is that the man never needed his money again, such are the misfortunes of war.

It is reasonable to assume that the abandoning of major construction work at the fort coincided with the crisis that led an officer to bury his gold. The suddenness of the attack on Corbridge is no proof that Hadrian's Wall was breached. The fact that the masons were working at the time of the alarm, and

171

that they dropped their tools on the spot, is more consistent with the North Britons having sailed into view.

The subsequent history of Corbridge has been lost. Grace Simpson says in volume five of *Britannia*: "The evidence for periods later than the storehouse was swept away entirely by Sir Charles Peers, Chief Inspector of Ancient Monuments, in order to obtain a flat lawn, easy to keep tidy."

Corbridge, as an example of preservation of a major site flowing with rich finds, has been a disaster. The comments of Grace Simpson, daughter of one of the principal excavators on the Roman wall, are echoed by those of M Brassington in volume six of *Britannia*. The old Ministry of Works "consolidated" those ruins at Corbridge Roman fort, Northumberland. Brassington, carrying out a reappraisal of the discovery there, in 1907, of a pottery shop by Leonard Woolley, found that "the whole structure has been rebuilt without using the original stones, and that the east wall of the unfinished building, underlying the pottery shop, has been placed some eight feet to the west of its original position. The roadway originally to the west of the building now appears on the eastern side."

A more general corollary to this, on a national scale, is that the supremacy of the Environment Department look has brought a certain sameness to the masonry of its preserved ruins, whether they are temples, abbeys or castles. The kindest

Second century stone carving of the Mother Goddesses, from Lincoln.

Photograph: Colin Graham

comment is that preserved ruins were often not quite what they seem.

An indication of the strains within the Roman province in the decade after 160 are that the state opted out of all, or part of, its monopoly in valuable metals. Perhaps the troops and officials could no longer be spared for its management. Imperial control appears to have been relaxed or removed from the lead industry after 170 for the pigs ceased to carry official stampings. Industry, such as it was, began passing into selected private hands while the state busied itself enlarging the army, a dual political process known today.

Eight thousand defeated Sarmatian horsemen, who had fought effectively against the Romans in the Dacian wars, were drafted into their captors' army in 175. Marcus Aurelius sent five and a half thousand of them to Britain, where they were garrisoned at Ribchester in Lancashire. In the opinion of David Breeze, writing in *Hadrian's Wall*: "They may have been required to support a hard-pressed provincial army, or Britain may simply have been an isolated place to which to send troops of uncertain loyalty."

Perennis, the administrator who controlled Rome and its empire during the reign of Commodus, is said in *The Later Caesars* to have intervened in the British troubles of 180 to 184:

"Yet in spite of his great power, because he had dismissed senators and put men of equestrian status in command of the troops in the British war, when the matter was made known by the legates of the army this same Perennis was suddenly declared a public enemy and given to the soldiers to be lynched."

Dio Cassius records that of all the wars of the time of Commodus "the greatest was the British war" and that the northern tribes "crossed the wall" – Hadrian's Wall rather than the Antonine Wall – that separated them from the Roman forts. "They did much damage, killing a certain *strategos*" – general – "and the troops that were with him". Commodus sent Ulpius

Marcellus to the province as governor and he "ruthlessly put down the barbarians".

The Later Caesars adds that "Commodus was named Britannicus by flatterers, although the Britons even wanted to choose an emperor in opposition to him." A coin was minted in 184 to celebrate the British victory – of Marcellus over the North Britons. In 185, two British legions were shipped across the Channel to put down a rebellion in Brittany. The soldiers resented being under the command of cavalrymen and a delegation of 1,500 marched on Rome. The changes were the responsibility of Perennis, the praetorian prefect. Commodus met the mutineers and handed over Perennis for them to kill.

In the 180s the ineptitude of Commodus had paralysed government in Rome, causing a famine which, although real enough for its victims, was mainly artificial as it resulted from state mismanagement rather than a shortage of crops.

In Britain, Germany, and Dacia, the *Lives of the Later Caesars* records "the provincials rejected his rule. All these troubles were settled by generals."

Publius Helvius Pertinax, a former governor of Syria and a member of the senate, was sent to Britain to replace Marcellus. To continue with Anthony Birley's translation in Penguin Classics: "On his arrival, he deterred the soldiers from any mutiny, though they wanted to make some other man emperor, preferably Pertinax himself. At this time Pertinax incurred the reproach of spitefulness, because he is said to have insinuated to Commodus that Antistius Burrus and Arrius Antoninus were making an attempt on the empire. He did in fact suppress the mutinies against Commodus in Britain, but came into immense danger, being almost killed in a mutiny of a legion – at any rate, he was left among the dead. This affair, of course, Pertinax punished very severely. As a result of this he sought to be excused from his legateship, saying that the legions were hostile to him because of his maintenance of discipline."

174

After governing Britain he was appointed proconsul of Africa, and was, on the last day of 192, chosen as emperor to succeed Commodus who had been assassinated. Quintus Aemilius Laetus, the prefect of the Praetorian Guard, had Commodus poisoned and then strangled – to the acclamation of the senate – and three months after the new emperor's accession he was to turn aside and let Pertinax face a similar mutiny. He was speared in the chest and then stabbed to death, but this time popular feeling was not with the killers. The former emperor's head was recovered for a token funeral by his successor, Julianus, and the following emperor, Septimius Severus, provided fulsome orations and himself accepted the name of Pertinax from the senate as a gesture of state recompense.

Decimus Clodius Septimius Albinus, Britain's governor from 192 to 197, weathered Rome's political upheavals from a safe distance, but he, too, had aspirations to higher power. However, he only had the support of three British legions and one in Spain. When the time came for him to relinquish his governorship after the statutory three years, in 196, he mustered an army and sailed to Gaul where he was proclaimed emperor. Politicians tend to cling to power when they are at the top for the only way out is down. Albinus was able to defeat local opposition but the crucial Rhine army remained on the sidelines and he was finally routed and beheaded by Severus the following year.

The Romans then bought peace from the north Britons. Dio Cassius wrote: "Since the Caledonians did not keep their promises and made ready to assist the Maeatae, and since at that time Severus was devoting himself to the Parthian war, Lupus" – Virius Lupus, governor of Britain from 197 – "was forced to purchase peace from the Maeatae for a great sum, receiving back a few prisoners."

175

An emperor carried the length
of Britain

LUCIUS SEPTIMIUS SEVERUS sent Heraclitus to Britain as governor at the start of the third century. The emperor himself spent his last years in the province (from 208 to 211) and it was to him that *Lives of the Later Caesars* credited the building of Hadrian's Wall; he was, however, only responsible for its reconstruction. Aelius Spartianus is credited as the writer but this is almost certainly a pseudonym.

"He fortified Britain – and this was the greatest glory of his reign – with a wall leading across the island to the ocean at each end; in recognition of this he also received the title Britannicus."

He was called to Britain, says the historian Herodian, by the then governor, Lucius Alfenus Senecio, who out of flattery or disaster confessed he needed more troops or the presence of the emperor himself.

The "barbarians had risen and were over-running the country, carrying off booty and causing great destruction." This was in 207 and Severus was happy to oblige not only with more manpower but also with the royal personage himself.

"Severus, by nature a lover of glory, heard this news with pleasure. He wished to add victory over the Britons to his victories in the east and the north. Even more he wished to remove his sons from Rome, so that they might be reformed by the discipline of military life, remote from the luxuries and pleasures of the capital. So he ordered preparations for an expedition to Britain. Although he was old and crippled with arthritis, he was more vigorous in mind than any youth."

He also, Dio Cassius adds to Herodian's account, "took along with him an immense sum of money". It was probably expected of an emperor that he should pay his way, and this one intended to achieve the impossible and conquer the whole of mainland Britain.

Herodian continues: "For most of the journey he was carried in a litter, nor did he ever stay long in one place. Having completed the journey with his sons at great speed, he crossed the ocean and advanced towards the enemy. Drawing troops from all sides he amassed a great army and prepared for the campaign."

There was a great expansion of Britain's capital at this time. London's city wall was built and enclosed an area of 330 acres; it was now the largest walled town in the country. Cirencester, which is second in size, was smaller by one hundred acres.

On the northern frontier the granaries at Corbridge were rebuilt once more and others constructed lower down the Tyne, at the fleet's fort by the Narrows, South Shields. These were the wharves that would launch the reoccupation of the Scottish lowlands. Lead seals have been discovered from the site of the Roman jetties at South Shields. They are stamped with the heads of Severus and his two sons, and an imperial mark "AVGG".

Corbridge and Dere Street were still the road link through the Borders, and the army retained its tenacious grip on the forts of Risingham, High Rochester, and Newstead, which seem to have held whilst all around were falling.

Newstead, always exceptional, was chosen as the staging post for the operation. To the north of it were four 165-acre camps, in which a huge army was marshalled. They had sufficient accommodation for a total of 180,000 men.

The daily food consumption of the basic regular complement of 25,000 men in the British frontier forces in the third century has been estimated by R W Davies – on the basis of three pounds of corn, barley, wheat and oats per soldier – at thirty-three and a half tons. This is an annual requirement of 12,227 tons, which would be vastly increased by such a campaign as Severus's where there were more soldiers and the need to stock new forts with a year's grain reserve. Allowance would also have to be made for inevitable wastage caused by transportation and by the onslaughts of war and mould.

And these North British needs were not unique. Each fort is said to have farmed its surrounding land, but it is doubtful if those beside the Roman wall ever made any headway towards self-sufficiency. Subsidies and fertilisers cannot bring corn out of that landscape even today. Mist and mould are the great levellers of the grain harvest and they are more catastrophic than any Russian drought.

But the diet of the Roman squaddy was not restricted merely to wheat and oats, as the *Lives of the Later Caesars* records: "Hadrian himself also used to live a soldier's life among the other ranks, and, following the example of Scipio Aemilianus, Metellus and Trajan, cheerfully ate in the open such camp food as bacon, cheese and sour wine".

Wheatmeal, for all that, is still the basis of pasta – which was being consumed in Pompeii at the moment of disaster – just as oats is for porridge. Caracalla, like Hadrian, is also recorded in *Lives of the Later Caesars* as sharing a soldier's life: "He set a frugal table, even going so far as to use wooden vessels for eating and drinking. He ate the bread that was available; with his own hand he would grind his personal corn ration, make it into a loaf, bake it in the ashes and eat it."

R W Davies, writing in volume two of *Britannia* in 1971, notes that this was wholemeal bread and adds, ahead of his time for dietary percipience: "Authorities both ancient and modern have shown that wholemeal bread is more palatable than white bread and has greater nutritional value, as it is rich in vitamins, especially B. At Trimalchio's banquet Habinnas said he preferred brown bread to white, because it was nourishing and prevented constipation."

The culinary excesses of civilised Rome, with its emphasis on fancy junk food, had also produced a greater awareness of healthy eating, as in our own time. Nowhere is this more skilfully satirised than in *Satyricon* by Petronius Arbiter (probably written in the first century AD) when Habinnas begins listing all the food he had eaten before arriving for dinner with Trimalchio.

"For the first course we had a pig crowned with sausages, and served with blood-puddings and very nicely done giblets, and of course beetroot and pure wholemeal bread – which I prefer to white myself: it's very strengthening and I don't regret it when I do my business."

Ancient wisdom, but it says something for history's repetitive nature that the alternative of refined non-fibrous white bread also posed problems for Roman society. Despite his gluttony, Habinnas showed more understanding of the necessity for dietary fibre than the two-year investigation carried out in post-World War Two Germany which led the British Medical Association to conclude that "both white and brown are equally good for you. There is nothing to choose between them."

Septimius Severus had brought detachments of the First Legion Italica from the Danubian provinces for the British campaigns of 208 to 211. A sandstone altar set up by a centurion from the legion, Publicius Maternus, was found in 1969 beneath a modern bus depot at Old Kirkpatrick, Dunbarton.

The account that follows is by Herodian, the Greek historian living in Italy who documented the chronicles of Rome from 180 to 238. It is quoted here from J C Mann's *Northern Frontier in Britain from Hadrian to Honorius*, which lists literary and epigraphic evidence. Herodian presents history with the rounded completeness that can make archaeology redundant:

"The Britons were disconcerted by the emperor's sudden

arrival, and learning of the size of the force collected against them, sent envoys to sue for peace, attempting to explain away the evil they had done. But Severus, seeking delay in order to avoid an early return to Rome and still wishing for a British victory in fact as well as in name, sent the envoys away empty handed and prepared for war. In particular, he saw to the provision of causeways in marshy places, so that the troops might both march and fight on a firm footing."

When the preparations had been made for the campaign, Severus left Geta, his nineteen-year-old second son, in command of the province and accompanied by his twenty-year-old elder son he entered Scotland.

"Taking Antoninus with him, Severus himself advanced against the barbarians." These are identified by Dio Cassius, the Roman politician and historian Dion Cassius Cocceianus – known to archaeologists, with unusual familiarity, by his shortened forename, Dio – who lived from about 155 to 235.

"There are two principal tribes of the Britons, the Caledonians and the Maeatae, and the names of the others have merged into these two. The Maeatae live close to the wall which divides the island in two" – by which Dio must mean Hadrian's rather than the Antonine Wall, as he claims Severus built the former – "and the Caledonians beyond them."

Herodian continues: "The army crossed over the rivers and fortifications which defined the limits of the Roman empire. Frequent skirmishes and battles occurred, and the barbarians retreated. They found it easy to slip away and, through knowledge of the terrain, to pass undetected through the woods and marshes. Roman unfamiliarity with the country served to prolong the war."

Dio Cassius adds that the advance of Severus through Caledonia was accompanied "by great hardships, cutting down forests, levelling hills, filling up swamps and bridging rivers". He goes on to tell of losses that reached disastrous proportions:

180

"He never fought a battle or even beheld the enemy in battle formation. But cattle and sheep were left deliberately for the soldiers to seize, so as to lure them on and wear them out. For the Romans suffered heavy losses in the marshes and were attacked when they were scattered. Unable to move they were killed by their own men to save them from capture. In all, some fifty thousand men died." That is the equivalent of five legions plus an equal number of auxiliaries. It would have made the campaign unacceptably costly and led to the extinction of numerous units, but there is no archaeological confirmation of the disappearance of any legion at this time.

The Severan campaign generally followed the course of Agricola's line of marching forts which, in turn, follow the foothills of the Grampians from Perth to Glenmellan (often misspelt Glenmailen by archaeologists), near the source of the River Ythan in Strathbogie. From Glenmellan the logical progression was to Strathisla and the valley of the Spey. Here, had they come this far, the mountains would have pushed the Roman army so close to the Moray Firth that they could be resupplied by sea. The narrowing coastal belt was probably not worth the further trouble, and Severus had already crossed most of the fertile and populated lands of north-east Scotland.

Dio Cassius wrote that Severus "did not stop until he had almost reached the end of the island". In the clear light before a storm you can look from the hills above the Spey to the grey mass of the mountains of Caithness, forty miles across the Moray Firth. Severus had almost reached the end of the island of Britain. He observed the differences of the sun's height in these parts, and the effect it had upon lengthening summer days and winter nights. Observations of this kind indicate a long campaign, which certainly stretched from 208 into 209 at least, and quite likely was not completed until the year 210.

During this time, Cassius notes, Severus was "carried

through most of the enemy country, in a covered litter, because of his illness". He returned southwards into the Roman province – "the friendly part of Britain", as Cassius puts it – "after compelling the Britons to come to terms and to cede not a small part of their territory."

By 211, however, the Maeatae north of Hadrian's Wall had flared up again and Severus prepared once more to cross the border – probably using the fleet this time to avoid weeks of unnecessary marching. But then the Caledonians joined the insurrection.

Severus, however, according to Herodian, was now confined to quarters because of his prolonged illness and his elder son, Antoninus, was given military command; he was less interested in waging war than the political opportunities for furthering his own career and therefore concentrated his energies on the manipulation of power.

Severus died at the imperial headquarters on 4 February 211, "not without some help, it is said, from Antoninus", comments Cassius. The *Lives of the Later Caesars* elaborates this somewhat: "He died at Eburacum (York) in Britain, having subdued the tribes which appeared hostile to Britain, in the eighteenth year of his reign, stricken by a very grave illness, now an old man." He was sixty-five.

Herodian says he was "worn out with grief, having surpassed all previous emperors in his military achievements". The last words of Septimius Severus, according to the same source, were reputed to have been: "I took over the republic in a disturbed condition everywhere, and I leave it pacified even among the Britons. Now an old man crippled in the feet, I bequeath to my Antonines, a stable empire if they will be good, a weak one if bad."

The account adds: "His body was carried from Britain as far as Rome, greatly revered by the provincials; although some say that it was only a golden urn containing the remains of Severus, and that this was laid in the sepulchre of the Antonines, since Septimius had been cremated in the place where he died."

He had achieved more than any other Roman commander in the history of the British frontier, in that peace of a sort was to hold for the rest of the century and not fall apart again until 305.

Coins of the next emperor, his younger son, Geta, proclaim the British victory, "Victoria Britannica". Coin issues of Severus and Caracalla show bridges on them which may have been prompted by the British campaign. That of Severus, issued in 208, has towers at each end and may represent the rebuilding of the important bridge over the Tyne at Corbridge. The other has a bridge of boats which the fleet constructed to enable an army to cross an estuary; this is the sort of operation that might have been mounted over the Forth and the Tay. Neptune and Oceanus are featured on coins from the year 209, which coincides with a time when the fleet was of paramount importance to the success of the British campaign.

Caracalla assumed control in York on his father's death and "began to murder all those around him". Herodian goes on to say that he then lost the support of the troops and signed a treaty with the barbarians "granting them peace and accepting their pledges of good faith". A reconciliation was reached between Caracalla and his brother and mother, and the family returned together with Severus's remains to Rome.

Marcus Aurelius Antoninus, nicknamed Caracalla from the long-hooded Gallic tunic that he adopted and brought into Roman fashion, became joint emperor with his brother Geta in 211. The following year he had Geta murdered and the praetorian guard proclaimed Caracalla sole emperor.

His father, Severus, had also made an impact upon the fashions of Rome: he had popularised the religious cult of Sarapis, the Egyptian god of the underworld, whom the Romans then widely adopted and credited with powers of healing. A fine classical head of Sarapis was found by J B P Karslake in the

183

garden of his house at Silchester Common, Hampshire. It had been cut with a drill in Portland stone and shows the god with curled hair and flowing moustache and beard. This has been described by Jocelyn Toynbee in *Art in Roman Britain* as the "very sensitively carved" work of a "first-rate continental sculptor". Major carvings in Portland stone are rare, and the same man seems also to have carved a head of Tutela, another work of superhuman proportions, a fragment of which has also been found at Silchester.

The reign of Severus had a lasting impact, too, in Britain; here it was the state infrastructure that was affected with the instigation by Severus of an attempt at regional decentralisation. Britain was now administered as two, and eventually four, provinces, producing references in classical accounts to "the Britains". Herodian implies the two provinces were established in 197; this was after the defeat of Albinus, and the intention must have been to reduce the possibilities of Britain again producing a separatist governor. Britannia Superior was administered from London, which still had a governor of consular rank, and Britannia Inferior from York, with a praetorian governor who doubled as the commander of the Sixth Legion.

Further north, the last units of the Roman army remained only temporarily in Scotland. A smashed monumental inscription from the rebuilt east gate of the fort at Carpow, on the Firth of Tay, is dated to 212 and the emperor Caracalla. It could not have stood there long as the evacuation of the Roman army from Scotland was completed in 215 or 216. With Carpow, and the phasing out of the last of the forts, must also have fallen the quasi-protectorates of Fife and the region between the two walls.

The one place that epitomises the opulence and fragility of mid-Roman Britain is the geothermal spa at the centre of the walled city of Bath. It drew rich patronage by the three-pronged infallible combination of bathing (the great Roman passion), comfort (water was not usually piping hot), and religion (the gods approved). The sick and the rich came and paid, and came back again, if they were well enough. If you think you are dying the cost becomes of diminishing importance. Bath's hot mineral waters, as approved by the Celtic water goddess Sulis Minerva, were presented in style; purely classical style – one of the few instances in the Roman province where there was no obvious concession to Celtic taste. The English obsession with class started at Bath.

Gaius Julius Solinus, writing about 230 in his *Collectanea rerum memorabilium*, described a perpetual fire burning in the temple to Minerva at Bath. It "never whitens into ash but as the flame fades turns into balls of rock". This was coal from the north Somerset field, which survived into the late twentieth century but is now closed and has been administratively transferred to Avon; in Roman times it was probably exploited from the surface by open pits. Coal was also used for home heating in the villas of Somerset, Gloucestershire, and Wiltshire.

An event of the mid third century had no immediate effect upon the comfortable living of these southern Britons but it laid another germ of unrest that would eventually swell to devastate the northern province. Bede, writing in the 720s, states that Caledonia, the ancient name for Scotland, was invaded in 258 by the Scotia from Ireland. The Scots had arrived in mainland Britain.

On the continent, Marcus Aurelius Claudius took the purple in Rome in 268 but he never ruled the province of Britannia. Control of the western arm of the empire, from the Rhine to Spain, was lost to an ambitious army officer, Victorinus, who asserted himself during 269 as a secessionist emperor, via numerous inscriptions and coins. He might have then gone on to take Rome but his ambitions died the following year in Cologne at the knife of one of his own officers.

Usurping a province

BRITAIN WAS ATTRACTIVE to prospective usurpers. It was protected from immediate imperial reaction by the Channel. Because of its special border problems the province was frequently given the Roman empire's top commanders who were able to assert a strong combination of personality and ability over units that were politically naive.

One powerful senator, Gaius Pius Esuvius Tetricus, was able to seize power in Britain, Gaul and northern Spain and declare himself emperor in 270 after the death of Marcus Aurelius Claudius. Unfortunately for him, his power-base was too provincial and control passed to Aurelian, who came into the job at a moment when a lesser man would have been incapable of preventing the imminent collapse of the western Roman empire.

This general unrest had the unusual effect of strengthening the stability of southern Britain. Wealthy refugees from Gallia Belgica were forced across the Channel by raids between 260 and 275. They and their descendants were to establish some, possibly most, of the prosperous fourth century villas in south-western England.

Lucius Domitius Aurelianus, the common soldier who rose to become emperor, drove the Goths back across the Danube and recovered Egypt. He reigned from 270 to 275, turning his attentions in 274 to the recovery of Gaul and Britain from Tetricus. After these successes Aurelian styled himself

Southern bastions of Portchester Castle, the only complete Roman fort in northern Europe.
Photograph: John Pitfield

Britannicus and began to fortify Rome, turning it into a walled city in preparation for troubled times. However, he was assassinated by officers of his own army.

During the time of Marcus Aurelius Probus, emperor from 276 to 282, the great fort at Portchester Castle was built beside Portsmouth Harbour, Hamphire. It is square, with sides 640 feet long and bastions projecting at each corner. There were also bastions at 120-foot intervals along the sides of the fort. Portchester is unique in being the only complete Roman fort in northern Europe with walls that stand to their full height, the crenellated main walls being twenty-five feet high with the bastions rising to thirty feet. These project twenty feet from the walls, with the outer face being rounded. The fort is built on a flat platform of gravel four feet above the high tide line, with the harbour beside the east side and running into a ditch just beyond the other walls. Though excavation of the internal timber buildings has failed to produce direct evidence of fleet occupation the location indicates it would have had the capacity to support, supply and service naval vessels, and could itself be supplied from the sea at times when this was necessary. Probus waged war against usurpers in Gaul, but was killed by his own mutinous soldiers in 282. Carinus, the emperor from 283 to 285, continued with the programme of fortification in the north-western sector of the empire.

The following year the Channel was providing both a refuge and a stepladder to power for a Roman opportunist. Marcus Aurelius Carausius was a 42-year-old former river pilot from Belgium who had helped Maximian put down the Gallic revolt of 286 and was then put in command of the Roman fleet at Boulogne controlling the shuttle-service to Britain. He was meant to fend off Frankish and Saxon pirates, but found he could prosper by their example. Instead of policing the Channel waters against raiders, in 287 he let the Franks and Saxons attack at will along the northern shores of Gaul and delayed their interception until the pirate boats were enriched and slowed by their loot. The stolen goods that were recovered were not returned to their owners, and, on hearing of the depths of corruption amongst the fleet at Boulogne, Maximian ordered the execution of Carausius. But Carausius had not lost the loyalty of the best-paid sailors in the fleet. He decided to cross to Britain where he called plunder by a different name, and, having usurped power in the province, declared himself emperor.

Maximian's original confidence in Carausius's ability with the navy was fully justified; the usurper was able to defeat the emperor's fleet. Not only did he retain control of Britain, but he also maintained his grip on the port of Boulogne, knowing that it was from there that any operation for the restoration of imperial control would have to be mounted.

Carausius issued his own, highly nationalistic, coinage in

large quantities – proclaiming "Restitutor Britanniae" and "Genius Britanniae" – and the province at least had the benefit, or otherwise, of a resident pseudo-emperor. To add insult to injury he adopted Maximian's names, Marcus Aurelius. His stylish propaganda war via the coinage extended to a quotation from Vergil, the only one ever to appear on a Roman coin. It is "Expectate veni" – "I came with expectation".

Carausius had six years of running the country – about average for a twentieth century British prime minister – before being murdered, by Allectus, in 293. It is reasonable to regard assassination as a legitimate political weapon when no other is available.

Allectus, however, was a treasury official promoted to praetorian prefect and he had little to offer. By the late summer of 296 the Roman fleet was massed on the River Seine. Constantius, who had been adopted as Caesar – the successor to the emperor – by Maximian in 292, planned the fourth Roman invasion of Britain; he had been given the government of Gaul.

Vergil has something appropriate to offer for the occasion, as Carausius, but probably not Allectus, would have realised. "Tendebantque manus ripae ulterioris amore" – "their hands outstretched in yearning for the farther shore".

Constantius split his forces into two fleets. The western detachments were massed in the mouth of the Seine under Asclepiodotus and took advantage of misty conditions to slip into Spithead and the Solent. Much to their relief they avoided the boats of Allectus – the remnants of the old Carausius fleet from Boulogne – for it contained the most experienced of the Channel boatmen.

Constantius was in command of the fleet in the main base at Boulogne and he may have taken them into the Channel as a feint to draw attention away from the Isle of Wight. It seems he then attempted a landing in Kent but deteriorating weather caused them to turn back to Boulogne.

Allectus tried to meet the invaders midway between London and the coast but he lacked a proper army – because of defections or confusion – and had to rely on barbarian mercenaries. These scratch forces were defeated somewhere near Silchester, and Allectus was killed.

Constantius sailed into London, arriving almost in William and Mary style to a mass of kneeling crowds; this was the most tactful way of welcoming a conqueror and is how the Saxons later received William the Bastard in 1066. There may also have been a genuine feeling of relief, for if it had not been for the coming of Constantius and his fleet the next visitors might well have been Frankish pirates.

Regional decentralisation came into fashion about 298, during the reign of joint emperors Diocletian and Maximian, and this led to a spawning of bureaucrats. Whatever the demerits in terms of inefficiency and duplication of work, there

Lincoln's north gate, the Newport Arch, before twentieth century demolition of most of its characterful surroundings. It was built about the end of the second century and was the only surviving Roman archway in Britain until a lorry pushed through it in 1964. The arch had to be completely removed but has since been restored to its original appearance. *Courtesy: National Monuments Record*

was now no going back on the changes for the new system gave the civil service a far more interesting career structure. The multiplicity of sub-provinces was to last until the end of the empire.

Diocletian split the two British provinces into four: Britannia Superior, previously ruled from London, became Britannia Maxima (London) and Britannia Prima (Cirencester); Britannia Inferior, the York part of the original province, was reconstituted as Britannia Secunda (York, the country's second city), and Britannia Flavia (Lincoln).

Flavius Valerius Constantius became emperor of western Europe in 305 when Maximian and Diocletian abdicated. The new emperor then returned to Britain, to campaign against the Picts who had spilled over the northern frontier.

The following year Constantius, then aged about fifty-six, lay dying in York and proclaimed his son, Flavius Valerius Aurelius Constantinus, the new Caesar: a wise precaution as Constantinus was one of six claimants to the throne. In a ceremony at York he was proclaimed Augustus, emperor of the western Roman empire. And as Constantine the Great he was to become the sole emperor of the west in 312, and in 324 he took power in the eastern empire, choosing Byzantium as his capital and renaming it after himself, Constantinople – city of Constantine. A large stone head of Constantine the Great, twice life-size, is on display in the museum at York.

He took the title Britannicus in 315, and David Breeze suggests, in *Hadrian's Wall*, that the generally accepted date of 297 for an attack on York should be revised to early in Constantine's reign as there "is no evidence for a Pictish invasion of north Britain in 297". York's defences were not rebuilt in 300.

Breeze dates the rebuilding of the legionary fortress there, with the elaborate polygonal Multangular Tower and other refinements, to later than 335. Such bastions, and the Multangular

Interior of the Multangular Tower at the west corner of the legionary fortress at York. It was built about AD 300 and is one of the most imposing structures of Roman Britain, though the top ten feet is mediaeval.

Courtesy: National Monuments Record

Tower and its adjacent fourth century wall are among the finest pieces of surviving masonry in Roman Britain, are in the late Roman Saxon-shore class and stylish enough to suit the status of the *Dux Britanniarum*, the commander of British land forces, who took over the fifty-acre fortress at York as his headquarters.

Religion was as important to most communities as defence, if not more so, and it was about this period that facilities at many temples were being expanded. The discovery of a third century semi-circular theatre two hundred and fifty feet wide, about five hundred feet from the Gosbecks temple – and facing away from it – on the outskirts of Colchester, raises the possibility that such structures were built close to other temples. Gosbecks theatre, according to its excavator Rosalind Dunnett in volume two of *Britannia*, was "clearly a religious building

192

designed to house a congregation to witness primarily religious rites, and as a meeting place for pilgrims to the cult centre".

At the Gosbecks site there was a timber stage with some twenty rows of seats eighty feet deep which backed up to a ten feet high wall. This wall was of Kentish ragstone and it was demolished in antiquity. The basic turfed slope left a D-shaped mound that is little more than four feet high.

The existence of such sites, for which there are plenty of Gallic parallels, would explain how audience participation was achieved in Roman and Romano-Celtic temples. It is reasonable to assume there would have been an area set aside for dancing or ritual display.

The most prestigious and costly grouping of religious buildings in Roman Britain was established on a streaming marsh beside the River Avon at the foot of the Cotswold Hills. The geothermal waters at Bath sprang from the ground at a temperature of 47°C (115°F), richly tainted from their contact with the earth's core by the traces of forty-three minerals. The water itself is ancient, having fallen on the Mendip Hills sometime during the last Ice Age, before 11,000 BC. Towards the end of the first century AD Roman engineers had constructed a stone reservoir over the sacred spring. This was an octagonal structure about six feet deep, which is now out of sight beneath the mediaeval King's Bath though it was reached by excavations that uncovered the baths in 1880 and stripped of its Roman lead to help meet the expenses of the exploration.

Around it, at the centre of a twenty-three acre walled town, were erected some of the most impressive monumental buildings north of the Alps. The name of the town, AQVAE SVLIS – *Aquae Sulis*, the waters of Sulis – points to the predominance of the native Celtic goddess Sulis whose attributes were combined with those of another healing deity, the classical Minerva. The baths were the temple and spa of Sulis Minerva. To the north of the Roman reservoir lay the sacrificial altar of the temple serving the baths, its two carved corners being restored in their original positions in 1982. One had been found in 1790, when the Pump Room was built during the creation of the Georgian spa. The second corner of the altar was discovered during excavations in 1965. A third, badly weathered, is in a buttress at the church of Compton Dando, a village eight miles west from Bath. Only the fourth corner remains lost. Animals were sacrificed on this altar by the temple priests.

Above them towered a classical tetrastyle pediment. Centred over the arch was a carving of two female figures supporting a roundel in which was probably a representation of the sun god, Sol. Some of the stones weigh a ton. Those that have so far been reassembled were discovered from three separate periods of excavation, in 1790, 1895 and 1981. Below gushed the sacred waters. Beside the altar and the pedimented doorway stood the façade of the Four Seasons, which is now displayed in the

Gilded bronze head of Minerva from a classical statue in the temple of Roman Bath, found beneath Stall Street in 1727.

Photograph: John Pitfield

museum at the Baths. The greatest single carving at Roman Bath is the gorgon-headed Medusa which was the centrepiece of the pediment above the main flight of steps into the temple. It was found in 1790 and has been described by Jocelyn Toynbee as "the perfect marriage of classical standards and traditions with Celtic taste and native inventiveness". The goddess Luna was also featured on a pediment, and other carvings have a recurrent hunting theme. In one Diana, the goddess of the chase, is finely sculptured with a recurved bow. In others a mastiff is carrying a roe deer, and a hound strains after a hare.

The Great Bath is the remarkable set-piece of this functional monument. It is of Edwardian municipal swimming baths size, still lined with Roman lead and fed by a direct supply of hot water from the Roman reservoir that enters along an open gully from the north-west corner. Until 1880 the Great Bath was

Gorgon-headed Medusa, the centrepiece of the classical pediment above the main steps into the temple at Bath.

Photograph: John Pitfield

Part of the vaulted roof that stood sixty feet above the main bath at Bath. The picture has been tilted to show the coursing at its correct angle.

Photograph: John Pitfield

covered by Georgian houses. The colonnades are a fanciful Victorian recreation, though the great Roman piers are obvious enough and supported something much more impressive. The bath was not originally open to the sky. In Roman times it was roofed with a huge barrel-vault, about sixty feet high, which was constructed with hollow box-tiles to minimise the weight and provide vents for the steam to escape. Part of this roof-arching is preserved beside the west end of the Great Bath, but it lies at an angle. When it was in place the tiles were coursed horizontally. Pilasters and columns which supported the roof lie in piles along the sides of the bath.

In the rooms to the east lay Turkish-style baths of varying temperatures. On the other side, towards the part of the baths covered by Stall Street, there were hot, dry sauna baths and the circular *frigidarium* or cold room, where the tradition of gifts to the gods (of modern archaeological funding) is maintained each day, including offerings to the dark waters of the world's small change. The original habit enabled the recovery of pewter, silver and bronze plate from the temple treasure. Each piece was scratched with the names of the temple's joint goddesses, *Sul Minerva*. A gilded bronze head of Minerva, from a full size cult-statue which stood in the temple, was found beneath Stall Street in 1727 and is now with the sacred plate in the museum at the Baths.

It is quite possible that there was some earlier Celtic shrine at Bath to the gods of the hot waters but the extent and scale of the Roman engineering and building makes it exceedingly unlikely that any traces can have survived. Other Cotswold sacred places have shown a direct progression from an Iron Age timber shrine into the masonry *cella* of a Roman temple. One

Roman Bath: the Great Bath with its hot water and big supports which originally carried a vaulted roof sixty feet high. The present open view brings in Bath Abbey, which is of seventh century origin. *Photograph: John Pitfield*

Processional mask found in a culvert of the Roman baths. It is made of lead.

Photograph: Colin Graham

such second century building, at Uley, Gloucestershire, had ancillary buildings with plastered and painted walls and was dignified by a great cult statue of the god Mercury which stood seven feet high. Its head and body fragments were found in 1978, finely carved from the local oolitic limestone with the kind of care that was usually reserved for marble. Votive offerings during the Iron Age included tools and food, a human thigh bone, and the foundation burials of three small children.

Christian and pagan revivals

CHRISTIANITY WAS ALMOST on the point of sweeping through Europe. Its existence had been permitted by Diocletian until the year 303 when, influenced probably by political allegations, he broke the traditional Roman tolerance of religions and issued an edict banning Christianity.

Believers were given the option of sacrificing to the emperor or being put to death; if they renounced their religion they would be freed. Diocletian himself was in poor health and losing power, and must have been quite relieved to face abdication in 305 and devote his remaining eight years to gardening.

In the time that followed, those Christians of the western empire, under Constantine the Great and Maxentius, were left in peace, whilst those of the eastern empire, under Gaius Galerius Valerius Maximianus (the man who had probably influenced Diocletian), were mutilated or killed. Cirencester has produced a Christian cryptogram on wall plates which must date from this period when the church lost its freedom. Ironically, however, the distinction of creating the first British Christian martyr must go to Constantine's father, Constantius, who in 304 (the year before he died in Britain) was responsible for the execution of Alban, who was later canonised. A Saxon text links St Alban's death with the time when Constantius was in Britain during the reign of Diocletian and Maximian.

In the extract the key words are emphasised: "*Caesar . . .*

Fourth century leaden vessel, presumed to be a Christian font, found at Icklingham, Suffolk, in 1939. It has Christian symbols, the Chi-Rho for Christ and "WA", alpha and omega.   *Photograph: Colin Graham*

without an order from the *emperors* commanded the persecution to cease, and reported to them that the slaughter of the saints was stimulating rather than suppressing the spread of Christianity." He therefore decided it was counter-productive to kill Christians, and none was murdered in the western empire during his short time as emperor, 305 to 306.

This account can be confidently applied to Constantius and his governorship in Britain; he was Caesar at this time, having been adopted as Maximian's successor in 292, and there were also joint emperors, Diocletian and Maximian. The quotation is also consistent with the absence of persecution during his reign in that part of the empire he controlled.

This matter needs to be emphasised as doubts over the dating have been cast by Sheppard Frere in his study of the Roman province, *Britannia*. Frere's attempt to backdate this event to 208 and the time of Geta, Severus's nineteen-year-old son, cannot be sustained. Geta, who was left in control of the province of York, was the emperor's second son with only half a claim to the succession, and it is doubtful if he would have had the maturity and standing to make a decision whose ramifications were a web of complexity. Furthermore, there were not two Augusti in his time, but one Augustus – Severus – who was on campaign with his other son, the twenty-year-old Antoninus. Although Antoninus was later to become emperor himself, this was shared jointly with his brother Geta; so maintenance of the 208 argument requires the evidence to confuse Geta's status from one date and Antoninus's from another.

In addition, St Alban was from Verulamium, the Roman city in Hertfordshire which now bears his name; he is therefore more likely to have come under the jurisdiction of Constantius (who governed Britannica Superior from London a hundred years later), than Geta, ruling Britannica Inferior from York.

But St Alban was only the first of many; other martyrs from this time included Aaron and Julius, and evidence, possibly, of the suppression of Christianity by the military rulers of Britain was discovered in 1974 in the ploughed Roman town of Durobrivae, near Water Newton, at Peterborough. The walled area had enclosed forty-four acres. It was surrounded by substantial suburbs spreading over two hundred and fifty acres and this made it one of the larger towns in Roman Britain. Close to its centre, A J Holmes found a hoard of twenty-seven silver objects, plus one item of gold, which had been recently smashed by the plough. They have since been restored and are now displayed in the British Museum. The Christian Chi-Rho monogram (the first letters of the Greek *Christos*) appears on them fifteen times.

This was church silver, of the late third or early fourth century, which could have been buried about 304 or 305. Styles known to have been popular later in the fourth century were absent from the vessels and plaques but, even so, the dating remains vague. All that can be said with certainty is the hoard is a clear two centuries earlier than church silver found in Turkey,

Silver strainer, buried about 304 at Water Newton, near Peterborough. The Chi-Rho symbol appears on the handle.

Courtesy: British Museum

making it the earliest collection of Christian silverware ever found.

Burial was deliberate as the handles had been removed from the chalice to enable it to fit into a tight space. One might more confidently link this with a time of Christian persecution but for another rich fourth century find in the ploughed town of Water Newton which was also made in 1974; a bowl was discovered which contained thirty Roman gold coins. Gold hoards of this kind are exceptionally rare. These were dated to 350, and were probably buried a year or two afterwards, but there is no record from this period of any upheavals in this area of the Fens which might have led to the coins being hidden. Their presence in the same town as the church silver may be coincidental, or both hoards may have been buried in response to the same dramatic event about the year 352. Obviously, neither owner returned.

An insight into the importance to the church of its chalice is contained in an account of the trial of Athanasius, acquitted of sacrilege in Nicomedia in 332. It was said there were "many cups in private houses and in the market, and there is no sacrilege in breaking any of these; but the mystic cup, which if it is deliberately broken involves the perpetrator in sacrilege, is found only in the possession of lawful priests." The rituals involved were standardised by a synod at Hippo in 393: "At the sacrament of the body and blood of Christ nothing is to be offered except bread, and wine mixed with water."

There is already an international appearance to the silver from Water Newton. The lettering is Latin and the names are those of the western empire, but K S Painter points out in *The Water Newton Early Christian Silver* that "the type of Chi-Rho device and the double-stroke lettering suggest an eastern origin of the workmanship". But the new religion was not above absorbing a little local flavour and the votive plaques are clearly pagan in type.

Christian persecution was not always one-sided. Painter

Water Newton gold disc and Christian silver plaques, with the Chi-Rho and alpha and omega, but the shapes are of pagan type.

Courtesy: British Museum

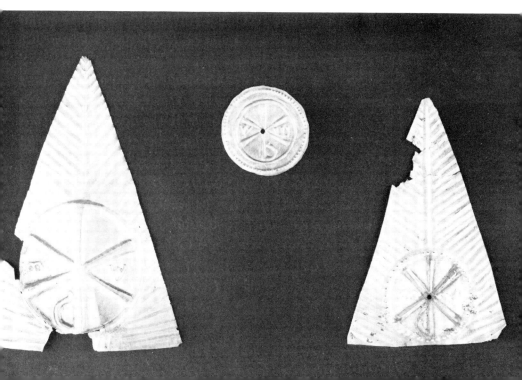

says: "One possible reason for hiding religious objects might be to protect them from damage by members of other cults. This is supported by evidence in Britain for the destruction of several of the five excavated temples of Mithras, probably by Christians."

A pagan temple at Caernarfon was abandoned in about 290 when its garrison pulled out. The troops who returned in 350 included Christian converts who set about smashing the altars that had been left, and then burnt the building down. Localised Christian vandalism, directed primarily at cult objects in temples, took place at two of the Hadrian's Wall forts between 310 and 320. It is reasonable to assume there were counter-attacks on Christian property.

The seven feet high statue of Mercury in the temple at Uley, Gloucestershire, was smashed in about 380. Its head and other fragments were then recovered by followers of the cult and buried in the precinct of the temple with reverence and an understanding of the god's appropriate offerings. The temple buildings were completely cleared and appropriated by the Christians. They then demolished the pagan *cella*, a distinctive religious building surrounded on three sides with an ambulatory, and replaced it with a timber structure; two altars to Mercury were incorporated in the new building. Dr Ann Ellison, its excavator, commented: "The deliberate clearance and apparent desecration of the pagan Roman temple and the placing of two altars within the post-temple building strongly indicates the impact of Christianity. The smashing of the statue of Mercury and the reuse of vital parts in the small but substantial building of the Theodosian period supports this interpretation."

This kind of strife was new to the western Roman world where people had previously accepted and tolerated many different religions and gods. The arrival of Christianity was different because its followers asserted an exclusive superiority, bringing a holy war against established beliefs and customs. The earliest known representation of the crucifixion, from a wall on the Palatine, Rome, is ironically a graffito showing Christ from the rear and with an ass's head.

Despite strong competition some pagan temples did well. More coins have been unearthed at Lamyatt Beacon, above the Fosse Way in Somerset, than on any other temple site in Britain. In all around fifteen thousand were found by excavation in 1958 and 1973 and by systematic unofficial looting during the period between. A coin in the hardcore of the flooring was of Marcus Aurelius Carausius, the usurper who declared himself emperor of Britain in 287.

The temple at Lamyatt dates from about the year 300, and finds have included votive spearheads, horse-and-rider brooches, and other jewellery featuring dogs and snakes. It remained in use into late Roman times and contained at least one life-sized statue, only the knee of which has been found.

Votive offerings in the vicinity of military camps tended to be predominantly state rather than personal property. Soldiers preferred to sacrifice army tools and fittings, and hang on to their own possessions. Most of the equipment they threw into such pits was quite usable, but then army stores were unlikely to provide much that was otherwise.

The wealthier classes could afford the luxury of buying their sacrifices, as happened at the Roman baths in Bath, where massive quantities of pewter and gemstones were thrown to the gods. Pewter, in this instance, was a readily available local purchase, for Somerset was the centre for its production in Britain. Amuletic substitutes included a wide range of bronze models of real-life objects, from jugs to boat-oars. Cash was always ultimately acceptable, particularly when no other appropriate offering was available. At Coventina's Well, Carrawburgh, more than thirteen thousand coins have been found which span the entire four centuries of Roman Britain.

Hilltop temples of the fourth century were often inside the

ramparts of prehistoric hillforts, as at Maiden Castle in Dorset, at South Cadbury and Brent Knoll in Somerset, Blaise Castle and Cadbury Tickenham in Avon, and at Lydney Park, Gloucestershire. More of these Roman implants must await discovery as the interiors of many of the western hillforts are still undisturbed.

The temple at South Cadbury was on the site of an Iron Age shrine, which raises the question whether the deserted hilltops were chosen for their traditional associations with the old religious and tribal centres. Or is the connection simply coincidental as, for example, in the West Country where most of the distinctive, isolated and flat-topped hills were already encircled by pre-Roman entrenchments? There were other temples which stood on fortless hills, however, so although this was not the sole criterion, even these apparently virgin outcrops may have held sacred associations with the past.

By far the most intriguing of the pseudo-religious objects from the fourth century temple ruins at Maiden Castle, Dorset, is a votive plaque with a female figure found by Edward Cunnington in excavations there between 1865 and 1884. In Mortimer Wheeler's view: "The thin bronze plaque, bearing in repoussé a crude figure of Minerva beneath a feathered gable and with slight fragments of a basal inscription, was found by Cunnington and belongs to a familiar class of votive reliefs."

Here, in his *Maiden Castle* excavation report, he took the evidence too far. To imply that the plaque is rough and primitive is retrogressive art criticism. The important feature of the figure is that she is outlined in native, Celtic fashion. But she was not seen by her discoverer nor by Wheeler as a piece of Romano-Celtic symbolism. They both introduced the Roman element and called her a Dorset interpretation of the classical goddess Minerva.

She was the consort of the war-god Mars, and the Maiden Castle figure does have the usual spear in one hand, and a Celtic shield in the other. Can this be regarded as conclusive proof that Maiden Castle worshipped Minerva?

Caesar found the Gauls had a goddess akin to Minerva, who was active in the field of healing, thermal waters and springs. In this way, the Minerva connection in a Celtic context brings us again to water deities. Minerva has associations with healing waters but it is impossible to split her classical and native presentations.

Anne Ross considers Minerva "is the classical representational type who is most popular in the south-western region, and yet it is clear that, in certain instances, at least, a native goddess underlies this rigidly classical figure". Sulis, for instance, doubles for Minerva as goddess of the sacred healing hot waters at Bath. Nodons, too, is represented as Mars in a piece of iconography found at Cockersand Moss. Minerva, then, can be seen as the consort of Nodons.

So either the Maiden Castle plaque is a native version of the Roman Minerva – shown naked and with a phallic head rising from her abdomen – or it is a separate Celtic goddess sharing (or merged with) some of the characteristic symbolism of Minerva.

It has, however, been pointed out that the figure may well not be female at all: the phallic head in the middle of the body may simply be another example of the Celtic practice of transferring the genitals to a different part of the body.

Whatever its deities, the Maiden Castle temple has been dated "not earlier than AD 367" and its position and period are shared with many other pagan shrines of Romano-Celtic England. As noted earlier, these temples were often on high spots, as at Lydney with its sweeping views over the Severn estuary, and the temple on Lamyatt Beacon above Bruton in Somerset.

Such solid masonry cubes as these with their Mediterranean verandahs may be attracting disproportionate attention as they are the buildings that survive to be noticed, whereas the purely

Celtic structures of wooden posts and wattle-and-daub walling have left only slight traces. The activities of some cults, however, led to the accumulation of objects at points where they are sometimes discovered. The water-cult, for instance, was generally widespread and compelling. Roman bronze votive oars have been found in the Thames mud, where they were thrown by travellers or boatmen.

On land there could also be strong reasons for having faith in the water gods, as at Winterborne Kingston, Dorset. Here a well was found in 1890 by J C Mansel-Pleydell which had a circle of eight burnt tiles placed at ten-inch intervals four feet from its edge. Inside this circle, at its centre, was a small sarsen stone and an iron knife. Nearby was a pit filled with burnt pottery, flint and ashes. In the well was found a thin strip of bronze with a simplistic outline of a hare punched on to it, and with two runic characters from the Celtic alphabet. There were also some coins from the first to the fourth centuries.

The precise location of the well is unknown but it is recorded as being near the two hundred-foot contour on Kingston Down beside a Roman road and cannot have been much more than half a mile from the Winterborne stream. It was eighty-five feet deep and about four feet in diameter.

Winterborne Kingston as a sacred place, with rites to the water-gods, is a significant choice. The stream at this point passes through what was, in prehistoric times, densely populated arable and ranched chalkland. It had the least dependable natural water supply in Dorset. Its stream is a true Winterborne (meaning "winter stream") and would fail to run in most summers, often not resuming its flow until November.

No stream in England can present a more complete seasonal contrast – in the middle of summer it can be completely dry, whereas in February it is full, gushing, and ten feet wide. Few better examples could be provided of a regular practical need for offerings to placate the water-gods.

Cults also developed around facial attributes, a notable example coming from the Wroxeter basilica where there seems to have been a shrine devoted to the eye. Some forty plaster eyes have been found with an average size of two inches though one, possibly representing the eye of a child, was only half an inch. Another of the Wroxeter eyes was in sheet gold and for a parallel to this oddity there is nothing nearer than the temple of Artemis at Ephesus which is a thousand years earlier.

The Wroxeter plasters place some stress on the pupil and tear duct, suggesting the cult could offer cures. If so, there could be a well nearby that awaits discovery – with coins and votive offerings at its bottom. For the "eyewells" of folklore show that people have for centuries sought out the water of certain medical wells to restore their sight. Sacred places such as these were once as commonplace as churches are today.

Cybele, the Asiatic Great Mother goddess of nature and

Castration forceps, used on the priests of Cybele and excessively worn, found in the Thames beside London Bridge.

Courtesy: British Museum

cultivation, was worshipped in Britain – or at least in cosmopolitan London. She was said to cross mountains on the back of a lion and representations of the goddess usually show her seated between a pair of the beasts. Followers of the cult were baptised in the sacrificial blood of bulls and rams, during a festival from 15 to 27 March that culminated with orgies of licentious joy. Her priests, however, were permanently excluded from such pleasures. Their celibacy was ensured through castration. Bronze forceps found in the River Thames beside London Bridge in 1840 were identified, by A G Francis in the *Proceedings* of the Royal Society of Medicine in 1926, as implements used in the castration of Cybele's priests. These forceps have the busts of Cybele and Attis protruding from the grips along with the planetary gods of the eight-day Roman week up the handles. They show signs of excessive wear and were skilfully repaired in Roman times. Francis suggested that this elaborate pair of nutcrackers, which are now in the British Museum, may have been thrown into the Thames "by an Early Christian iconoclast, perhaps during a raid on the temple".

The phallic pendant was the popular talisman of Roman London. John Aubrey, the seventeenth century antiquary, records in his *Monumenta Britannica*: "In digging for the foundations of London after the great conflagration" – the fire of 1666 – "there were found several little priapuses of copper, which they wore about their necks. Elias Ashmole Esq hath some of them among his cimelia (treasures)." Aubrey notes that they were worn by women "for fertility's sake" or against bewitchment.

He sketched the phallic tip of a pendant and showed a ring at the opposite end through which it would have been attached to a chain. The twentieth century parallel to these charms are the horn amulets, made in ivory, coral or plastic, which are produced and widely worn in southern Italy.

Although Aubrey, the first field archaeologist, was well

aware of their purpose, as are millions of Italians, by 1978 it was necessary for British scholars to be reminded by Dr R G Penn in a paper entitled *Attribution of function: a cautionary tale*, published in the journal *Antiquity*.

Penn quoted the description of a pendant found at Kirmington, Humberside: "A bronze instrument 7.5 cm long having a good patina and with a gently curved thick handle with a claw-like end. One end of the claw is broken and originally would have been much more of a full circle. Although small, the instrument fits comfortably in the hand with the thumb and forefinger at the base of the claw and feels designed for some form of lever action." It was suggested the pendant was a dental tool, for removing teeth.

The British Museum then confessed that it was "a puzzling item . . . not able to suggest what its function may have been. However, it appears to be post-mediaeval. The Department of Prehistoric and Romano-British Antiquities have informed me that it is not of Roman origin. There remains the possibility that this item may have had a use connected with a rural trade or craft. In this respect the Museum of English Rural Life, Reading, may be worth consulting."

Ralph Merrifield, at the Museum of London, was the one who recognised the bronze instantly "as a phallic pendant of Roman date and very similar to one in the possession of the museum, found at Angel Court and still attached to a chain". Mr Merrifield was quite certain that the so-called 'claw' was "originally a complete circle and had been broken by erosion or by severe wear and tear".

Dr Penn then noticed that such pendants were still on general sale in London, in shops of the Carnaby Street variety. He later spotted a similar pendant on the neck of the actor Sylvester Stallone, on the cover of *The Sunday Times Magazine* for 20 March 1977. He commented: "The description of Mr Stallone as 'The Italian Stallion' gives further proof of the

211

phallic symbolism of the pendant and an unexpected link with his possible fellow countrymen in early Britain." It is a cautionary tale, of how the Roman phallic pendant was restored to its place in British archaeology.

There is also confusion at times in some of the older archaeological reports about distinguishing marks on the bases of pieces of Roman pottery. How this came about was explained simply by J S Wacher in the *Archaeological Review* of 1973: "The typical whorl on the base of a wheel-made pot is caused when it is cut from the wheel by a *twisted* wire; a straight wire will leave no mark." Misinterpretation extends from artefacts to buildings and trees – and probably just about everything else.

R H Hodgkin, in his standard work *A History of the Anglo-Saxons*, states that the sites of local temples in Norway and Iceland have been excavated and "within the long building, divided somewhat like a church, in the inner or holier place where stood the images of the god, the blood of slaughtered animals flowed freely." In this account he refers to a drawing of the "Site of the Temple at Hofstathir" in Iceland, but Tom Lethbridge added this note of caution: "In the foreground is the sanctuary. Beyond is the hall, with stone supports of a double row of pillars, length about 36 metres; breadth five to eight metres. Unfortunately, after all that lavish prose, the building illustrated is not a temple at all but a farmhouse."

Pitfalls also litter the history of Roman Britain. They even extend to the trees of our primaeval countryside, but as there were only twenty distinct species and their pollen spores last for thousands of years as proof of their existence, any debate on the subject is really unnecessary. Translations of Caesar's *Gallic War* maintain that the beech was absent from Britain, whereas it is, and was then, the most common tree of the forest canopy in the regions through which the dictator passed. Lethbridge slips up here, and says that Caesar thought it absent because he did not see any. The problem has arisen because although *fagus* is the modern botanical name for the beech, in Caesar's context it refers to the sweet chestnut which, two thousand years ago, had not been introduced to these islands.

Hornbeam is another tree said to have been missing from Britain but, in fact, pieces of its wood were found in 1925 in pre-Roman levels at Ham Hill, Somerset, and "in deposits in which objects of the earliest part of the Iron Age were discovered". It was also found in 1922 at a depth of seven feet in the silting of the Bronze Age ditch at Avebury, Wiltshire, three inches below a beaker-period pot. The hornbeam was firmly established as an indigenous tree by Miller Christy, writing in the *Journal of Ecology*, who pointed out that its nuts had been found at much earlier levels. Despite this, and the fact that it is the principal tree of Epping Forest, hornbeam is still not included by many local councils in road landscape planting programmes on the erroneous grounds that it is not a native species.

The attribution of function is an exercise in the avoidance of pitfalls. In *The Idea of a Town*, which is subtitled with an explanatory synopsis, "the anthropology of urban form in Rome, Italy and the Ancient World", Professor Joseph Rykwert correctly asserts that the most important ceremonial in Roman surveying was that of marking an ownership boundary by ploughing. He is summarised by one of his reviewers, Patrick Nuttgens: "The plough is of course a male symbol and the earth a female one. The copious illustrations even include a rather tasteless American cartoon showing a farmer ploughing the land with his penis, presumably included to ridicule the argument. The town is both male and female – a symbol of strength and fertility."

It is possible to introduce sexual meaning into the act of ploughing, but in the context of Roman planning it was the established and most practical method of conveniently fixing a boundary. Unlike marker posts, a ploughed line is impossible to shift and leaves an impression that it is there until replaced by

213

something more permanent. The associated ceremonial is to emphasise the importance that property and its ownership held in Roman society. The conveyancing of property in British society is the one form of legal mumbo-jumbo that has held out against all reforms and is still maintained as a complex ritual.

The *agrimensores*, Roman surveyors, used simple equipment to lay down in the ground the base plan of a town and divide it into plots, and if there was any mystique it was simply to enhance their professional status and disguise the fact that decisions (as with modern conveyancing) were based upon a firmly practical set of considerations. Observance of ritual, where it serves a lasting purpose, is carried out to establish this fact on men's minds, and is not its own justification. Ritual belongs as much to the devices of law and the mechanics of ownership as it does to the conventional religious and sexual context. It is right to bring sex back into the matter of the pendants, but equally correct to exclude it from land surveying.

The first symbol to be adopted by the Christians was the eight-segmented sphere, the sign of the double-cross, with equal distance between its arms. This symbol was universal throughout the Indo-European world from Buddhist stupas in Burma to chunky Celtic brooches of enamelled bronze, one of which was amongst a cargo of imported jewellery tailored for Celtic taste shipwrecked in the Scillies on its way into the country. Another, from the River Avon at Bristol, also looks like a miniature ship's wheel. What originated as a symbol of the sky-god became synonymous with the 'X' of Christ's execution (distinct from, and more accurate than, the upright later versions) and finished up as a general mark of divinity.

The Indo-European connection is sometimes purely coincidental. The "buddhic" pose of some Celtic gods does not have eastern origins but came about for the simple reason, as classical writers confirm, that the Celts did not use chairs but squatted on the ground.

The great turning point for Christianity came in 312. Constantine ousted Maxentius from Rome and was welcomed by the senate as the Supreme Augustus, ruler of the western Roman empire. He had the strength to be conciliatory, which a Christian story proclaims was due to a vision he had of a cross of light in the sky and the message: "In this sign shalt thou conquer". In 313, by an edict issued from Milan, Constantine restored full legal rights to the Christians, guaranteed them his future protection, and gave back confiscated property.

The following year they began to exercise their new freedom and the bishop of York was amongst the group of Britons attending the council of the church held at Arles, in southern France. Three of the British provinces were represented by a bishop, but the fourth man was probably ill as two delegates, a priest and deacon, went in his place.

A mosaic featuring a bust either of Christ or Constantine was

Christian soldier: the labarum, a Roman cavalry standard surmounted by the monogram of Christ, was adopted by Constantine the Great and appears here on a gold coin of the eastern empire. *Photograph: Colin Graham*

The head of Christ – or the emperor Constantine – with pomegranates either side, at the centre of a Roman floor discovered at Hinton St Mary, Dorset, in 1963.

Photograph: Colin Graham

The firmly non-Christian aspect of the Hinton St Mary mosaic from Dorset – Bellerophon spearing the Chimaera.

Photograph: Colin Graham

found beneath the blacksmith's shed at Hinton St Mary, Dorset, in 1963. It was lifted and restored and is now the centrepiece of the Romano-British collection in the British Museum. It is a mosaic of a thirty to forty-year-old beardless man (as was Christ in the western empire, though not the east) with the Chi-Rho monogram behind his head and pomegranates either side – the fruits of eternal life. It was this eternal life that "God Incarnate had promised", to quote Jocelyn Toynbee. The god Bellerophon is featured as well, spearing the Chimaera. The pavement also depicts collared hounds hunting stags, both of them animals which feature on zoomorphic Celtic brooches found at Ham Hill, to the west of the Blackmore Vale.

In *The Riddle of the Labarum*, George Pitt-Rivers suggested that the head is not of Christ but of the emperor Constantine the Great, youthful and unbearded, with Chi-Rho to signify he had saved the adherents of his adopted religion from torture and premature eternity. The Chi-Rho was Constantine's standard, the personal *labarum* with which he had conquered the empire, which was carried and guarded by an élite of fifty guards.

Chi-Rho monogram on a Roman pottery oil lamp of the late third or early fourth century, one of the earliest representations of the Christian symbol on a household object.

Photograph: John Pitfield

I have noticed that busts of Constantine show a cleft chin – which is also a distinctive feature of the Hinton St Mary head. These Kirk Douglas chins are uncommon in Roman art. There is also the coincidence that Constantine's busts and the head on the Roman floor share the same hairstyle.

More importantly, there is positive evidence that Constantine combined his portrait with the Christian symbol. Eusebius of Nicomedia, the patriarch of Constantinople in 339, writes in his *Life of Constantine* that the emperor set up a painting of himself and his sons at the front of the palace in Constantinople. This portrait incorporated the Chi-Rho monogram behind Constantine's head – as in the Dorset mosaic.

George Pitt-Rivers was depressed that the archaeological world never gave serious consideration to his opinions and this rejection led to the eventual dispersal of his famous grandfather's private collections. In taking on the establishment he gave a caution, relevant here too, that Dorset was not Constantinople:

"The Roman civilisation of Britain was only skin deep. It influenced first the tribal aristocracies and later those landed classes whose estates were grouped round villas, and these only in a purely material sense. It never seriously affected the culture of the bulk of the Celtic population. In the villages and poorer quarters of the towns, as my grandfather's excavations helped to demonstrate, the only sign of Romanisation was the use of such externals as Roman pottery and coins."

Whether or not the Hinton St Mary floor represents Christ or Constantine, the point is that by inclusion of the Chi-Rho monogram the owner of the villa was making an open statement endorsing Christianity. This was an intellectual religion of wealthy homes, and the monogram appears at Frampton, Chedworth, and Lullingstone. These were not the kind of people to be confused by the meaning of a trendy symbol. To have Chi-Rho on your floor was about as non-committal as a ban-the-bomb sign woven into a 1950s carpet.

Count of the Saxon Shore

THE ROMAN EMPIRE had a new confidence both in religion and its own survival. It was probably during the reign of Constantine that the defence of Britain was reorganised on a naval basis. This involved the construction of a multiplicity of shore forts of the type that had been built in about 280 at Richborough, the supply point for the original Roman landings in Britain and the vital port responsible for protecting the key shipping route to the continent.

The proliferation of these forts can only be attributed to a strong reign such as Constantine's, though it is also true that his successor, Constans, was equally aware of the potential of sea-power for, in the 340s, he issued a medallion of himself in a ship and the message "Bononia Oceanen" – the Boulogne sea-crossing.

This medallion commemorates the expedition mounted to Britain in the winter of 342–43, when the Picts were attacking from the north. It shows a galley with rowers; Victory stands on the prow and there are two standards at the stern. Constans himself dominates the scene: he is wearing military dress and holding his shield and, standing on the side of the boat, is about to hurl his spear into a naked North Briton swimming towards the bow. This projects at the waterline – for ramming other vessels. In the background is a lighthouse, similar to the eighty-foot *pharos* which was built at Dover in the second century, the

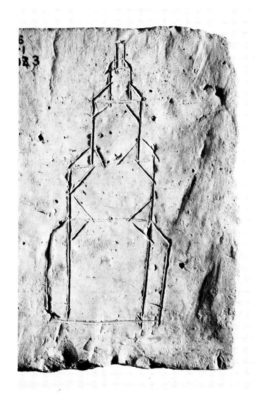

Drawing of a lighthouse,
inscribed on a tile in
Roman London.
Courtesy: British Museum

flint core of which still stands to a height of forty-three feet, with another twenty feet of mediaeval work added above. It functioned as a beacon, along with another that still stood on the western harbour heights until the seventeenth century. Such structures typified a major military port and the representation of one on the medallion was intended to convey the magnitude of the threat to the security of the state.

The fourth century Latin writer Julius Firmicus Maternus extravagantly praised Constans for his endeavours: "In the season of winter thou hast trodden the swelling and raging waves of the ocean, a deed never before accomplished, nor ever again to happen – under your oars hath trembled the flood of the sea almost unknown to us. And the Briton has gazed, appalled, at the unexpected sight of an emperor."

However, if Constans had fortified the Saxon shore then we

220

might expect to be told something of it, and there is a certain amount of positive evidence that his predecessor was responsible.

The commander of the forts had a title that was introduced by Constantine, that of *comes* (count), and he became therefore *comes litoris Saxonici*, the Count of the Saxon Shore. His army equivalent in Britain was *comes Britanniarum* – Count of the Britains (that is, the British provinces) – but this post does not seem to have become fully established until about 370 when Gratian and Valentinian were joint emperors.

Other activity which can be effectively dated is likely to be contemporaneous with the construction of the coastal forts. In the 330s, coinciding with the refortification of York, the bastions – apparently eighteen of them – were added to

The Roman pharos, lighthouse, beside St Mary's church at Dover Castle, Kent. The lower forty-five feet is genuine Roman masonry, though much of the facing stone has been lost. Originally it towered in eight stages, each set back about a foot on the previous one, to a height of eighty feet. The present top stage is mediaeval.

Courtesy: National Monuments Record

London's city wall. The most recent discovery of a previously unknown bastion was at Crosswall, north of Fenchurch Street Station, in 1980. The riverside wall was also built after 330, and determined efforts were being made to ensure that other major towns could also withstand sudden attack.

The forts of the Saxon-facing shore were built either side of the Thames estuary, at Reculver in Kent and at Bradwell in Essex. The northern bulge of East Anglia was covered from Walton Castle, between the Stour and Deben estuaries, and Burgh Castle, on the Yare. Patrols from Brancaster sailed the mouth of the Wash to protect the rich farmlands of the Fens.

Kent, however, was the front-line state which pointed directly towards the Saxon threat, and four forts on its peninsula are only fifteen miles apart. Dover and Lympne faced the Straits. The spacing between them was then increased to forty miles, to Pevensey, Sussex, and then to eighty miles (nautically speaking), to the westward outpost at Portchester, Hampshire, which has survived as the most complete single structure of Roman Britain. It was cleared of squatters and brought back into military use. Offshore, there was a fourth century fort at Carisbrooke in the centre of the Isle of Wight; its "inland" position suggests the Romans feared the island might be invaded and occupied, so it was placed at an equal distance from all shores.

The count also prepared defences which the Saxons were never to reach: Cardiff Castle, in the Romanised corner of Wales, was a massive shore fort and its patrols intercepted Irish pirates attracted into the Bristol Channel by the rich villa-lands of Somerset and the Severn estuary; an important villa at Ely, near Cardiff, had been overwhelmed and destroyed about 325. These were hazardous waters at the best of times. Conditions in the Bristol Channel are alarmingly changeable, for it is open to the south-westerly depressions that move in from the Atlantic. The tidal range, at forty feet, is the second greatest in the world;

caused by the funnelling effect of the narrowing estuary, it results in strong currents.

Roman craft must have made frequent use of their estuary out-stations at Barry, Swansea, and Carmarthen. There were also Roman wharves on the Somerset side of the coast at Sea Mills, on the Avon, at Bristol in the Axe estuary – the port for the Mendip lead and silver mines – and in all probability at Down End, Puriton, on the mouth of the River Parrett; Roman coins have been found there, at the west end of the Roman road along the Polden Hills, which is the nearest firm ground to Bridgwater Bay.

The boats were *scafae exploratoria*, fast-moving scout craft with camouflaged sails, and the men who used them would have evolved a set of traditions and beliefs as different from those of the squaddy invasion forces as our modern navies have from the armies. Mortimer Wheeler found indications of the men's religion in the 1930s, when a link was discovered between a unit of the British inshore fleet and the god, Nodons, at Lydney Park, beside the Severn estuary in Gloucestershire. A mosaic unearthed there, in the Temple of Nodons which had been built after 367 – nothing was found that predated the year 364 – had the inscription PR. REL. This has been taken to stand for *Praefectus Reliquationis Classis*, the supplies officer of the western fleet, and to indicate that its home waters were in the Bristol Channel.

The most probable translation for the full wording on the mosaic is given in Anne Rainey's *Mosaics in Roman Britain*: "To the god Nodons, Titus Flavius Senilis, officer in charge of the supply depot of the fleet, laid this pavement out of money offerings, the work being in charge of Victorinus, interpreter on the governor's staff." The main mosaic, which has been destroyed, was suitably nautical with a frieze of fish and dolphins.

Effective use of Roman seapower must have depended upon sightings and signals from semaphore stations. Roger J A

Wilson writes, in *Roman Remains in Britain*: "Cardiff cannot have stood alone and must have been linked with a series of signal-posts to give warnings of imminent pirate raids."

The finest viewpoint in these waters is the two hundred and fifty foot high rocky island of Steep Holm, six miles off each coast and midway between Cardiff and the port the Romans used for the lead mines. There is no other point in the Bristol Channel with a panorama that stretches the full seventy miles from the coast of Devon at Ilfracombe along the entire seaboard east to the Severn Bridge, at that time a ferry crossing. Its coverage of the English coastline of the Bristol Channel is unlimited and, on the Welsh side, the view runs from Barry to the Black Mountains. Even small boats can be pinpointed at a considerable distance and their speed and direction accurately gauged. Gun emplacements litter the island cliffs and show its strategic value was recognised both in Victorian times and during the Second World War. Steep Holm had the additional attraction for the Romans in that it has a clear view to the mouth of Cardiff harbour, the approaches to their main base.

Excavations in the late 1970s around the island's mediaeval St Michael's priory revealed that the builders of Victorian fortifications, in 1866, disturbed a considerable quantity of Roman material, including coins of Constantine. Indications are that Steep Holm was occupied in the first and fourth centuries, the two periods when the coast needed watching, and at its western end – the side with the direct view to Cardiff – is a large mound of stones which was converted by the Victorians into a shell-store. Archaeologists led by Stanley and Joan Rendell have recovered the neck of a large first century amphora from this mound, which may once have contained olive oil, and they believe the spot was probably a Roman signal station.

Another series of signal stations also gave warning of raids from the Picts. It ran along the north Yorkshire coast with stations every ten miles or so at Huntcliff, Goldsborough,

Ravenscar, Scarborough, and Filey. Huntcliff, the most northerly and therefore the most vulnerable, was raided from the sea – probably on a day when hill-fog lay across the clifftop – and the bodies of its men, women and children thrown down the well.

On the west coast the sector that caused concern was the north-west corner of Wales facing St George's Channel and Dublin Bay. This was a problem not so much for its own sake but because of its location to the west of the rich Welsh metal mines and the city of Chester. A naval fort at Caernarfon had an out-station on Anglesey to watch for raiders trying to slip around the north coast of the island.

It is simpler to list those areas of the coast that were not giving special concern by the middle of the third century. There were three only. Cumbria and north Lancashire do not seem to have been threatened from Galloway at this stage, but they came under attack in 367. Cornwall, south Devon, and Dorset needed no protection. The Humber coast was considered to be out of the range of both the Picts from the north and the Saxons from the south-east.

The raiders of the east coast came in light keeled boats that were about twenty feet in length and had pointed bows and blunt sterns; made from cow-hide stretched over willow frames, they had a crew of three. These were the standard sea-going craft of non-Roman Britain. They were still in use into the twentieth century by the South Aran islanders off Galway Bay; known as curraghs, they carried cattle safely bedded on seaweed and took potatoes to coasting steamers. In 1853, C H Hartshorne wrote in *Early Reminiscences of the Great Isle of Aran*: "Such is the dexterity with which it is usually managed, that it (the curragh) will land from ships in distress through the roughest breakers, and cross over to the mainland, when vessels of every other class are unserviceable."

Giraldus Cambrensis described the versatility of hide-covered craft in his twelfth century *Topographia Hiberniae* – "Hiberniae" was the Romanised name for Ireland – "Some sailors told me that having once been driven by a violent storm during Lent to the northern islands and the unexplored expanse of sea off Connaught, they lay for shelter off a small island. Soon after the storm abated they noticed a small skiff rowing towards them. It was narrow and oblong and made of wattled boughs, covered with hides of beasts. In it were two men without any clothing except broad belts round their waists. They had long yellow hair, like the Irish, falling below their shoulders. Finding that the men were from some part of Connaught and could speak the Irish language, the sailors took them on board. They said they had never before seen a ship built of timber."

James Hornell gave the specifications for these craft in his *British Coracles and Irish Curraghs*, published in 1938:

"Equipment is of the simplest – a pair of oars for each man and an extra one for the steersman, are present in all curraghs. In long ones a short mast hoisting a low and relatively long lug sail is set right in the bows. The form of the ten feet oars is similar to that of Connemara except that the bull (pivoting block) is triangular in shape. The sail is without shrouds or stays. Apart from the halliard, the only ropes controlling it are the tack which is led to a point near the stern, and the sheet, carried aft to be passed around the last thwart."

Hornell found the Connemara curraghs had their protective amulets: "A small bottle filled originally with holy water but often found empty is invariably suspended by a string from some part right in the bows. It is a sacred amulet against misfortune." The fishermen told him of a storm a few years earlier when almost the whole of the island fleet was caught in a hurricane, with many drowned and all the wooden boats wrecked. The single curragh with them was the only vessel that returned to the shore.

The incredible versatility and endurance of the leather boat was demonstrated in 1976 and 1977 when Tim Severin and a crew of four attempted to prove that the sixth century Irish St Brendan "discovered" America. Oxhides, dressed with various fats known to have been used in mediaeval times, covered a structure of ash-wood. Timber for masts and oars was hand-picked from the tough north-facing sides of the ash trees, and heartwood of oak was turned into gunwales. This was all bound together with leather thongs dressed in alum, a system known at least in Roman times. Although an American bi-centennial silver dollar was set under the mainmast as a good-luck talisman, a phial of holy water was also carried, inside the double gunwale, "as does every Dingle curragh, however small". In all, the Brendan voyage successfully covered four and a half thousand miles, braving dangerous pack ice, gale-force winds, icebergs, sub-zero temperatures, and some of the foulest weather the planet can offer. Experiments showed the leather had a tensile strength of two tons per square inch.

Despite pressure on the northern coast of Britain from seaborne Picts, the decade that began with the year 330 was a time free from molestation for many – and some surely pros-pered. Even the occasional new industry started up. Typical of those taking advantage of this lull in the troubles would have been the people in Yorkshire engaged in jet-carving; this became fashionable in the third and fourth centuries around Whitby, where workshops have been found, as the raw material was readily available from beaches in the area. It produced fine jewellery, beads, medallions, and carvings of animals and figures. One of the most sensitive of the latter is the figurine found at Levens Park, Westmorland, which shows a tearful face wearing a mantle and wiping her left eye. With it was a coin dating from about 330. Jet objects have been found in the Rhineland and appear to have been exported from Britain.

The beginning of 343 produced a crisis of alarming propor-tions and the emperor Constans himself was forced to intervene. Forts north of Hadrian's Wall had been overwhelmed and destroyed. Padarn Pesrut, a former senior commander, was brought out of retirement and given a commission over a special force known as the Areani, or Arcani.

Seven years later, Magnentius plotted against Constans, causing his death in 350. Flavius Popilius Magnentius became emperor in his place, but at the cost of a civil war. This led to losses amongst the British garrison and Magnentius himself was soon in deep trouble. He was defeated by Constantius II at Mursa in 351 and fled to Gaul where he took his own life two years later.

Christianity, meanwhile, continued its gradual infiltration of Roman life, and several British bishops were among the four hundred attending the church council at Rimini in 359. On the other hand there was a considerable revival of the Celtic religions and numerous rural temples were established on hilltops and beside rivers. They received a certain amount of encouragement from the next emperor.

Flavius Claudius Julianus was proclaimed emperor by his troops in 361 and, the following year, he sent Lupicinus to Britain to counter a growing number of raids from the Picts and the Scots. Julianus was an implacable opponent of Christianity and had publicly declared his conversion to paganism. He led an expedition against the Persians in 363 and was killed in a desert battle beyond Ctesiphon. In the chaos that followed, the major barbarian incursions of 365 led to the *barbarica conspiratio*, the Barbarian Conspiracy that threatened the heartlands of Roman Britain in 367.

The finest surviving Roman floor at Littlecote, in the Kennet valley east of Marlborough, is from the pagan revival in the time of Julianus – Julian the Apostate – and conveniently happens to be the most closely dated Roman pavement in the country. Three coins were discovered in its core during the rebuilding of the floor in the 1970s, dating its original construction to within a year of 360. Bryn Walters, the director of the Littlecote

The floor of the Orphic temple at Littlecote, Wiltshire, dated to 360, which is regarded as the finest mosaic in Britain.

Photograph: Tony Pritchard

Roman Research Trust, commented: "To find one would have been unusual. To find three is an utter miracle. It is the closest dated pavement in Britain."

The Littlecote floor is forty-one feet by twenty-eight feet, featuring Orpheus – whose powers of song were such that he could move trees and rocks and tame the wild beasts – encircled by four galloping horses each with a frenzied female dancer. It was an Orphic temple, the religious room of the house and the precinct to its bathroom. The floor and the house were only in use for about ten years before some event caused them to be abandoned. The buildings, however, must have survived in a reasonable condition as the bath house appears to have been brought back into use in the eleventh century, and the nine-acre Roman site was covered by a mediaeval village until 1400.

The third abandonment of the pavement came after its discovery and excavation in the 1720s. Pieces were known to

229

have been disturbed and smashed and the Victoria County History wrote it off: "believed subsequently destroyed". This would have been its fate, except that William George, the steward of the estate, left a set of large-scale drawings coloured with immense care to show the position of each cube in the mosaic. This crucial information, and the equally important backing of D W Wills of the tobacco family, owner of Littlecote House, enabled the complete reconstruction of the floor to its original perfection. The work of the Littlecote team has led to the discovery of still more villas in the upper Kennet valley, from a handful in 1972 to thirty-three by 1982. Some are of national importance, including one where tesserae cubes are in every molehill across nine acres of shooting preserve and indicate the densest concentration of Roman flooring ever found in Britain. At another, near Rudge Farm, a wealth of past finds points to the need for excavations before the land is subjected to deep ploughing. Littlecote itself has earlier associated buildings across several acres and the long term programme is to restore them into a spectacular Roman setting, under a replica villa rather than the usual school-like modern canopies. Already the first steps have been taken towards restoring the contemporary environment, by re-digging the ancient channel of the Kennet and diverting the river so it now flows along its Roman course.

The barbarian conspiracy

THE GREAT *barbarica conspiratio*, the Barbarian Conspiracy of co-ordinated attacks against Roman Britain in June 367, was recorded by the contemporary historian, Ammianus Marcellinus. The emperor Valentinian was at Rheims when he heard of these attacks and immediately set off for Boulogne. However, he fell ill on the way and was forced to spend several weeks in Amiens.

Then two of his three leading generals in Gaul, Severus and Jovinus, crossed the Channel and sent back an urgent request for reinforcements. Theodosius therefore sailed from Boulogne with a field force of about six hundred men experienced in rapid cross-country campaigns and trained to cope speedily with rivers and other obstacles. They won back the crippled province in 368 and 369, having spent the winter of 368–69 in London; this field force was part of the emperor's personal army. By the time they arrived in Britain, Valentinian had proclaimed his son Gratian as Augustus, with a share of government, on 24 August, 367.

Theodosius redisposed forces in Britain in 369, abandoning the major fort at Portchester on the northern edge of Portsmouth Harbour and moving its units six miles up the deep-water Hampshire creeks to Clausentum on a bend in the River Itchen at Bitterne, Southampton. The new choice was a compromise that could provide a central base for the indented Hampshire coastline, from the head of Southampton Water, and fell in line with a decision that it was desirable, where practical, that forts should be sited beside main settlements.

Roman legislation in the second half of the fourth century enabled temples and tombs to be demolished for the emergency repair of town defences and this led, probably in 367, to the graveyard at Chester, for example, being robbed of its stones for the strengthening of the fortress walls. Such desecration ironically preserved a hundred inscriptions, the first of which was rediscovered during work on the North Wall in 1883. These are displayed at the Grosvenor Museum in the town, and many more must be still entombed in the walls, particularly in the stretch beside the Deanery Field.

The ferrying of Roman soldiers and stores across estuaries was carried out by small shallow-draught *barcae* operated by a unit of *Numerus Barcariorum*. These are certainly known to have been stationed on the Tyne at South Shields and on the Lune at Lancaster, where a nine-acre fort of the Saxon-shore type was built by Count Theodosius after the disasters of 367; it was operational into the fifth century, a potsherd from this date of north African red slipware having been found in excavations.

In these troubled times the duties of the ferrymen were

The Mildenhall treasure, found in the early 1940s on the edge of the Fens in Suffolk, on display at the British Museum. Its magnificent fourth century silver was probably buried to conceal it from Saxon raiders. That succeeded, but the owners never retrieved it.

Photograph: Colin Graham

Eighteen-and-a-quarter pound silver dish, two feet in diameter – the heaviest item in the Mildenhall Treasure which was found in Suffolk during the 1939 War. The centre head is Neptune or Oceanus, surrounded by nereids riding sea monsters. The outer frieze features the triumph of Bacchus, god of wine, over Hercules. Silenus and Pan also appear, with maenads and satyrs.

Photograph: Colin Graham

probably extended into the operational field, their light vessels being used to patrol and intercept raiders. The men of the *Numerus Barcariorum* at Lancaster dedicated an altar to the war-god Mars which was found in 1794 at Halton-on-Lune, three miles up the estuary. In two other carvings found near Lancaster, at Cockersand Moss, the Celtic god Nodons had been synthesised with the classical god Mars as *Deo Marti Nodonti*; Nodons had a wide range of powers that included nautical affairs.

There was also a bureaucratic solution to the disaster area around Lancaster – when in doubt create another layer of government. A fifth Roman state was therefore carved out of

Middle quality home-produced pottery, with thumb pots from the New Forest kilns and a Castor ware beaker with leaf pattern applied in barbotine.

Photograph: John Pitfield

the already subdivided British province in 369; this became Britannia Valentia, honouring the emperors Valentinian and Valens. It appears to have been detached from the territory governed from York and took in Carlisle and Hadrian's Wall, the area through which the barbarian knife had sliced in 367.

The names of the sub-provinces survive through the Roman obsession with documentation: P BR S, for instance, stamped on wood, drainpipes or lead seals, denoted *Provinciae Britanniae Superioris* – the property of the London-ruled province of Britannia Superior.

Art managed improvements in these difficult times, as it frequently does. Debris from workshops and about nine kilns were found at Little Baldon Farm, Oxfordshire, in October 1970, after the South Oxfordshire Hunt had galloped across a ploughed field. Someone noticed a scatter of potsherds and

234

picked up the neck of a flagon on which was a finely moulded face. The orange ware had a blue-grey core and, following this discovery, Julian Munby searched through museum collections to find another fifteen colour-coated faces which had been made in the same area, all recovered in a late fourth century context from sites as far apart as the Temple of Nodons at Lydney Park, Gloucestershire, to the shore fort of Richborough, Kent. His findings are in volume six of *Britannia*. These flagon-neck faces from the Oxfordshire kilns have Celtic touches to the styling and elaborately patterned hair, and are much more complex than the faces that appear on Castor and Colchester products. What Munby calls the "Baldon design" represents the continuation of Celtic art, Romanised but distinctive, and at its finest level. The faces were made as little plaques and then attached to the rim of the flagons.

By the year 385 overall security in Britain must have been

Face-pot from North Africa, imitating Samian ware and setting the trend for highly decorated pottery. There is a hunting scene around the base.

Photograph: John Pitfield

successfully tightened as some of the troops of the occupation were shipped to the continent. The finding of very few coins in Britain of Magnus Maximus, it has been suggested by P J Casey, was due to the withdrawal during his reign of British garrisons for campaigns in Gaul. As a result of this far fewer crates of soldiers' wages were shipped into the province and there was also, as a consequence, less need for small change.

Magnus Maximus, who was Spanish-born but based in Britain, organised the killing of the emperor Gratian in 383 and himself reigned until 388. A ninth century pillar at Valle Crucis Abbey records the claims of a Welsh family to descent from Maximus, whom other sources credited with two wives and several sons and daughters. Shortly after his death, one of his sons, Victor, was assassinated. But perhaps the most distinguished relative of Magnus Maximus was his son-in-law Vortigern, who was to become king of Britain in the fifth century.

Christianity now began to establish a substantial urban following, but one as fraught with internal dissension as a modern British political party at its annual conference in October. Saint Victricius, bishop of Rouen, crossed the Channel towards the end of the fourth century to intervene in doctrinal rows and attempt to patch them up.

The Chi-Rho initials, representing the first letters of Christ's name in Greek, *Christos*, appear on oil lamps and from three, otherwise unmarked, slabs found at Chedworth, Gloucestershire; Chi was the Greek *X* and Rho the Greek *P*.

The cemeteries of the first British Christians lie outside the Roman town walls. This is confirmed by St Chrysostom who stated in a sermon in 403 that such communities had their burial grounds outside the walls of cities. So, too, did the Roman pagans, with their masses of roadside graves, for space had once been at too high a premium to allow any religion room for burials inside walled defences.

The **Romano-Christian cemetery at Poundbury, Dorchester, during excavations in 1973.**
Photograph: Colin Graham

Howard Pell was the assistant director in 1973 of the dig that uncovered the largest collection of Roman Christian graves ever excavated in the British Isles, dating from 325 to 420. This took place on the chalk hillside of a factory estate overlooking the River Frome, and facing towards the wall of Durnovaria (Roman Dorchester) and its present-day administrative office block at County Hall.

Pell was fighting at the time for another year's continued exploration, as he told the *Dorset County Magazine*: "A transformer sub-station is to be built here by the Southern Electricity Board who say they must have a level platform for their buildings. This will be shelved twelve feet deep into the hillside and go through graves. Some of their buildings are to be put on untouched areas which we have not excavated." Ten years later the land is still a vacant plot.

Pell was proud of the latest discoveries which were besmirched by the impending abandonment of the investigations:

"We definitely need another season because this is the largest Roman cemetery ever excavated in Britain and we are finding the precedents which others will compare in the future. It's not that there aren't cemeteries elsewhere, it's just no one has bothered digging them before. This has not been booty hunting as there is no treasure to be found – all we get is hard knowledge."

Surprisingly, in the final week of the 1973 dig came the only definite evidence of Saxon continuity on the site. A fifteen-foot square depression overlying a handful of the 1,068 mapped-out Roman graves was identified as an early to middle Saxon *grubenhaus*, a pagan building dating somewhere between AD 500 and 700. It was sunk eighteen inches to two feet into the chalk and perhaps had floorboards. The collapsed floor yielded Poundbury's only domestic finds of the year – four fragments of loomweights. The excavators were baffled not to find pieces of pottery or any rubbish pits in association with the *grubenhaus*. It was the furthest west such a hut had been found in Britain.

Pell's appeal eventually received national recognition and the dig was extended, bringing the total of 760 skeletons at that time to ultimately well over a thousand. They were to confirm the evolution of the human skull in the past sixteen hundred years. The majority of Dorchester's Roman population had teeth with edge to edge bite – buck teeth, in other words. Today it is the reverse and most people have smaller mouths with overbite.

Genetic and racial similarities and the medical state of Dorchester's population are also being analysed. Without a thousand skulls, Pell kept insisting, the sample would be in-sufficiently representative for any real conclusions to be made.

"The bigger the number of skeletons raised, the more valid the statistics," he pointed out. "Early in the season we lost two heads to the skull-thieves and that was a bad enough waste."

All the exciting finds of 1973 came as the dig was preparing to close. Rex Clive of Minterne Magna uncovered a lead coffin containing the first evidence ever found that the wealthy wives of fourth century Roman Britain lived elegantly with sophisticated hair styles. The lady was aged about forty with chestnut hair, worn in three plaits about seven to eight inches long, and heaped on her crown. Like the others at Poundbury, she was most likely a Romanised Celt of native stock, but one of the lucky élite who were the new aristocracy. Her hair preservation was a total freak and came about only because of an accident of conditions inside her gypsum-packed coffin. Ancient hair is very rare. None of the other eighteen gypsum burials in lead and stone coffins revealed more than just the tufts of facial or pubic hair; so hers was of sufficient importance to attract Environment Department scientists who came to remove her coiffure under sterile conditions and take it to London for treatment and preservation. Hers was the first woman's hair of the Roman period from anywhere in western Europe to have styling. Dorchester had provided an internationally important discovery.

Burying corpses packed in gypsum is a north African practice previously found in Britain at London and York though Poundbury is the first dig to uncover it in a Christian context. Gypsum is found on the Dorset coast at Worbarrow and Portland. It was dehydrated by roasting, then packed as a white powder around the corpse to absorb body fluids. When a coffin is opened, the gypsum has shrunk into soft blocks of plaster-like substance carrying the imprint of the weave of the corpse cloth.

One of the lead coffins contained a child, of three or four, and here Pell interpreted the discoveries for his archaeologist and holidaymaker audience as he opened its shrine on a hot Sunday morning.

"There's no hair but it's the best piece of shroud we have found," he said, attempting a little Mortimer Wheeler showmanship.

"For some reason the bones are better preserved than

usual." He picked at the centre of the body-dust and called for a plastic bag for his samples: "I'm looking for seeds and things in the stomach, but there's nothing. He must have died of starvation!" More likely the poor child vomited before he died, but there was something anaesthetically remote about the proceedings, and no one would say anything that insensitive.

Pell's general opinion on the find: "Quite a nice one, good gypsum packing." Both gypsum and bones are lifted into a succession of brown cardboard boxes addressed with *On Her Majesty's Service* official-paid labels to the County Museum in Dorchester. Pell takes most time with the head: "Teeth will be very, very small but they are most important." The whole operation took half an hour. "The Department of the Environment staff men would have taken a day," Pell said. "They are always stopping for cups of tea."

Digging Christian graves needs limitless enthusiasm as all the bodies lie in east-facing rows without grave goods, clothing or the sort of surprises that make archaeology exciting. So for those working on the site there was little except the consolation they were doing something of national importance as they dug under a constant chalk glare which made them grimace for days with heatstroke, "snow-blindness", and headache.

Howard Pell described the conditions: "The glare is unbelievable. It's never dull and you can even read out there by moonlight. In July the temperature was 97°F and the light-meter reading for my camera shot to fifteen. That was out in the open, but it's out there where we work. There's no shade and it nearly became the first nudie dig ever."

The graveyard has thrown new insight into the minds of the early Christians. In the earlier part of the cemetery, everyone is buried alike, or almost, with the only concession to wealth and class being in the treatment of the coffin. Those with status were packed in gypsum powder and then had their lead coffin placed inside a wooden coffin with special nails that had a raised head. At a funeral there would have been no outward difference between a lead coffin disguised in wood and the ordinary wooden coffin, except for the number of pallbearers. As the lead industry of the Mendips declined, the upper classes turned instead to attractive two-piece coffins hewn from huge one-ton blocks of Ham-stone with clean yellow surfaces that still ripple new and fresh with tool marks. Sometimes the poorer people mimicked the aristocracy by edging their coffins with rubble.

All this distinction was an underground matter as no post-holes or stones have been found above the graves, and if there were any markers they could only have been low mounds. But equality after death became a principle of the past. The latter half of the cemetery saw the introduction of the first above-ground mausoleum and altogether ten have so far been found. They were strongly built, roofed with stone slates, and covered inside with wall paintings showing figures four feet high holding wands of office. These buildings may have been adapted by the Saxons into houses and surrounded by palisades and trenches.

The crammed nature of the cemetery is striking. The area under investigation had 1,068 graves in only about an acre and the whole cemetery, before it was disturbed, extended to four acres with four thousand graves. This raised questions because the same deliberate layout policy was followed from the first grave to the four thousandth. All had been dug with equal care and no Christian grave disturbed or cut across another even though they are only inches apart. Why are burials packed together? As no parallels exist, Pell cannot turn to other places and reply that they always were. Plenty of space lay around Poundbury and could have been consecrated and the grave-yard extended, as would happen today in a modern cemetery if the ground were available. In fact, in its growth from 320 onwards, more land was probably commandeered but the bodies were still packed equally tightly. This suggests that the early Christians saw themselves meeting in death as a single community, body next to body and family next to family, rather than being separated for the convenience of the grave diggers.

Dorchester in the fourth century was the thirteenth largest town in Roman Britain, a tribal capital, and estimated to have had a five thousand population. Many died young and the provisional figures from Poundbury show the average life-span can have been little over thirty. That means the century must have witnessed more than fifteen thousand burials – four thousand of them are at Poundbury, but where are the rest?

Answers to a multiplicity of questions are coming only slowly. It was not until 1972 that proof came that the Poundbury cemetery was Christian. An inscription was discovered cast in the lead on the underside of a coffin facing towards the inmate's head: IND IN. It was meant to spell out IN DNI. The letters were reversed as they were scratched in sand in a moulding tray, in an attempted mirror image which was partially successful. Whoever did this was literate and his Roman capitals have serifs. Translated they say: "In the name of the Master (God)."

In 1971 a man was discovered buried with his hands on the skulls of two children at his side. Immediately above their bones were the charred remains of a door. The laying of hands on the head is a gesture of comfort and suggests the man was their father. Probably they died with a volatile disease and the burning of the bodies was a precaution against the infection spreading.

Though virtually all the site is Christian there was also a small contemporary pagan cemetery. Pell explained: "The two religions were living and burying side by side with a fence in between. All the Christians face east in orderly lines with no grave goods, except for a one per cent minority who have a bracelet or coin as double insurance. But in contrast with the great Christian respect for the dead, on the other side of the fence in the pagan cemetery the bodies are mixed up, facing in

242

all directions, some crouched and unstraightened, and others even upside down."

The two pagan bodies facing downwards were the only two burials with jet, brought from Whitby, and this is the furthest south or west any has been found in Britain.

Virtually all the Christians buried with token grave goods, in a pagan hangover, are in one tiny lower corner of the cemetery which is dated by six coins, all Constantine the First with little wear, minted just before 320. These were people born pagan and converted. Their grave goods were buried with the body, rather than on it, which would be totally pagan, and the same care in digging and placing the grave was taken as with the other Christian burials. If anything, it is surprising the transitional period was so short, and restricted to a single decade (315 to 325), as it suggests rapid and wholesale conversion of the majority of the community, whereas the undertones of the old religion might be expected to have lingered longer. Possibly the early death-age meant a quicker turnover of beliefs.

Personal jewellery from Dorchester – bronze and glass bracelets, rings and beads. *Photograph: John Pitfield*

One of the bronze coins was under a man's tongue as Charon's fee to ferry his soul across the Styx. The biggest collection of grave goods with a Christian burial was uncovered by Steve Lewis of Dorchester beside a child of about eight in the last fortnight of the dig. She was buried with several items of second-hand jewellery, most of it broken and repaired long before it was buried. With her, too, was a small lathe-turned toy of Kimmeridge shale, Dorset's imitation jet, and polished bone. Also at her feet was a five-and-a-half inch long bone pin, far longer than any ever found elsewhere.

Today, in a limited sense, there is more acceptance of grave goods than was shown by the Dorchester Christians after they had left their transitional phase. The main period of the cemetery, 325 to 420, produced no grave goods, whereas in modern times toys are still occasionally placed in children's coffins, and jewellery and other sentimental items with adults. Women are often buried with their wedding rings.

Even this may be a mild reversion to former practice rather than a continuous survival from deep in the past. Country people into recent years have been strongly averse to any jewellery whatsoever – warning that it would disturb the soul. The Victorian collector of folklore, S A Baring-Gould, heard from a Yorkshireman whose mother had died that when the woman who laid her out was told to leave the wedding ring in place, she retorted: "You mun no send her to God wi' trinkets about her."

Usually, for the archaeologist at Poundbury, all that came from a grave except bones were a few slithers of calcified wood and a handful of nails that marked the corners of the coffin. More than five thousand nails were unearthed by 1973. Otherwise, all traces of the wood had gone and usually only well-preserved orange bones protruded from chalk bedrock. Two of the wooden coffins had iron corner braces, preserving in their rust some splinters of elm wood. One grave turned up seven.

"Always a magical number," said Pell. Could he have missed the eighth, though? "Not a chance. You just can't lose something like this. They are huge things, six inches wide. Corner braces were used to support the coffin, if it had loose planks, or to make it look better than the rest."

Seven planets are said by astrologers to govern both the universe and man. The mausoleums at Poundbury are also in a magical layout with a quincunx (repeating five-spot of a dice) pattern which has parallels in ancient Babylon. The coffin with the magically missing corner brace was another of the burials in the collection "no later than 325" containing Dorchester's (and perhaps Dorset's) first Christian converts.

Shortly before this, when the cemetery first came into use, part of the ground was cleared of scattered hutments and some bread-ovens from these habitations have survived. Earlier finds from the site include a casual smattering of Neolithic and Bronze Age pottery and tools from semi-nomadic occupants, and in about 1300 BC there was a small farmstead which left quantities of ox bones, a rectangular house twenty-five feet long by sixteen feet wide, and several granaries raised on posts. The limits of the cemetery extended uphill to the outer, eastern rampart of the Iron Age defences at Poundbury Camp. Here are the earliest Roman remains.

The prehistoric defences of the deserted fort were slighted early in the Roman colonisation to carry a section of a twelve-mile aqueduct which took water from near Notton Mill on the River Frome to the fountains and public baths of Roman Dorchester. Often, aqueducts were major engineering works that were years in the making, and failed to work when completed. Dorchester's must have taken twenty years and was operational by AD 90. The excavators inspected a section on the edge of the hill-fort and found it was an open channel six feet across with a clay lining, though the latter was probably only a precaution to prevent leakage where the watercourse passed over the instability of former earthworks. It even worked – there were the shells of hundreds of freshwater snails. Maximum discharge capacity of the Dorchester aqueduct has been calculated at 12,958,000 gallons a day.

Poundbury cemetery provided the first evidence for the continuity of civilisation at Dorchester after the collapse of Roman rule. Certainly, there was an extensive Saxon settlement inside a maze of palisade trenches on the slopes of Poundbury within sight of the Roman walls, including huts and probably converted mausoleums. The position of this settlement suggests it is either overspill from the reoccupied top of Poundbury Camp or, equally likely, one of a scattering of habitations that included buildings inside the area of the old Roman walls. Nothing has been found to indicate there was a Saxon Dorchester, and yet this is British archaeology's weakest period and digs have even consistently failed to come up with anything except the most sparse material from a Saxon London despite the embarrassing mass of contemporary literature calling the city "a mart of many peoples coming by land and sea" and "a famous place and a royal town". Later, London's Roman walls were repaired and the city was probably surrounded by multiple ditches and entered by stone gates in the last centuries of the Saxons when it held out against the prolonged attacks of the Danes and was described as "protected on the left side by the walls, on the right side by the river, it neither fears enemies nor dreads being taken by storm".

Even William the Conqueror acknowledged its strength and threatened to "raze the bastions to the ground, and bring down the proud town in rubble". Yet for all this there is the most slender of archaeological evidence for London as a Saxon city.

Dorchester, as the hub of a prehistoric and Roman road system that continued as the basis of communications, has a logical claim to a presumption of survival. The discovery in the final days of the Poundbury dig of the Saxon *grubenhaus* shows that a scientific excavation which had been in progress from 1966 to 1973 could nearly fail to reveal a crucial stage in the site's development. Until then the director, Christopher Green, had looked upon the buildings overlying the cemetery "as suggesting a sub-Roman rather than an early Saxon context". There are no second chances in rescue archaeology.

Eventually, when Green's work reaches publication, Dorchester should emerge to the excitement of the archaeological world as the earliest, and largest, proven Christian community in Britain. Until now the new religion has been dismissed as making little impression on the Romano-British people who were said to have reverted to paganism in the late fourth century, for which Dorchester has also provided proof in the form of a temple (though well away from the city walls) standing on the top of Maiden Castle.

The scope and complexity of Roman Dorchester is widening. Already in this century County Hall and the library have been planted on the least disturbed sector of the Roman town, though it came to light only in 1980 that the library's construction had also been used as camouflage for the secret building of an underground nuclear fall-out shelter, intended for the use of Dorset's minor officials.

But the future's notable discoveries may come from under buildings awaiting destruction above the best-preserved Roman levels in the centre of the town. Their demolition will almost certainly reveal Roman buildings and streets. As for the heart of the Roman town, the forum lies under Lloyds Bank and extends south-west below gardens as a flint-gravelled surface spreading over one hundred and twenty-five feet. Dorchester is at last starting to live up to Thomas Hardy's dreams, for he wrote that his Casterbridge "announced old Rome in every street, alley, and precinct".

The existence of Poundbury cemetery was first realised when the army built a camp across the site in 1940, dug foundation and drainage trenches through dozens of skeletons, and only stopped when they hit stone or lead coffins. Second World War army debris found by the present excavators included emergency ration tins, a half-full cough medicine bottle, and a French fly-button. It does not quite amount to the military archaeology of the twentieth century, but First World War finds added more interest. There was then a German prisoner-of-war camp at Poundbury and from this period came an empty tin of Turkish-blend Graf v Koenigsmarck "flack gold-tipped" cigarettes. The dig also produced a French bayonet holder of 1914 vintage. But the star find is a German bullet carved into a tin whistle.

Poundbury is not the only site in Britain where the influence of Christianity on burial customs has been observed. Rendlesham, four miles from Sutton Hoo in Suffolk's Deben valley, provides evidence of a pagan Saxon burial ground that passed into Christian care. Pre-Christian cremation urns have been dug up in quantity on Hoo Hill where there happens to be an outlying strip of glebe land which has been owned by the church for as long as records exist. There is no obvious reason why the church should want such a detached and isolated piece of ground, and it becomes plausible to suggest the first Christians at Rendlesham adopted the graveyard according to the spirit of Pope Gregory's edict of the fifth century advocating the christianisation of pagan sanctuaries.

Fourth and fifth century burials from elsewhere in Britain are frequently in the Christian manner and style, with bodies laid from east to west and without grave goods. Thirty-four such inhumations were found beside the M4 motorway at Beacon Hill, Oxfordshire, in 1972.

Gravel excavations that same year cut through a cemetery with a thousand graves at Queensford Mill, Dorchester, also in the same county. These, too, were predominantly set out from east to west. A boundary ditch had enclosed the plot; late

Roman pottery was found in the silting of the ditch, and radio carbon testing of a bone sample provided a date of 420, plus or minus a hundred years.

There is still no certain discovery of a Roman town church in Britain. The only contender is at Silchester, but this temple-like building has the reverse of the expected orientation and was abandoned by about 385, a time when churches were being opened rather than closed. A timber-framed building dating from about 400 in the Saxon-shore fort at Richborough does, however, seem to be a church, with a font and outside baptistry.

There is always the problem of deliberate Christian adoption of pagan buildings, emphasising that this was not simply an alternative religion but a complete replacement. Pope Gregory's letter sent via Bishop Mellitus to Saint Augustine's British mission suggests that "the temples of the idols in the said country ought not to be broken, but the idols alone which be in them; that holy water be made and sprinkled about the said temples, altars built, relics placed: for if the temples be well

High-class pagan tomb, from The Minories, London. *Courtesy: British Museum*

built, it is needful that they be altered from the worshipping of devils into the service of the true God."

The Venerable Bede's quotation from this letter also points out that some objectionable habits were also allowed to remain as long as they could be rendered devoid of meaning. Gregory insisted that people "no more sacrifice animals to the devil but kill them to the refreshing of themselves" – an invitation from the father of modern blood sports. At least he perpetuated a bizarre assortment of hobby-horse dances, well rituals, and holy day treks to the sacred sites of the old religion. Harold Bayley records how, at the time of the First World War, the villagers of Avebury "still toil to the summit of Silbury Hill" on Palm Sunday "to consume fig cakes and drink sugared water".

Just as temples became churches, so some of the secular earthworks became venues for the fairs that were the key form of economic and social intercourse for mediaeval rural society. Yarnbury Castle, a large hillfort in Wiltshire, was thus transformed into the pound for a sheep fair. Here, the abandoned fortress offered instant sheep-penning.

There was also a far greater number of fairs held not inside, or even near, any ancient monument. Taking Dorset as an example, George Cooke listed forty-four fairs in his *Topographical and Statistical Description* of the county in 1810. Only those at Lambert's Castle, Woodbury Hill, and Poundbury, were in hillforts – yet these were the major fairs and probably amongst those with the longest history. This was reflected in their size. That at Woodbury Hill, overlooking the village of Bere Regis, started on 18 September and continued for a further five days with "all sorts of cattle, horses, hops, cheese, cloth, haberdashery, and all sort of goods".

Likewise, the overlapping and continuity between Roman buildings and major Christian churches does not always follow an expected pattern. In Dorset, there are two such confirmed examples, excluding churches around Dorchester where rebuilding of any sort stands a high chance of interfering with Roman foundations. In Victorian times, an area of Roman flooring was found at Wimborne Minster during renovations. Sherborne Abbey is another Dorset example of a Saxon church, then of cathedral status, on the ruins of a Roman house. P D Carpenter told a meeting of antiquaries in 1891 how a portion of *tesserae* paving had been found under the abbey "some time ago".

While considering these examples, however, it must also be taken into account that at least another six of the principal Dorset monastic centres have not produced any such remains; and it must be borne in mind that anyone beginning church construction work in the vicinity of a substantial Roman building would have to be unduly dim-witted not to appreciate the possibilities that the older site provided for a dry, level base, and abundant hardcore.

Roman stones could be re-used in other ways. Standing at a roadside above the eight hundred foot contour on the northern edge of the Dorset Downs, overlooking Batcombe and the country far into Somerset, stands the Cross-in-Hand. This pillar of lichen-encrusted limestone is just under four feet high. The track beside it coincides with a parish boundary and has the feel of a pre-Roman ridgeway. Past speculation, including that by Thomas Hardy, has tended to regard the Cross-in-Hand as part of a pre-Norman wayside cross. Yet its shape is that of a carved column, a baluster shaft removed from a nearby Roman villa and set into the ground by the Saxons to mark the parish boundary of Batcombe with Sydling St Nicholas. There is a circular moulding below the bowl-shaped top and this is probably repeated on the base, underground. Someone has suggested that the stone "tends to become a square". Its buried part will have preserved the genuine shape as it has not been exposed to the weather and centuries of erosion.

One of the difficulties reconciling archaeology with our

received ideas of history is that the coin evidence does not fit too well with the general theory of economic decline in late Roman Britain, to the extent that eighty per cent of coins found on continuously occupied sites date from 259 to the year 402; there was a notable bulge in the mid-fourth century, from 330 to 360. A high proportion of Roman small change of this period in Britain was locally made in the province, with the irregular issues making up a third of Constantinian coins from 330 to 348.

Despite this, some problems were natural rather than monetarist. Toward the end of the fourth century there were difficulties at ports and in the canal and drainage systems of the Humber and the Wash, caused by the change in sea level which had been gradually rising since the beginning of the previous century.

Sub-Roman Britain

FLAVIUS CLAUDIUS CONSTANINUS usurped power and proclaimed himself emperor in 407, gaining control first in Britain, then across the Channel in Gaul, and finally in Spain. This produced the famous statement by Honorius, the emperor, which Victorian historians considered as signifying the cut-off point between Rome and Britain. In 410, facing an emergency at the heart of empire, he told the Britons they were on their own.

In the words of the *Anglo-Saxon Chronicle*: "In this year Rome was destroyed by the Goths, eleven hundred and ten years after it was built. Then after the kings of the Romans never reigned in Britain. Altogether they had reigned there 470 years since Gaius Julius first came to the land."

But perhaps it was not quite that final. The situation changed in 411 when Constantius (the third, emperor in 421) fought and defeated Constaninus. The rebel leader was taken prisoner and brought to Ravenna where he was executed.

Even the *Anglo-Saxon Chronicle* is no authority for the finality of the situation in 410. Eight years later, it records: "In this year the Romans collected all the treasures which were in Britain, and hid some in the ground, so that no one could find them afterwards, and took some with them into Gaul." Eight years is a long time for treasure to be left in a vacuum, and on this basis alone the 410 statement can be shown to be premature.

Honorius, the last emperor of Roman Britain.

Photograph: Colin Graham

Secondly, the publicised and propagandised act of burying their valuables must have brought some sort of temporary respite to the Romans in Britain. Having removed the goods from view, as it were, there was now less risk of greedy Saxons crossing the channel in search of treasure.

Reports of the death of Roman Britain were greatly exaggerated but, then, society was changing all over Europe. The late Roman empire saw the decline of community life and the rise of feudalism in its place.

The poet Claudius Rutilius Namatianus, sailing from Rome towards Genoa in 416, observed that Palo and Santa Severa were "today large country estates, in earlier days small towns". His voyage took place six years after Alaric and the Visigoths had sacked Rome. Sidney Perowive writes in *The End of the Roman World* that these ranches were managed by "rural tycoons", having palatial villas with "their own baths, and

254

pillared porticoes in profusion". One of these, on the scale of a vast palace, was at Piazza Armarina in Sicily.

Towns, which had been "the very cells of the empire's life", were being killed by corruption, inflation and extreme taxation. As well as these, however, was the problem that individual talent was restrained by the legal obligation for sons to follow their fathers' trades, and Diocletian's command that citizens could not move from the district where they enrolled.

There are many parallels with eighteenth century England where a general pattern of decline on one hand was matched by the appearance on the other of lavish country houses set in equally massive estates. These were also dependent on the near-slavery of service workers trapped in their "stations in life", after the wealth and control of the countryside had polarised and been taken into the hands of a privileged few. Many of these great country houses mushroomed across the sites of previous village or small-town communities. Usually the landscaped parkland has disguised most of the traces of the earlier free societies, but the one enduring pointer to the past is the former parish church, of a size disproportionate to the needs of the house; this often ceased even to be a public church and became merely a private chapel for the owners of the estate.

The collapse of the rural economy in Roman Britain following the Pictish incursions of 367 was due to the inability of villa owners to prevent the desertion of their slaves. Without this labour force – and there was no capital for any other – the complex estates could no longer function. Wealthy villa occupants were no more able to harvest corn from their extensive holdings than the families of equally large country houses were able to gather the Southern cotton after the American Civil War. The debris of their wealth might provide sufficient comforts for the transition into first generation townspeople but exhausted capital is a poor provider for the future.

Slavery was as vital for the continuation of Roman feudalism as it was in eighteenth century England for the creation of the biggest estates that the country had seen since the dissolution of the monasteries. The major difference was that the new rich of the English countryside could live on excesses from both sides of the Atlantic. Having found in West Africa a native trade in slaves, and transplanted this labour to the sugar fields of the Caribbean, they gave the world millions of gallons of rum each year. This external income was the prop to the English country houses, the means to pay for its architecture and art, and the provider for its captive service labour. Colonial rum was to outlive the abolition of slavery (which made little difference as the free slaves could neither return "home" nor give up work) and at the height of Victorian England seven-and-a-half million gallons a year were being imported into the country.

Wealthy Romans in Britain, or Romanised Celts as they almost all were, had no similar overseas support. The military assistance extended to Britain was no substitute for economic stability and prosperity. Even to police the country and maintain the status quo – for you could always send a soldier after a debtor – was only possible if the military were underemployed. But from AD 367 they had become the guards on the front-line of empire and there would no longer be soldiers to throw stones idly in the streets. The people were now self-governing.

Neither could the province itself rely upon additional assistance from Rome, after the directive Honorius had sent telling the people to defend themselves. Although it is convenient to consider the year 410 as marking the end of Roman Britain, the emperor himself certainly did not regard the renunciation as total for the province still belonged to Rome and was defended by units of the imperial forces.

The *Notitia Dignitatum* is an official Roman garrison list of about 395, up-dated into the 420s; these alterations, which were made directly onto the original vellum in the form of deletions and additions, make it highly unlikely that the work is an imaginative fake. The *Notitia* is a tedious and boring official file, not a public statement, and its compilers and users would have been bureaucrats and clerks. Archaeologists have ignored and misinterpreted it for so long that this, as Captain John Hester Ward says in volume four of *Britannia*, is tantamount to "acceptance of the premise that the Roman Chancery was so childishly incompetent that it kept long-obsolete material intermixed with current data in a non-public, official working document". What confirms its authenticity is its very detail and attention to specifics.

Fifteen forts of Hadrian's Wall are listed geographically, from east to west, but with the addition of Uxellodunum – a wall fort between two deep-cut valleys to the north-east of Carlisle. Its later restoration to the list, Captain Ward says, is the clue to the location of the northern breakthrough that took place in the period after 410. The Picts needed to achieve only one breach in the wall to enable them to sweep south, and the *Notitia Dignitatum* listings show that the other forts were also maintained and hung on to their garrisons.

It would have been common sense for the Picts to have left them alone. In the whole of history no line has ever been defensible. Linear defences can never be successful because from the moment they are breached all those deployed elsewhere along the line become prisoners of their fixed positions and can play no further part in the conflict. The burden of halting the enemy advance has to fall on additional forces forming a rearguard and, if they fail, the defenders of the original fortifications can be mopped up by the invader at leisure; in the case of Hadrian's Wall this would have been costly in terms both of casualties and time – and absolutely unnecessary. A barbarian force would lack the application and incentive to carry out the highly organised routines of siege warfare which, as the English Civil War of the seventeenth century demonstrated, could drag on from months into years. Even in modern times, with the assumption of evenly matched armaments, military thinking is that it takes a three-to-one advantage for attackers to succeed in taking fortified positions. There was nothing of value in the forts to attract potential invaders, only units of trained soldiers. The prospect of southern loot must have been a lot more enticing.

After the Roman fleet had landed in the Tyne and relieved the beleaguered wall the one gap in the list was restored. The *Notitia Dignitatum* gives the posting to Uxellodunum of the *Cohors I Hispanorum*, a unit of the British garrison known from Maryport and Netherby in previous centuries. Further additions to the list show the re-establishment of coast defences along the Solway Firth, including Gabrosentum, Tunnocelum, and Glannaventa. These were also returned to commission under British units, including two that had held the same positions earlier in their history which indicates there had been no major losses of manpower as a result of the attack on the wall. Its defenders were not wiped out, but stayed inside their fortresses.

In 428 there were still two legions in Britain which a governmental memorandum shows to have been the Sixth at York and the Second at Richborough. There was a mobile reserve with the emphasis on fast light scout-craft each with forty rowers and camouflaged with the colours of the sea painted on their hulls and sails.

Even forts of the Saxon shore were still being held and the main displacement of forces – towards the east – suggest it was from there that the principal threat was feared. Peace, however, was sufficiently unbroken for St Germanus to return to Britain in 447 and argue Christian ethics with the prosperous citizens of St Albans.

The coastal forts, nearer to danger than the inland towns, did not start to fall for several decades. The first to be stormed was not one of the expected North Sea bastions but Anderida

Reverse of a gold coin of Honorius, showing the centuries-old Roman dream of victory over a trampled barbarian.

Photograph: Colin Graham

(Pevensey) around the Straits on the Channel coast. Its collapse in 491 was a setback and a precedent, but not the loss of a nation. Both Britain as an entity and its second-tier administration of regional capitals survived fundamentally unscathed throughout the fifth century.

Life in the countryside especially had changed during this period, and with a decline in wealth there was a reduction in the types and levels of exploitation, the discomforts and tensions bringing about a different unity. Overall the country was becoming a freer society, with less government for the people and self rule for the state.

On the other hand, these were not conditions in which the size of the population could expand and so the country's birth

259

rate fell with consequent reductions in society's production and consumption. An increasingly urban population, unlike the unsophisticated agricultural communities, does not provide ready recruits for military service and the towns failed to develop alternative systems of home defence using civilian guards; even central government in Rome had never worked out a form of conscription that might have averted the progressive slide towards a totally mercenary army. It had been drifting that way for centuries. At the height of its power Rome conquered with a force of aliens, Italians comprising only twenty per cent of the Roman army at the time of Vespasian's capture of Britain. By the end of the second century this had declined to one in a hundred, giving rise to a provincially-dominated officer corps as well as a provincial monopoly of the common soldiery. In much the same way the British held India with an army of Indians and predominantly Indian civil servants, a principle perfected at home in protecting the property of the English middle classes with a police force provided by the working class. Such systems may be inherently unsafe but it says much for the skill and administration of Rome and its emperors that a ninety-nine per cent colonial army was able to hold the empire together for a further two centuries. This would be an achievement for any state at any time in history, so it is all the more remarkable for one commonly believed to have been riddled with corruption and decay.

The decline of the Roman empire can be more convincingly attributed to those reasons which had led to its original expansion. Italy is an impoverished land, requiring food, minerals and commodities from outside its natural borders. An empire under pressure, producing these items in reducing quantity and at growing cost, was bound to feel the results of retraction. When the ramifications of change led to deprivation and adjustment inside Italy then the fabric of empire could only be weakened. Ultimately, it was not the will to govern that was lost but the means, and responsibility without power is the point at which government ceases to be effective.

As the structure of empire was stripped of secular meaning it became the skeleton for the apparatus of the most successful of all European religions. The great British contribution to Christian theology was articulated by Pelagius, a monk born in the south-east of the country in the early 350s. He argued for man's basic right of independent thought, and wrote a work *On Free Will* – refuting the Augustinian doctrine of predestination, by asserting the individual's freedom of choice to do good or evil. With Celstius, another preacher of Christian unorthodoxy, he went to Africa after the Goths sacked Rome in 410 and met Augustine. The two preachers were later cleared in Jerusalem of heresy but incurred the opposition of the emperor Theodosius. Pelagius, condemned by the Carthage councils of 416 and 418, was banished from Rome. He died about 420 but his thoughts lived on.

Pelagius had argued against the concept of original sin, declaring baptism unnecessary, and this thinking was developed by his disciple, Celstius: "Sin is not born with man. It is an act of will which he may be led to commit by his individual imperfection, but it is not a necessary result of the essential imperfection of mankind." The assertion of the individual's responsibility for his own actions, and its corollary that life was a god-given span during which man walked alone, was a pattern of Celtic thought that ran counter to the whole Mediterranean tradition; this had assumed for centuries that all human acts were initiated and controlled by one god or another.

Vortigern, the first post-Roman king of Britain, eventually adopted Pelagianism, and with it a stance that rejected the totality of divine right and the authority upon which Roman power was now based. This rejection on the part of British intellectual thinking was responsible for the second, certainly, of two visits made to this country by Germanus in the 420s,

261

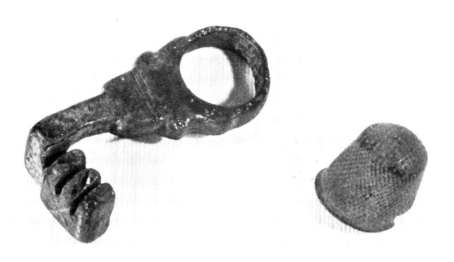

Roman key and thimble – about the only domestic items that are unchanged after all these years.
Photograph: John Pitfield

who was able to argue a specific, rather than purely conceptual, instance of Pelagianism as the king, Vortigern, was indulging in an incestuous relationship.

The debate over Pelagianism, and its subsequent modification into semi-Pelagianism, was the greatest upheaval within the British church's brief history, and it was not to be exceeded for another thousand years when the institution itself was nationalised by Henry VIII. A revival of paganism at the close of Roman rule meant that the church, itself divided, was not yet synonymous with state authority and there was total religious freedom in early fifth century Britain, a position which – with the wretched persistence of blasphemy laws – has never quite been matched to this day.

Another major difference between British and Mediterranean attitudes concerned the role of women in the early church. Female deacons were acceptable in Britain and Brittany, though without formal status, and this ultimately brought a letter of protest from the orthodox bishops of Tours. British tribes had also happily accepted women as their rulers, the last of whom were Boudica and Cartismandua, and as druidic priestesses, though their position in the church was more a reflection of the place of women in society generally. Two Breton priests received the letter of condemnation from Tours about 520: "You continue to carry from hut to hut among your countrymen certain tables on which you celebrate the divine sacrifice of the mass with the assistance of women whom you call *conhospitae*. While you distribute the Eucharist, they take the chalice and administer the blood of Christ to the people. This is an innovation, an unprecedented innovation."

Irish druids shaved the front of their heads, from ear to ear, leaving a quiff across the forehead. Something similar happened with the tonsure of the British Christian priesthood, which also allowed long hair at the back of the neck. This style was considered aberrant by the continental bishops as the orthodox Saint Peter's tonsure required only token shaving at the crown of the scalp. Despite such opposition the British form continued here and in Brittany until the ninth century.

The British church was also in dispute from 457 over the date for the Easter festival, the most important of the year; ironically, its name is pagan, deriving from the Saxon goddess Eostre who had her festival in April. The church council held at Nice in 325 had arranged the date on the basis of the eighty-four year cycle of Augustalis which placed Easter between the fourteenth and twentieth days of the lunar month, thereby establishing it in the period 28 March to 21 April. Then in 457 the system was changed to the 532-year cycle of Victorius of Aquitaine but the church in Britain continued to follow the previous calculations – as they did when Rome changed it all once again in the sixth century. By 631, the celebration of Easter in Ireland and Rome was adrift by a whole month.

Individually, these disputes might not amount to much though minor religious differences tend to generate disproportionate friction to the extent that there is often less hostility amongst people holding totally different beliefs than there is between those who differ ideologically within the same sect.

Jean Markale shows in *Celtic Civilisation* that these differences reflect the independence and remoteness of the Celtic Christian church, and a determined resistance to the rules of Rome which British emigrants transplanted to Brittany and Galicia. Dissident Christianity in the British Isles might have evolved into something unique but those independent minds and their coastal monasteries were snuffed out by the Vikings. When they were rebuilt there was a reversion to, and a restoration of, orthodoxy.

Vortigern, who was born probably about 365 of Romanised Christian stock from Gloucester, was the British king from 426. He it was who is said to have allowed Saxon immigrants to settle in the country in 430, though his sons were to resist the Saxon advance, and he favoured a Roman style of authority and government.

Guoirancgon, the civil governor in control of Kent, had his region withdrawn from him and handed to the Saxon Hengest as part of an accommodation over a bridal price for Hronwen. John Hester Ward discusses this in volume three of *Britannia*: "Vortigern was in this episode exercising power over a civil governor in such a manner as to strengthen the picture of him as a *Vicarius Britanniae* heading a Roman governmental system that was still in tolerable working order."

Vortigern was usurped by Aurelius Ambrosius in 438, by which time he was an old man, and his son, Cattigern, was killed in Hengest's first victory, about the year 441. The attacks against the Saxons were led by another of Vortigern's sons, Vortimir, who died in about 442 after his fourth battle. Cattigern's own son, Cadell Ddyrnllug, seized the throne of Powys with the assistance of St Germanus during the saint's second British visit in the 440s. All early literary sources accept that Britain was still a province of Rome up to the rise to power of Vortigern, and its administration remained unchanged during his rule.

Early Celtic Christian inscriptions dating from around the period 450 to 650 have a western distribution, with a concentration in Wales and the West Country, and outlying examples from Wareham in Dorset (five), Silchester, and Wroxeter. The pattern is similar to the spread of imported pottery from Africa and the eastern Mediterranean during the same period which, as with the inscriptions, also turns up in Scotland. This indicates which areas were last to come under the Anglo-Saxon influence.

Coins of the late fifth century were found by General Augustus Pitt-Rivers in the great chalk and timber entrenchments of the Wansdyke in Wiltshire and Bokerley Dyke in Dorset. The Wansdyke was a fifty mile barrier, from Avon to Berkshire, requiring manpower on a huge scale. Even allowing for local control over individual sections there had to be a higher command behind the strategy and organisation. These were the last frontiers to Saxon invasion, thrown up by the Celtic communities of the grainlands of the southern chalk. The farmers of the Iron Age had won through as farmers of Rome and soon they would become the producers of grain for Saxon Wessex. These conspicuous earthworks led to St Gildas giving a post-Roman dating for the turf-built Antonine Wall: he confused it with the extensive linear earthworks of the Wansdyke and Bokerley Dyke and therefore reasonably assumed they were all from this period.

Aurelius Ambrosius led the British forces in a counter attack that checked the Saxon advance in about 490 – or the troops were led in his name. Perhaps he has come down to us as the legendary King Arthur and this was the battle of Mount Badon – or perhaps Arthur was a genuine historical figure and the battle he won is that attributed to him in the year 520. In all probability the leader of the victorious army was Arthur, and the date could just as easily have been 490; for although Ambrosius was the titular head of the country at the time, there is the evidence of Nennius that Arthur was of lesser rank but won command of the army in the field through his unrivalled abilities.

The name Arthur is not recorded before the second half of the sixth century, when those boys named after a new national hero would have grown old and were dying. The problem would not arise if Gildas, a Welsh monk writing at Glastonbury about 540 of the siege of *mons Badonicus* – "when took place almost the last and not the least slaughter of our cruel foes" – had bothered to name the victorious British commander. But sermons have always been high on morals and low on facts. What is lacking from his *De Excidio Britanniae* is hinted at by a Welsh poet, probably Aneirin, in *The Gododdin*, which dates from the end of the sixth century. A warrior in the poem "glutted the black ravens" – with enemy dead – "but he was no Arthur".

Nennius, a Welsh monk writing two centuries later, compiled a history of Britain. He had access to chronicles that have not survived and his *Historia Brittonum* was used by Geoffrey of Monmouth, along with a book of Breton legends that are otherwise lost, for his own *Historia Regum Britanniae*. Nennius writes of the Saxons: "Then Arthur and the kings of the Britons fought against them; and though there were many more noble than he, he was twelve times chosen commander and won the battles."

Attempts at geographically locating the decisive battle have not progressed beyond the inspired hunch of our first field archaeologist, John Aubrey, writing in his *Monumenta Britannica* in about 1680; this work has only now been published, three hundred years later. In it, Aubrey suggests the Mount Badon battle was connected with a siege of Bath, and that it took place on Banner Down at Batheaston. It shows a better sense of history than the alternative argument that Mount Badon was fought at Badbury Rings, Dorset.

Bath lay at the edge of the Wansdyke frontier, and as a monument to conspicuous consumption and a focal point for rich settlements, it was equally a place to attack and defend; in addition, the movement of a potential enemy would be restricted by the deep gorge-like slopes.

The Dorset choice lies southwards from both of the main fifth century defensive lines. To reach this point hundreds of square miles of densely populated farmland would already have been lost; in fact, just about the whole country would have fallen, and there have been enough archaeological digs in the settlements of Wiltshire and Dorset to show that this kind of widespread upheaval and devastation simply did not happen. A commander would not be revered as a hero for the next fifteen hundred years if the face-saving final victory for himself and his men came only after an army of occupation had visited itself upon every home in the land.

The inheritors of Roman society in Britain had one last weapon that was to prove ultimately more effective than the sword: the island pacified and absorbed its Saxon immigrants by allowing Christianity to subvert their culture and beliefs. Through religion the influence of Rome upon the hearts and minds of man was able to spread far beyond the lands reached by the legions.

The *Anglo-Saxon Chronicle* writes of 596: "In this year Pope Gregory sent Augustine to Britain with a good number of monks, who preached God's word to the English peoples." London had survived as well as the rest of the country, for in 601 Gregory designated it the primary see of England.

A late or sub-Roman mausoleum, which originally held a large stone or lead coffin, is the earliest surviving remains from the early Christian complex that later became Wells Cathedral, Somerset. It was discovered in 1981 as excavations there were being wound up. Only the debased Roman capitals ETI survived from its burial inscription. Continental parallels, particularly at Xanten on the Rhine, point to such structures containing the bodies of Romano-Christian martyrs. In the age of Saxon Wessex the bones were removed from the Wells mausoleum and possibly shared between other churches as relics, though the name of no local saint survives in documents or tradition. The mausoleum was then used as an ossuary and rebuilt as a later Saxon family burial chamber. By the tenth century it had been enlarged into a two-roomed lady chapel, dedicated to St Mary. By 1210 this had been demolished and the area incorporated into the eastern extension of the cathedral. Wells has the longest known direct succession of Christian buildings in Britain that take the religion back to its Roman roots.

The church even conquered those places where the legions had required thousands of men for four centuries. The *Chronicle* records in 601: "Bishop Paulinus converted Edwin, king of the Northumbrians, to baptism". The only hiccup in the programme was the reversion of the East Saxons to paganism in 616, but this only lasted a generation. By 654 there were churchmen in London once more and, from that point, the episcopal succession was never interrupted.

It is a power that any secular leader must envy, less noticeable now, perhaps, but remarkably undiminished by the passing of one and a half thousand years. Not long ago it was unthinkable that one man in the Vatican could inspire the open resurgence of Polish nationalism, but as this is precisely what happened at the beginning of the 1980s, it must be assumed that the Roman empire has never died.

But for a real glimpse of the type of society and beliefs once found in the old empire you have to look further beyond the imperial frontiers. Hinduism, the faith of non-Moslem peoples of the Europid race of northern India – the same branch of humanity as the bulk of Europeans – is the closest equivalent to the Roman religion in today's world. Romans, like the Hindu, had gods and rituals for all classes and occasions.

Index

Romans are designated here by their family name (*gens*), with the exception of some rulers and public figures who are listed under names by which they are generally known.